بسم الله الرحمن الرحيم

٣

Zaatari

الزعتري

Culinary Traditions of the World's Largest Syrian Refugee Camp

KAREN E. FISHER

Food photography by Alex Lau with Jason LeCras
Arabic text translated by Mohammed Shwamra and Salah Aldin Falioun

GOOSE LANE EDITIONS

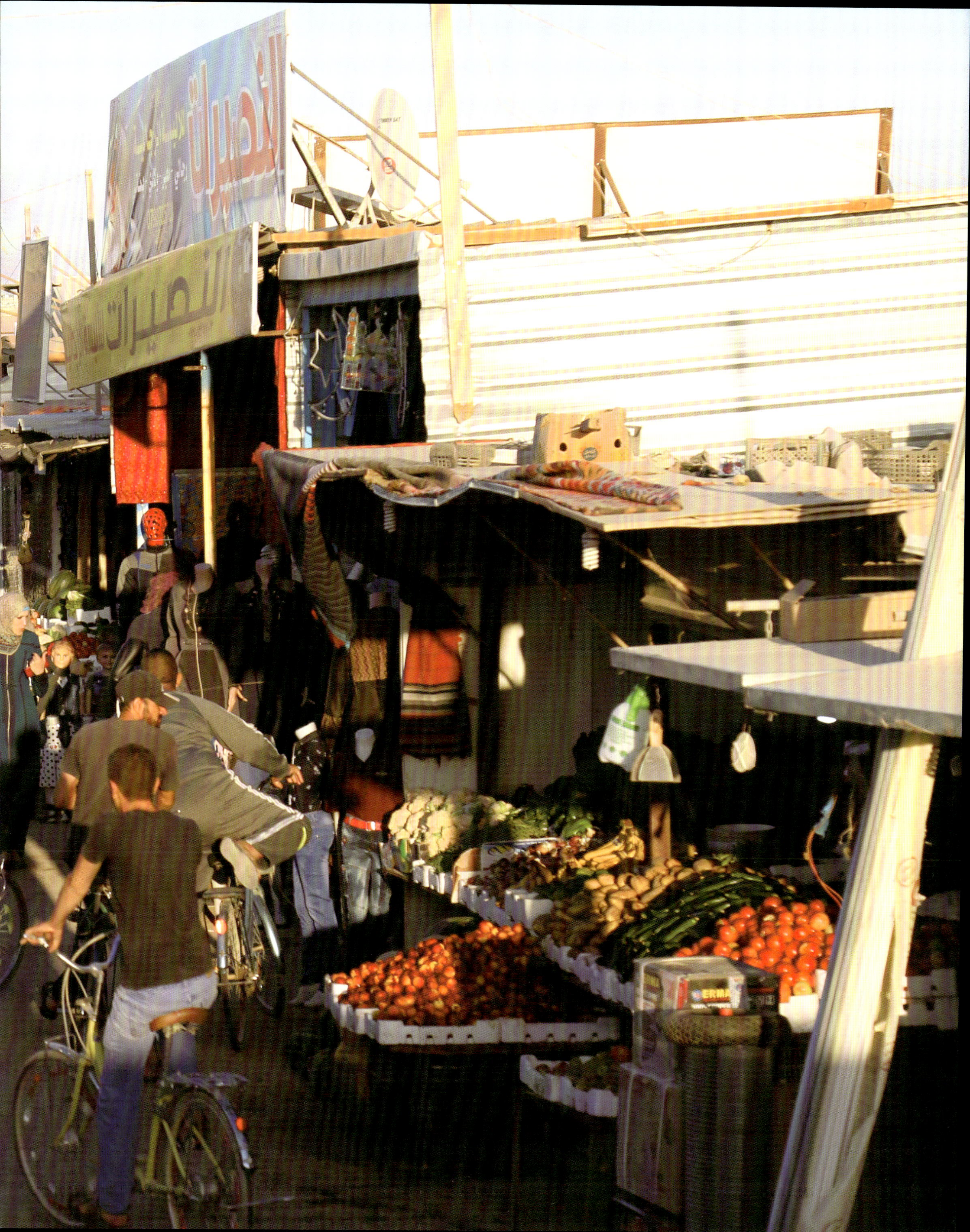
النصيرات
النصيرات

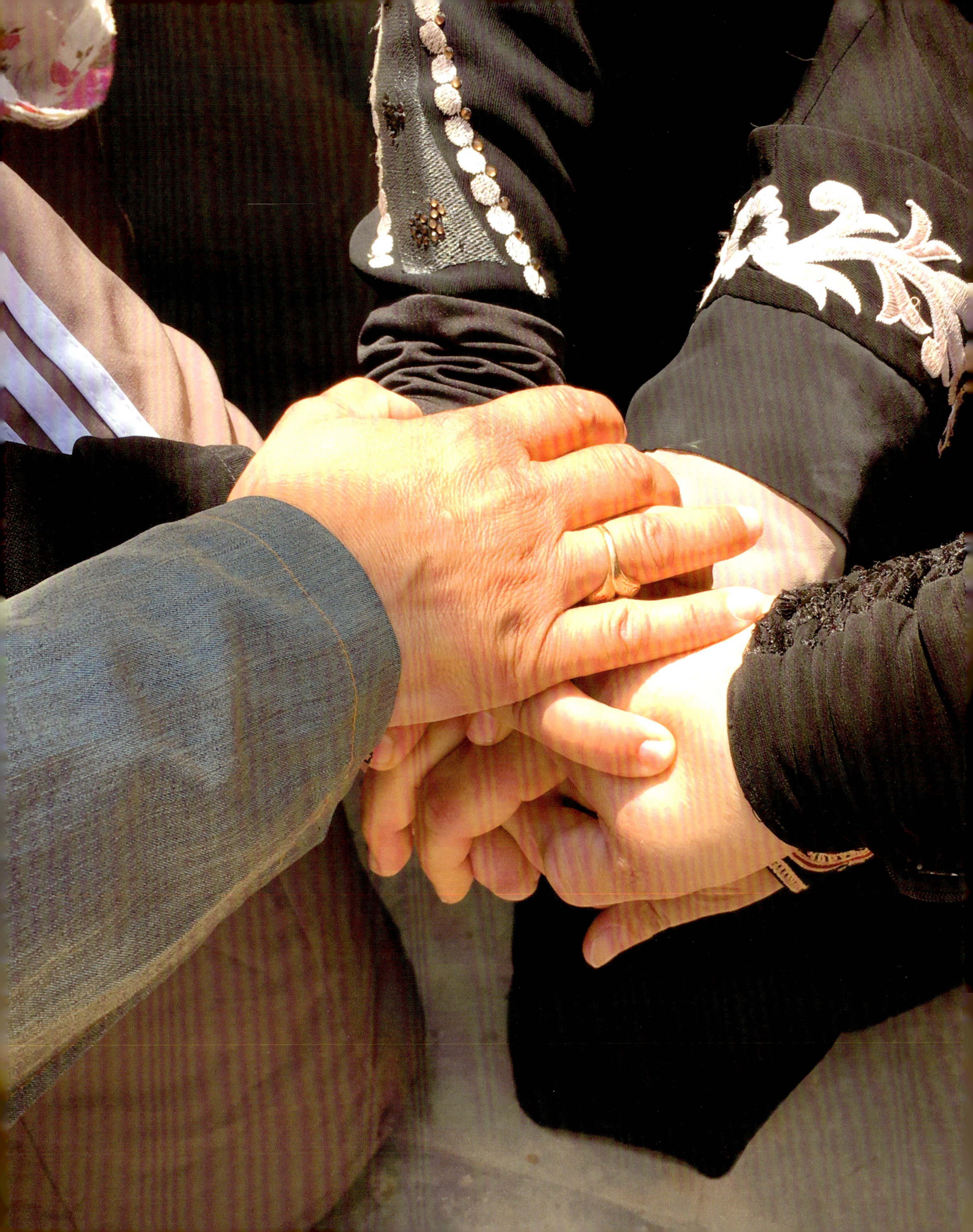

Contents

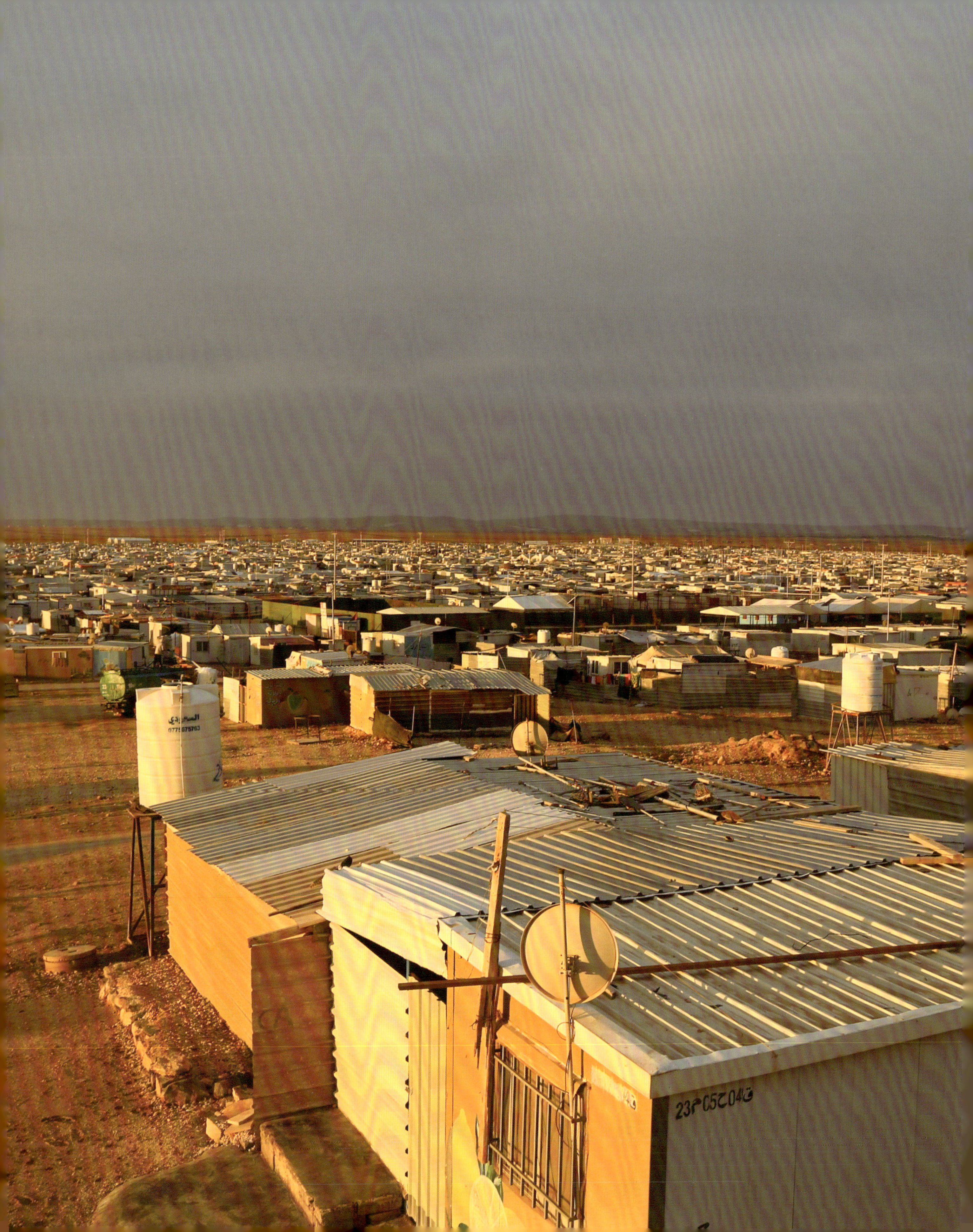

Foreword

No one chooses to leave their home and become a refugee. When war and persecution forced millions of Syrians to become refugees, most of them did not carry anything but the clothes on their backs. More than half a million Syrians arrived in Jordan to find safety and over eighty thousand of them made their home in Zaatari Camp. Originally a site to provide new arrivals with emergency relief, Zaatari has since evolved into a thriving community.

When I close my eyes to recall the sights and sounds of Zaatari, I hear the braying donkey, I imagine children running around after school and the hustle and bustle of the market, and I smell the amazing flavours of meals being prepared in thousands of homes. The smell drifts across the rows of white caravans, the standard shelters that house refugee families in the camp.

Food plays a central role in the camp's economy. Fresh produce is available in the supermarket, where refugees redeem their food rations and in the many shops lining the Shams Élysées, Zaatari's famous market street. Quite a few refugees find casual work in farms to the east of Zaatari in the fertile Jordan Valley, using their farming skills to earn a small income. And some families in the camp have begun to grow hydroponic vegetables in their homes, producing ever more varieties.

Food is what brings us all together; it plays an essential part in the community at large, perhaps more so in Zaatari than in other communities. With the camp now hosting refugees for more than 10 years, there are Syrian children born here who have never set foot in their homeland. They experience Syria through the memories of their parents, their cultural traditions, and the taste and smell of the food they eat every day. It is their mothers who cook those meals with great passion and a deep respect for their family recipes, handed down for generations. It is therefore no surprise that we want to dedicate this book to the women of Zaatari, to honour their perseverance and resilience.

Through their extensive engagement with the inhabitants of Zaatari, Karen and her refugee team have succeeded in offering an intimate portrait of what life is like in Zaatari. The initiative to compile this book has grown organically and found its shape over time, never turning away from the initial ambition to have the residents of Zaatari tell their own story. The many storylines show how food has a central place in Zaatari life, both as a ritual in and of itself—be it a simple breakfast or a coffee between friends—and as a key part of major

Maqloubeh, p. 120

community events like weddings and funerals. The book freely mixes traditions, heritage, religion, the Arabic language and artistic expression—and wraps it all up with many delicious recipes for everyone to try at home. And it is the astounding images in the book that show just how important it is to retain the connection with our homes, even more so when continued conflict and persecution in their country of origin prevents refugees in Zaatari and elsewhere from returning back home.

Food is comfort, food is memories, and food is shared experience. In Zaatari, wisdom is passed on in the shape of food, and traditions are protected in the company of those sharing a meal. It is a privilege for us in UNHCR and all the partners working in Zaatari to play a small part in safeguarding the delectable culinary traditions of Syria.

—Dominik Bartsch, UNHCR Representative to Jordan

Maamoul, p. 162

Mural by Jonathan Darby

Introduction

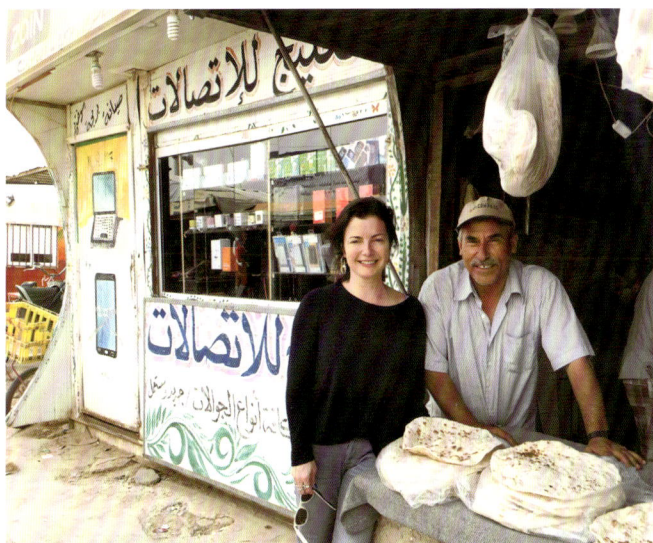

"*Sabah al-Khair* (Good Morning)," we exchange over drumming *tarab* music and bustle as Abu Ali works the brass *rakwah* (coffee pot) atop the flame, expertly stirring my *qahwa sada* (sugarless Turkish coffee). In seconds, my perfect little cup is ready to motor my day—super hot with heady foam and fragrant cardamom. Six sips, or maybe eight, and I'm hitting the grainy sludge. Rules you remember: hold the cup by the rim, never stir the coffee, and never drink the sludge.

My stomach has been growly since Amman, anticipating *ftoor* (breakfast) at Zaatari Camp near the Syrian border, past the camels and sheep, herders in *dishdashah* robes and *shemagh* (red- or black-checkered head scarves) worn by men everywhere. Syrians are known as the best cooks in the Arab world, and for me, eating in Zaatari Camp is proof. Humour and pride are essential ingredients to cooking in a place like Zaatari. We often joke that even though we are in a refugee camp, we eat as if we were at one of the world's most exclusive restaurants. Started in 2012 for people fleeing the Syrian war, Zaatari is a closed refugee camp that cannot be entered without an invitation and security clearance. A field ethnographer since January 2015, I fell in love with the food as quickly as I did the people.

Ftoor is high art. I bypass the lure of handmade, savoury *mana'eesh* flatbreads—*zaatar* with olive oil, cheese, *muhammara*, spinach—so many kinds, hot from the *souk* (market) ovens, vibrant vegetable stalls and spice shops, and head towards the caravans and Umm Mohammad's house. We women greet the Syrian way, rhythmically with a right handshake and kiss to right cheek followed by two kisses to the left cheek, a brief pause, then one more kiss, and maybe a fifth. Children's hands accept my gift of maple-sugar candies from home. *Chai wa naana* (sweet black tea with mint, p. 234) is ready and we start to cook.

The aroma of sweet frying onion wafts out from the tiny kitchen. My eyes are drawn to a pyre removing the skin of eggplants, unleashing their smokiness for *mutabbal* (p. 33). It is dark, as the electricity won't come on until evening, but the desert sun finds us, as does the *shamal* wind, sometimes clamouring, sometimes whistling through the space under the thin metal roof. *Wallah*, we swear by God, it's good we're inside and away from the *haboob* (giant sandstorms) today.

Chattering in Arabic about camp news and about family in Daraa, the cradle of the revolution in southern Syria where most are from, Umm Mohammad's sister and daughters work together in an organized, synchronized manner,

Ftoor (breakfast)

exemplifying *karme*: people generous to guests through food. They seamlessly work together without cookbooks, tables and chairs, measuring spoons, scales, appliances, or modern gadgetry. Their tools are their hands, their gauges are their senses, and their recipes are as old as ancient Syria. *Zaatar* (Arabic for thyme)—a favourite spice blend of dried thyme, sesame seeds, oregano, marjoram, salt, and sometimes sumac, for which Aleppo and Palestine are famous—is Zaatari Camp's namesake.

"*Yallah*, let's go, Karen," and I join them in the main room rolling grape leaves for *yabraq* (parcels of fragrant lamb and rice, p. 157) bundled into the big pot for steaming. All cooking is social, with food presented on large trays, with an eye to beauty. In the spotless kitchen, where all the ingredients and cookware are perfectly organized and the shelves are adorned Arabi-style with gold fringes, we make *ful mudammas* (p. 144), a stalwart bean stew drizzled with spicy oil, cumin, and tomato for breaking the long fasting days of Ramadan but enjoyed at breakfast year long, and *tesqieh* (p. 148), a Daraa comfort food of tahini, chickpeas and fried bread layered into gooey bliss.

The caravan floor transforms into our *soufra* (table) as a cloth is laid for us to dine the Bedouin desert way when nomads carried food wrapped in leather or cloth, which they untied and spread out on the ground. Scholars say floor sitting is traditional as it entails bowing your head and is more social; tables, bowls, and cutlery are ostentatious. Umm Mohammad snips the yabraq, unleashing their steam, dressing each platter with fragrant local lemons. Spoons for tesqieh and ful, and stacks of *khubz* bread, home-cured olives, lemon wedges, *zaatar*, *jibneh* (cheese), and *laban* (yogurt) signal "Let's eat!"

Sharing tapestried cushions and bolsters that are used at night for sleeping, we say *Bismillah* (in the name of God) and dig in, tearing the pillowy, thin bread to scoop, make little parcels, dip: all ways of eating. In the desert, where water is scarce, we waste not and Muslims consider all food a gift from God. In truth, dining Arabi-style—sitting on the floor and eating by hand from shared platters—brings people closer together, a tradition continued by Syria's farming communities and brought to Zaatari, deepened by necessity where few people have furniture. Even in Amman, if you're meant returning to Syria, to an earlier time, refrigerating without modernity, jury-rigging generators and pumps to stave off winter freeze and spring floods, against which caravans' metal walls and camp roads offer little protection, and using herbs and other foods that keep the body healthy and are said to cure afflictions.

My red notebook—fat with stories, lore, and wisdom—smells like Zaatari. I began it in January 2015 when I arrived from Seattle, and it's now expanded into several volumes, with people—children and those with disabilities included—writing in Arabic and doodling. My writing is the least legible. I'm a professor of information science at the University of Washington, a design ethnographer by way of librarianship, and a long way from my island home of Newfoundland in eastern Canada. If Zaatari had a guest book, I'd peg as the only Newfoundlander.

This book "happened" organically, *Mashallah*, by the will of God and the people. On my first visit, asking how young people used mobile phones and the Internet, girls drew pictures of themselves baking cakes to help war orphans feel better. People kept diaries about life in Syria and Zaatari and about their hopes for the future, pasting in photos taken with instant cameras. This was a way of revealing what life is like 24-7 from the community's perspective. The diary of

with the right people they will lead you to restaurants with private, caravan-size rooms for experiencing the old Arabi way of dining.

Kitchens everywhere are the best places for news, gossip, truly being with others. Everyone at camp has a story. There are eighty-three thousand stories, one for every person. Umm Mohammad fled to Jordan with her children and sister in 2012, just after Zaatari opened, when it was a collection of tents and people cooked over an open flame or the Bedouin desert way, in ovens tunnelled in the sand, making dishes like *mandi*—fresh chicken or lamb slow-cooked with herbs, the rendered juices falling onto rice suspended underneath and flavouring vegetables above, or *abood*—a Bedouin ash-covered bread, baked in a fire pit. People had few belongings, they were suffering from war trauma, and families were scattered, with many trapped or detained in Syria. It took coordinated efforts by the Syrian refugees, the UN Refugee Agency (UNHCR), the UN World Food Programme, aid agencies,, and the Kingdom of Jordan to arrive at where Zaatari is today: a community of resilience, pride, and identity.

People brought to Zaatari many of the old ways of Syria that most thought had been long forgotten: ways of cooking, healing, and especially eking out a living in the barren desert. In a sense, leaving Syria and surviving the war also

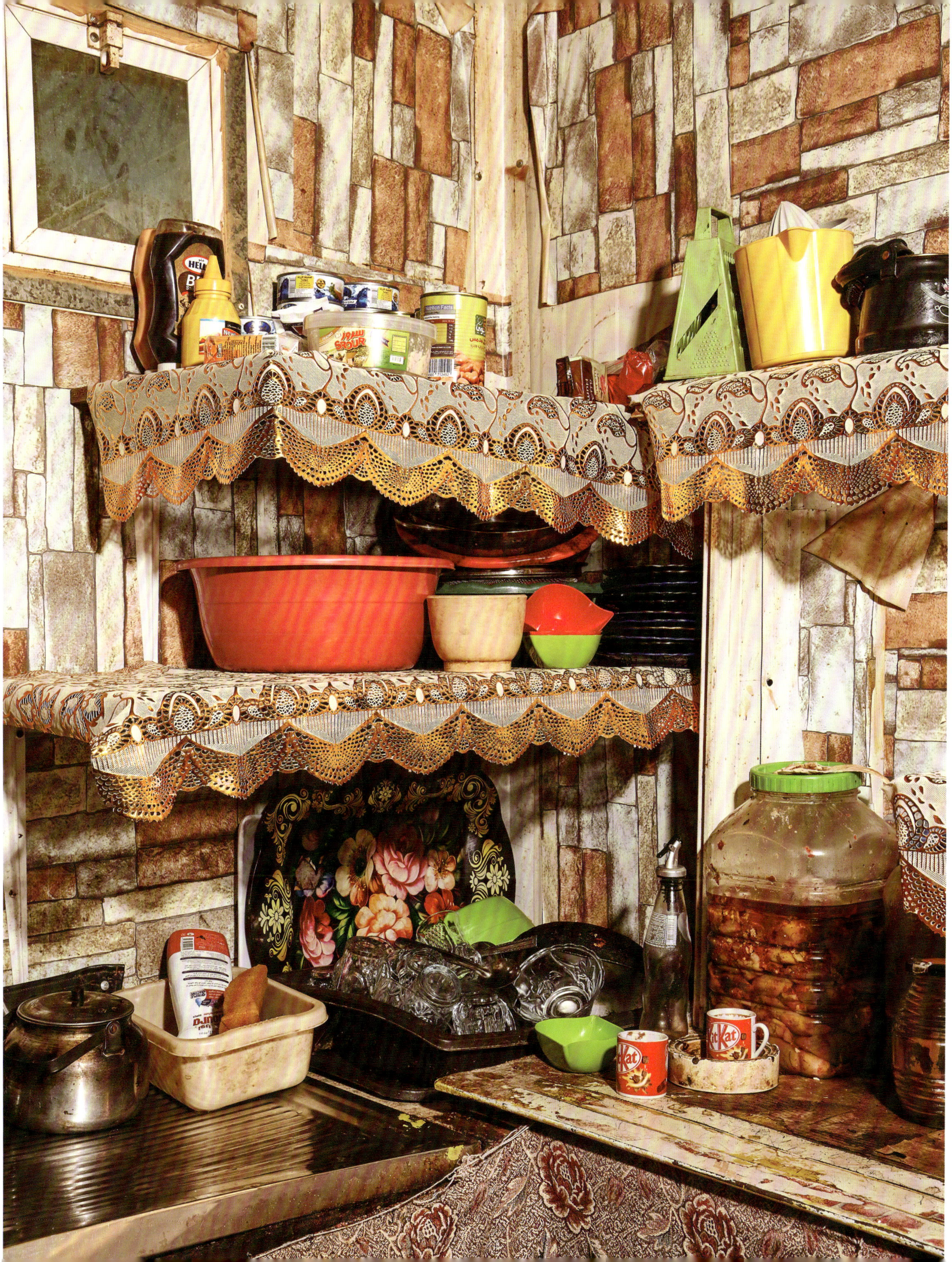

Ghada' (lunch)

sixteen-year-old Nour, written in English, contains my first recipe and was the inspiration for this book. It deserves to be in an archive instead of in my office in Seattle.

Ghada' is lunch, the biggest, most important meal of the day, served mid-afternoon, and everyone gathers for it. Leading up to ghada', vendors hawk produce by donkey cart through Zaatari's dusty roads, calling out their wares against a background of the muezzins' adhan, the Muslim call to prayer, which resounds beautifully from the many masjid (mosques) five times a day. Zaatari is vast, over thirteen hundred acres divided into twelve districts, each with a theme. It is an array of colourful bespoke caravans and hidden fountain gardens, community centres, a few schools, and a hospital—surrounded by the Ring Road and then desert beckoning to Jordan's Bedouin border with Syria. The border is recent in Arab time: one hundred years ago, Syria, Jordan, Palestine, Lebanon, and parts of Turkey were one region—Greater Syria.

At around three p.m., ghada', heavy with aromas from home, brings camp to a standstill, and Little Syria—and more specifically, Little Daraa emerges via the dishes set out as soufras throughout the camp, such as Shish barak (Old Man's Ear, p. 131), delicate meat-filled pastries gently poached in yogurt with a hint of tomato or majestic mleihi, choice lamb or chicken atop Bedouin kethi sauce made from dried homemade yogurt, adding a creamy, salty zest

to the bulgur base. Maybe you will find horaa osba'o (lentils with pomegranate, sumac, and fried crispy onion, p. 112), or Mahshi (stuffed zucchini or cabbage leaves, pp. 100, 103, and 105), or my favourite: Rgagah, oven-baked layers of thin Bedouin dough woven with pulled chicken, spices, and onion (p. 136). Salads are near ubiquitous at ghada', with lemony bright Fattoush studded with pomegranate seeds, seasoned with sharp sumac and cooling mint, or perhaps freshly-made Tabbouleh with parsley, tomato, mint, and bulgur (p. 56). "Sahtain wa afiya" echoes across camp as people wish each other double health and blessing, enjoyment of their food before and after eating. In the evening, neighbours visit for coffee and sweets—nutty baqlawah (p. 186) or cream puddings such as mahalabia (p. 218) with syrup, rosewater, mastic, and nuts. Over narghile (water pipes), games of Tarneeb (cards) and Tawilat al-Zahr (Syria's famous hand-tooled backgammon game) are played along with singing, accompanied by the lute-like oud and tabla (hand drums). Leftover khubz is hung outside in thanks to Allah for his mercy.

The souks have amazing street food—golden crispy falafel with fluffy insides, savoured as finger delicacies glistening with dark, earthy sumac, popped in hot oil or smashed with condiments in sandwiches; juicy chicken as garlicky shish tawook or lamb shawarma with homemade pickles and tahini sauce wrapped in paper-thin, saj-baked shraak; and lamb shoqaf grilled open air, luring you from blocks away—all prepared and sold by men. But the best food is found inside the caravans, made by the women.

I asked UNHCR if we could do a cookbook, building on our missions identifying community assets and strengths. The cookbook would document and preserve indigenous food practices handed down through the generations. Our recipes would be different from those in other Syrian cookbooks, and certainly Arab cookbooks, as they would reflect people's origins in mostly southern Syria and modifications necessitated by cooking in camp. Next day, we started the cookbook.

Writing a cookbook was not a simple matter. I met with women to ask if they wanted to do it. They wholeheartedly said "tmam" (yes), but the next questions were What is a cookbook? What is a recipe? How do we start? There were no examples, no one had fled the war with cookbooks—and no one had cookbooks anyway, because they all had learned from their mothers and grandmothers.

We gradually built the cookbook through gatherings, in homes and elsewhere, and the discussions were deep. We pondered: what goes into a recipe? Zaatari women prepare

The women wanted to be referenced by the Arab convention of Umm (mother of) or Anseh (aunt of) followed by the child or niece/nephew's name, and the men as Abu (father of), both to protect their identity as refugees and to shield them from the regime. Children were similarly assigned an alias for their first name. For each recipe, the contributor's home village or town is noted.

In the stories, few discuss the war, due to sensitivity and painful memories. A single click on Google reveals atrocities, how protests began in March 2011, when teenagers in Daraa, inspired by the Arab Spring, were arrested for writing "Your turn, Doctor" on their school wall—anti-regime graffiti referencing Syrian president Bashar al-Assad, a doctor who trained in ophthalmology. At the time of writing in early 2023, over thirteen million Syrians are displaced worldwide and internally—over half of Syria's pre-war population of twenty-one million. Nearly one million have died and hundreds of thousands are missing, disappeared into Assad's prisons. The 2015 painting (below) by camp artist Iyad Sabbagh poignantly captures the feelings of refugees.

Having agreed on the recipe style, the women and I began identifying recipes like food detectives as word of the cookbook spread quickly across camp. One highlight was a workshop held in August 2016. Normally, a large workshop in Zaatari might include twenty-five people. This workshop drew one hundred and forty people, and the temperature was 42°C (108°F), and we were inside a canvas tent. More notable still, men participated in this workshop. Zaatari, like

food in large quantities and cook socially, using not measuring spoons but rather their eyes and hands, while jar lids, coffee cups, and glasses become quantifiers and qualifiers. This is a place where approximations such as "the size of a chicken head" are not only used, but understood.

Our recipes are modified to serve four to six people. Then there was the challenge of specifying ingredients, such as spices, use of Maggi—a seasoning found in both powdered and liquid form that is common in kitchens throughout much of the world outside of North America— and methods such as "put on the fire," "cook until done," or "reach a golden colour." Meat and chicken are butchered following *halal* practices, and always cooked the same day for freshness and to save space, often first tenderized by boiling in salted water. The women had to agree on explicit terminology, tacit knowledge that they had never before described. We wanted to share the details necessary to find success in your home kitchen, while maintaining authenticity and reflecting the culinary brain trust found here, in Zaatari.

Iyad Sabbagh's painting poignantly captures the feelings of refugees.

much of the Arab world, is a gendered society where women and men perform separate activities, and when an activity is mixed, they sit apart: women on one side, men on the other. Together, we brainstormed the cookbook sections, posted notes on the walls of the tent, and then organized the recipes for each section.

Men also participated in the inaugural Zaatari Camp Best Chef Contest. Like many things Zaatari, the contest was organized on the fly (Yallah!) and came together magically (Wallah!), designed by the community with the support of UNHCR, the aid organization Blumont, and UN Women. The community set the rules (team entries, double-blind judging, hot dishes judged first) and the prizes promoted food safety, time saving, and energy efficiency such as pressure cookers, large cooking pots, and electric fryers. Participants received welcome gifts such as oven mitts and silicone spatulas. To fanfare, nine judges drawn from the community and aid agencies announced the winners, with a first-place tie between *Maqloubeh* (a show-stopping dish of rice, meat and vegetables topped with fried nuts that is ceremoniously flipped upside down before serving, p. 120) and *Basbousa* (a luscious semolina cake filled with rose-scented cream and doused in citrus syrup, p. 189). While awaiting the results, the community staged a breakout talent show, sharing the microphone to sing and recite poetry and Quranic verse.

Over two thousand Syrians handwrote pages as the cookbook morphed into *Zaatari: Culinary Traditions of the World's Largest Syrian Refugee Camp*. Food transcends cultures and boundaries of gender, age, ability, and trauma. Food heals the soul, confers dignity, and offers hope. Camp artist Mohammed Amaari illustrated each page of heavy linen paper in watercolours, reflecting its theme, often using subtle humour—a work of art illuminating the collective creativity. Many of the pages are multi-authored, such as those on Arab medicine or where a person with vast knowledge but low literacy is assisted by a friend or an aid worker.

As the book progressed, people added stories from Syria and Zaatari, poetry—highly regarded in the Arab world—or art. Stories of girls planning their futures as surgeons, scientists, and human rights lawyers; single mothers supporting their children and parents; disabled young men designing wheelchairs to handle Zaatari's roads; boys juggling school and work to help their families; men in the souks who could teach entrepreneurship at any Ivy League college; elders teaching the traditions of old Syria to children born in the camp. Six years ago, if you asked a child where they were from, they would say Syria; now they proudly shout, Zaatari Camp!

Mohammed Amaari's illustrated recipe page

Since August 2012, more than 670,000 Syrians have registered as refugees in Jordan. The Jordanian government estimates there are up to 1.3 million Syrian refugees in the country as many refugees have not registered officially with the government. Some refugees stay in Zaatari or one of the other camps, others have moved to a village or a city. People wrote of their journey and the early days when Zaatari comprised tents with dirt floors housing fifteen thousand people; its high point of one hundred and fifty-six thousand people in 2013; and the transition from tents to caravans, from central water sites, communal kitchens, and public wash centres to home plumbing and electricity and the expansion of schools and community centres. Most Syrians across Jordan have a memory of Zaatari, and I hear of refugees wishing to return to the camp or having done so.

I learned about food the Zaatari way by cooking with women in their homes, visiting souk food stands, the Made in Zaatari catering kitchen, and the UN World Food Programme (WFP) school lunch preparation centre. Where there was food, so was I. Across Jordan, I collected beautiful, hand-etched antique brass and silver dishware, cooking

pots, falafel presses, and silver-laden *dalal* (brass qahwa coffee urns) with leather-wrapped handles; ornate serving trays of all sizes, *safertas* (stacking pots for ferrying lunches), silver *haj* vases, *ataar* perfume infusers, and antique glassware in blue and red hues. Antique wooden moulds for making cookies like *maamoul* (p. 162) or breads during Eid. Misshapen Bedouin wooden bowls lovingly melded with scrap metal joined my growing collection of handmade furniture, mirrors, and boxes with distinctive silver-lined Islamic mosaic finishes. Treasures made near extinct by war and time, and used in our food photography along with dishware in people's homes.

Ancient cookbooks—the tenth-century *al-Baghdadi Cookbook* by Ibn Sayyar al-Warraq, the Ayyubidian thirteenth-century (1226) *Kitâb al-Tabîkh* by al-Baghdadi, and the fifteenth-century *Kitab al-Tibakha* by Ibn al-Mubarrid of Damascus—reveal Syria's rich culinary history, hearkening back to the Silk Road trade route—which brought not only ingredients but also the culinary practices that go with

them—and the Islamic Golden Age of empire, science, and medicine. These books offer advice on fresh foods, herbal cures, and cooking for royalty or family with spices and aromatics such as rose essence and nuts. I learned how Zaatari cooking that can be traced from Bedouin heritage to villages and cities in Syria, routed through Yemen, Iraq, Palestine, and Persia (Iran), was adapted to camp constraints, with such practices as dyeing peanuts and coconut green to replace expensive pistachios and using corn oil instead of the beloved fresh hand-pressed olive oil from family farms and homemade *saman* (ghee) for everyday cooking. Wartime food practices echo throughout history. Think World War II and how cooking changed with substitutes for butter, eggs, milk, flour, coffee, meat, and vegetables, heralding the packaged, fast-food industry of today.

The land we now call Syria used to be a part of Mesopotamia, a fertile region including parts of what are now Iran,

Leaving Syria

In the dark skies of our crisis, the clouds of hope appear more than any other clouds. I remember that day, nine years ago, when suitcases were piled on the roof of the car. We weren't going on a pleasure trip. My parents, little siblings, and I left after a big argument about whether to stay under the danger of war or leave without our beloved things. I didn't know why my dad was pushing us so hard to leave. It might have been because he had gotten used to the bitter taste of exile after being away for such a long time, or because he overworked himself from worrying about us until we finally surrendered and left, like millions of others.

I gathered my luggage and my memories, and said goodbye to my room, my house, my school, and my notebooks. I wanted to hug these things, but I walked away with a heavy heart. My sorrow was shared by everyone as the car lazily moved towards refuge in Jordan. The desert road under the burning sun, while I contemplated the fear of the unknown, was seared in my mind as we crossed Syrian territories, scattering pieces of ourselves behind. "Please, God, let this be a dream and let me wake from it," I kept telling myself, but this time we were the refugees and this was as clear as daylight.

When we arrived at Zaatari Camp, I was on the brink of losing my young mind. We came here escaping death only to realize despair was still everywhere—etched and tattooed on the faces of others who had just arrived. My heart sought a glimmer of hope, something to sustain us.

Hope came from UNHCR and WFP to the lines and lines of people. The fieldworkers distributed blankets and food and provided shelter. They served so many people with unwavering kindness, people deeply suffering from war trauma—especially the children, the old, and the very hurt. People kept arriving and everyone was exhausted.

"We will go," said my father as we followed a fieldworker. Where? I asked myself, but the question melted in my mind's big emptiness. What are we doing here exactly? Is this happening for real? Or is it my treacherous imagination? Many questions, and my young mind couldn't answer any. We were led to a tent. I had heard that people who went to the camp would live in tents, but hearing about something is totally different from living in it. Tears ran down my swollen cheeks, shed for my family who were supposed to be living happily in the countryside.

Days and weeks passed, challenged by bitter cold, rain, and the flames of the burning sun. With God's mercy, we adapted. People thought the stay would be short, maybe a few weeks, certainly not years. While SRAD (Syrian Refugee Affairs Directorate) and UNHCR administered the camp, UN agencies, international and local partners, and the Jordanian government worked together

to replace the tents with caravans and built infrastructure for water, electricity, and solar, schools and community centers. Our early needs resonated like the desert itself, where water and electricity are scarce. But after realization set in, we didn't give up, despite the overwhelming grief and sadness. We overcame our defeats; we created our own difference.

I have learned that people need healing in many ways to rid the suffering and breaches inside. Some use writing and art, others use sports like running and other practices to heal.

In Zaatari Camp I noticed that people also rely on our beloved food and culture from Syria, especially from Daraa. Preparing and garnishing food Syrian style as aromas fill the streets at night and our hearts fill with warmth and happiness help us hold fast to our homeland. These are my Syrian people of Zaatari Camp. We rose from the ashes. From our long exile, we light the candles of hope with the simplest ways from home.

—AMJAD AL-MASSRI

Old Clocks
AMJAD AL-MASSRI

I lacerate my chest three times a day	أشُقُّ صدري ثلاثَ مراتٍ في اليوم
Looking for myself there	وأبحثُ عنّي هناك
Only to find some old clocks	فلا أجدُ غيرَ ساعاتٍ قديمة
Pointing to some old nights	تُشيرُ إلى مساءاتٍ بعيدة
I look closely, everything is blurry	أمعنُ النّظر، كلَّ شيءٍ ضبابي
Reproachful messages	رسائل عتاب
Frayed relationships	علاقات مهترئة
Unuttered insults	شتائمُ لم أقلها لأحد
Withered eyes	عيونٌ ذابلة
Lost battles	معارك خاسرة
And shoddy poems.	وقصائد ركيكة
I couldn't find myself there...	ولا أجدُني هناك
I returned with many questions in my head	فأُقفلُ راجعاً وفي رأسِي تساؤلات كثيرة
Questions about me, about you, and about the songs	عنّي وعنكِ، وعن الأغنيات
Questions about two kids shriveled on waiting chairs	عن طفلين ذبلا على كراسي الإنتظار
And they didn't get the infection of being close.	ولم تُصبهما عدوى الإقتراب.

Syrian Welcome

Bismillah al-Rahman al-Rahim
In the Name of God, the Merciful, the Compassionate

Salaam, peace, and blessings from Allah upon you. On behalf of the people of Zaatari Camp, it pleases us to welcome you and introduce you to our book about the most renowned foods and traditions from Syria that we brought to Zaatari. We are also happy to share stories of our lives, of our resilience as Syrians, and what makes us human, like you, our readers.

Our goal was not just to make a cookbook that tackles ingredients and preparation and inspires you to cook, but also to document what binds together our present and our history. Syrian cuisine is deeply rooted in the people, culture, and natural bounty of each region, making it distinctive and prized worldwide.

Syrian cooking is an art, but it is also a science: foods are prepared with love and for beauty, with the nutrients necessary for good health. Much knowledge comes to us from the Holy Quran, such as the properties of dates, honey, milk, olives, grapes, and grains; and we follow the seasons that are best for preparing and serving foods. The Syrian cook always prepares large amounts, as families are big and blessings come from sharing with people in need.

When we arrived at Zaatari from Syria we started anew. Cooking the foods from home is what has kept us together, even though our homes were destroyed and our families dispersed. As we make our foods, children learn the stories of our past and dream of the future.

Between your hands lie the heartbeats of thousands of people. May your hearts beat with ours and may you join us at our table. *Sahtain wa afiya* (double your health and well-being, may your eyes eat before your stomach)!

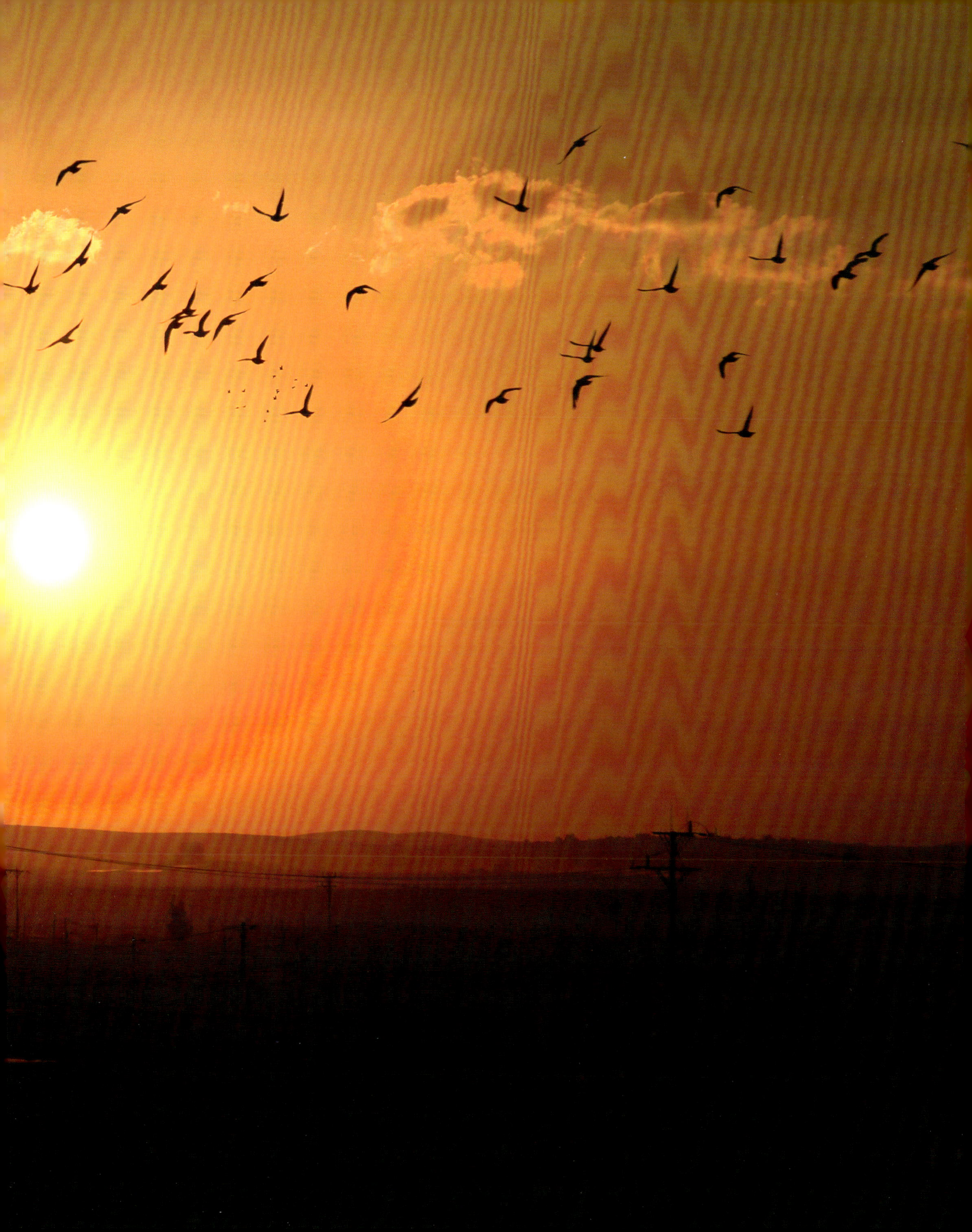

Arabic Coffee

Ahlan wa Sahlan, Welcome! At Zaatari, coffee—qahwa—is ubiquitous, deeply entrenched in Syrian culture. While coffee trees originated in Ethiopia, coffee as a drink was enthusiastically celebrated and drunk in the mid-1400s by Sufi monks in Yemen. Coffee spread across the Arab world, and was brought in 1544 to the Ottomans in Istanbul by two Syrian traders, Shams of Damascus and Hakem of Aleppo, who opened a coffee shop. Displaced by the war, many Syrians are again introducing Syrian-style coffee to the world.

At Zaatari we serve two types of qahwa: Arabic, a slowly-prepared, cardamom flavoured watery coffee which is served to welcome guests and on special occasions; and Turkish (p. 237), which is dark, prepared quickly and served at any time but especially at the end of a meal—after chai (tea).

Making and serving Arabic qahwa is usually men's domain and a high art, whether enjoyed Bedouin-style, outside over an open fire, or in the home *madafa* (entertaining area). Qahwa is distinguished by its preparation, taste, and custom of serving. According to Abu Ahmed from district 1, both Bedouin and at-home traditions begin with the preparation of *tashreba* (the starter base), which lasts for days, replenished with roasted coffee and water. Bedouin-style qahwa has its roots in ancient hospitality traditions—when strangers could stay or seek refuge in any home and the host would be obligated to provide hospitality for three days and/or ten meals.

Bedouin qahwa begins with the preparation of a fire pit and the placement of a warming *manqal* (a large, deep-footed brass tray) beside the fire. Green or dark coffee beans are roasted until deep red, and ground in a *mehbash* (a heavy, narrow wooden pot with wooden mortar)—the rhythmic pounding traditionally accompanied by Bedouin song. The beans are then transferred to a rectangular wooden bowl to cool. After, the ground beans are added to pots of water and boiled for an hour, creating the base. Meanwhile more pots of water are added to the fire.

If the coffee is to be drunk immediately, a quart of tashreba is boiled in a kettle with a spoonful of coffee with ground cardamom. After it rests, it is served in a special ornate urn, called *dallah* (plural *dalal*), Arabic for "friendliness, openness, and sociability from drinking coffee together." Al Raslaniyah, made by the Raslan family, is considered by many to be the best producer of dalal, but these are hard to find because of the war. Damascene-style dalal have a gracefully curved Arabesque body and handle; Bedouin-style dalal have a lantern-shaped body and a straight leather handle, often silver-woven, made for both left- and right-handed pourers. For Bedouin gatherings, many dalal are prepared, in anticipation of hours of music, singing, poetry recitation, and conversation by the fire.

Holding the dallah in his left hand and *finjeen* (small cups, often gold or silver with an Arabesque design) in his right, the host pours and tests the first cup. The qahwa is then served to the senior guest from the right side in finjeen filled half way at most (if filled to the top, it means the host wants you to leave!). If you want more, extend your cup, keeping it still; if you're finished, shake your cup. A polite guest always accepts more, but stops at three cups. As guests enjoy the first round, more is prepared. A glass of water is served with both Arabic and Turkish coffee. If a guest drinks the water before tasting the coffee, it means they are hungry. If a guest drinks the water after drinking the coffee, it signals that they did not like the taste of the coffee.

In traditional Bedouin culture, the three cups were highly contractual: the first cup cemented an agreement that the host would welcome the guest for three days and that the guest would not steal from the house. The guest was under no obligation to provide any information except his name. The second cup was an agreement that the guest would, if needed, fight on behalf of the host. The third cup meant the host would defend the guest.

At Zaatari, men greet you outside their homes holding dalal and finjeens and welcome you inside their madafa, for more, to share news, stories, poetry, and joy.

Tamur (dates) is the classic accompaniment for weddings, funerals, and other important occasions. Qahwa is believed ideal for adjusting everyone's mood, and the person who serves coffee is seen as a generous host. True Arabic coffee, like Turkish coffee, has no sugar; hence, dates, sweets, and nuts are served alongside it.

Tashreba
(coffee starter base)

ABU QASSEM, Ghouta, Syria

3.5 oz (100 g) green coffee beans

3 quarts (3 l) of water

Roast green coffee beans over medium heat in a heavy skillet until dark red in colour, then grind or pound to a fine grind and let cool.

Heat water, add the coffee, and boil for 1 hour. Refrigerated, the coffee will last a week.

To make coffee with tashreba:

1 cup (125 g) tashreba

3 cups (750 ml) water

2 tbsp roasted coffee beans

1 tbsp ground cardamom

cardamom pods (optional)

saffron threads (optional)

Put tashreba in a pot and add water, roasted coffee, and ground cardamom.

Heat at a low simmer for 30 minutes. Pour into a brass dallah or a thermos and serve with a few cardamom pods or saffron threads in each coffee cup.

Coffee without an Appointment

How would sadness climb the neighbouring trees of a sun?

Having this question in mind, I wore the coat of my sorrow tonight, and surrendered to the fugitive tears from a hole in the branches of my heart, to listen to a pigeon's sound carrying the pain of my tears, and slowly sip my coffee of anxiety.

Oh, dear pen, wipe out the titles of my happiness and tell how many tears I shed, how many ghosts of sorrow I killed; that the balm is bitter but it's a cure, and we must have our sadness meals with satisfaction. We prepare the most elaborate bowls and cups, and wear the best clothes in its presence.

Sadness—oh, sir—is necessary. Doesn't it make the woman more beautiful? When her eyes are full of tears, don't they resemble two birds wet with rain?

Sadness is necessary to welcome the coming joy like a child who lays Eid clothes next to his head, waiting for the morning celebration. Sadness is when the light is suddenly switched off and we turn to the sky and see the stars hidden from our sight by the shadow of man-made lights.

With sorrow I wash my sins to welcome a new pure immaculate blessing, pure as a teardrop. ✦

—RAGHAD, Damascus

Artist unknown.

Sabah al-Khair, Join Us for Ftoor

"Although we are women and housewives, we know the importance of breakfast for the body, because it gives energy and calories, and when the family gathers breakfast becomes tastier. Most important is how you arrange and garnish the food, because the eye eats before the mouth. With best greetings, I love peace." —UMM MOMINA, Tasil

On my first visit to Zaatari, I stayed in Mafraq, a neighbouring town, and the first evening we ventured out to find food. At the bakery, surprise worked both ways when I requested "one," thinking I was getting one piece of bread to sample, and received one kilogram, their smallest order. At Zaatari, around ten a.m. every day children hurry home with kilos of bread for ftoor. As Umm Maysaa explained over making *ejjeh* (fritters), "Every home has its own traditions, depending on what the family likes. There are specific habits for breakfast, lunch, dinner, snacks, and sweets. What is important is that it is homemade food that I prepare myself, not from any market. A simple Daraa breakfast may be just *mezze* (small dishes) of *makdous houran* (pickled, stuffed baby eggplant) *zaytun* and *mouneh* (olives and pickles), *labneh modahbara* (preserved yogurt balls, p. 258) zaatar, olive oil, and homemade bread, sometimes with *jazmaz* (an egg dish, p. 35)—always delicious."

A simple ftoor based on the Quran is key to a good long life. Elders lead their families in starting the day with Turkish coffee and one or three *tamur* (dates)—never an even number—followed by spoonfuls of local olive oil, honey, and *habat albaraka* (pulverized black nigella seeds) for optimum health. Fascinated, I have learned how dates are mentioned more than any other food in the Quran and are highly nutritious. A spoonful of rosewater stirred into a glass of water is also taken daily, for its antioxidants. Local honey is valued for its anti-allergens and other properties—reminiscent of prized Yemeni Sidr honey described in the Quran (16 An Nahl, The Honey). Habat albaraka, also sprinkled on salads and other foods, is believed to help heal all diseases except death.

Over the years I have cherished ftoor, learning how to make the many specialties. Sometimes it might be a large gathering with family returning from early-hours work or a small gathering of women and children. Sometimes we enjoy ftoor at a community centre such as Questscope, International Medical Corps, or UN Women, where people share or prepare food. Such ftoor are especially fun—Syrians are the ultimate foodies, as everyone has tons of photos of homemade food and family farms in Daraa on their mobiles, and discussing the origins, making, and enjoyment of food is a daily pastime. The people prize nothing more than hand-tilled olives, cheese and foods from home that occasionally reach camp. With Turkish coffee and Syrian music, the taste brightened by smiles of home is sublime.

Roll up your sleeves and join me in preparing ftoor favourites. Some recipes to round out your mezze are in the Zaatari Pantry chapter, while others are in Ramadan, as they are specially made for *Iftar* (to break the fast) and *suhoor* (an early morning meal, before the sun comes, and fasting begins).

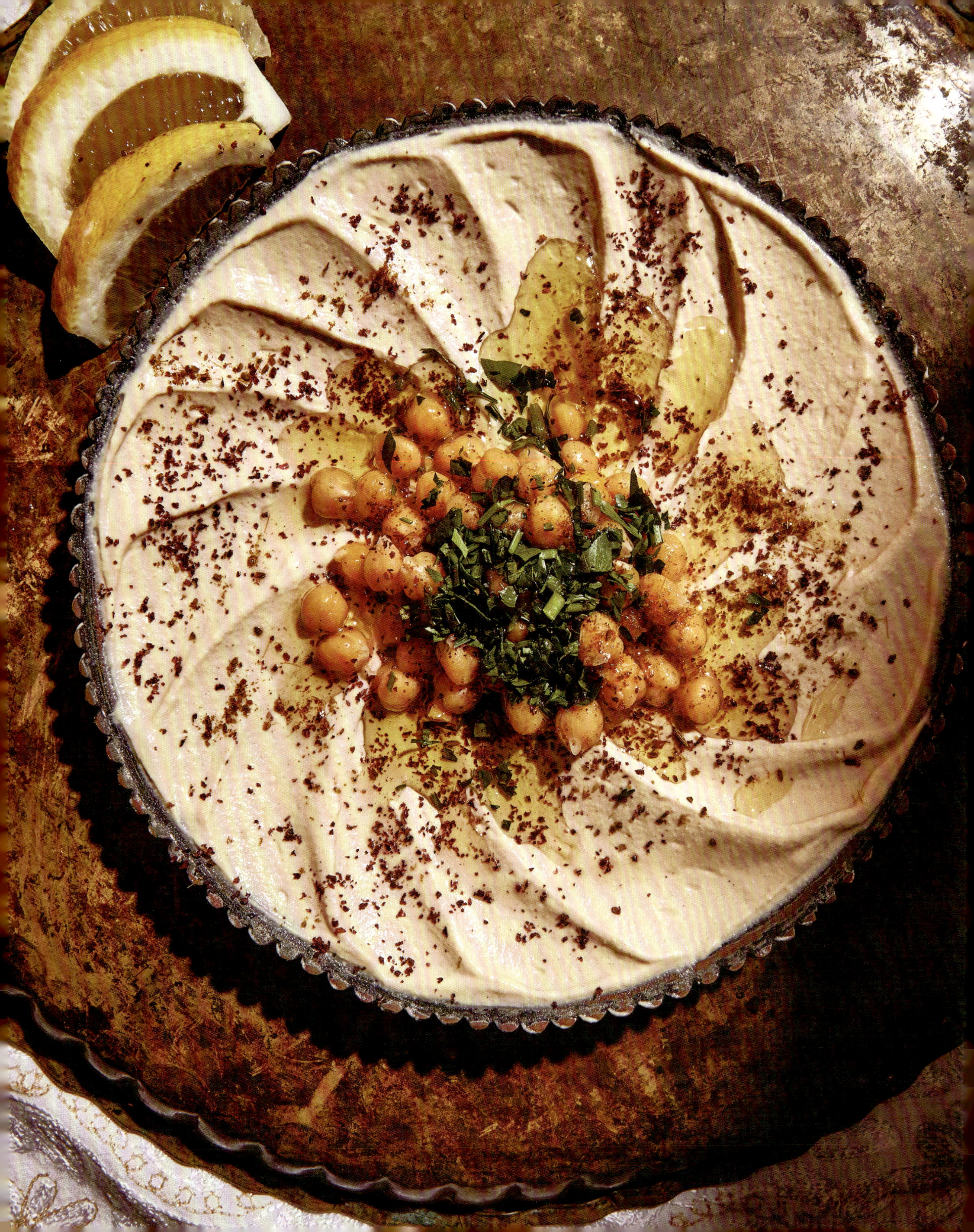

Hummus

ABU ABDULLAH, Daraa

Everyone loves hummus! Although the word itself is Arabic for chickpeas, the eponymous dish (and the legume) is pronounced *HOOM-uhs*. It's the most ubiquitous dish at Zaatari, appearing at every ftoor and mezze, in fattehs, as snacks, snuggled inside soft, warm bread, and more. At home, I love to toast khubz over a gas flame, open the pocket, and fill it with homemade hummus and sliced cucumber drizzled with olive oil and sprinkled with zaatar or sumac. True confession: my golden retriever, who accompanied me to Amman from Seattle, also loves hummus.

Hence, our quest for the best hummus in camp. I noticed that people from Zaatari often skipped hummus at events and restaurants outside camp, their hummus radar so finely tuned. I showed the women of camp the recipes we received; they looked strikingly similar to me, but the women replied, "OK but *lah*, not the best." When I asked around, it became clear that Abu Abdullah's hummus at his restaurant in the Shams Élysées was the best, hands down; it was legend. Was it the spices? Did he roast the chickpeas—as some recipes are rumoured—to get such a flavour? Was it the technique in how he blended it all together?

But what of the recipe? Now I'm thinking it would be easier to find the Sword of Saladin, founder of the Ayyubid dynasty.

Alhumdillah, we prevailed. Abu Abdullah's base 4.4 lb (2 kg) of chickpeas yields 24 lb (11 kg) of hummus! Here's a more manageable home version. Golden rule: hummus is always served in a shallow bowl, drizzled with lots of green olive oil, scooped using khubz.

❖

Place the chickpeas in a large bowl and cover with water. Soak for 7–8 hours in summer or 10 hours in winter. Drain and rinse well.

Transfer the chickpeas to a large pot, cover with 6 inches (15 cm) of water, and bring to a boil. Reduce the heat and add the oil and baking soda—the chickpeas will swell. Leave for 2 hours on low heat. Drain, rinse well, and spread out to cool. Reserve one third of the chickpeas for garnish.

Using a blender, blend the chickpeas with cold water until very smooth. Add the tahini, salt, and lemon salt in batches, alternating with a little ice until the hummus is very smooth.

Transfer to a bowl and refrigerate.

To serve, dollop onto a shallow bowl, make a well with the back of a spoon and pour in olive oil. Top with the remaining chickpeas and place lemon wedges alongside. If desired, garnish the sides of the bowl with sumac and top with pine nuts. Serve with khubz.

1 ¼ cups (300 g) dried chickpeas

1 tsp olive oil

1 tsp baking soda

3 tbsp (45 ml) cold water

1 cup (250 ml) tahini

1 tsp salt

1 tsp lemon salt

ice

Garnish options: olive oil, lemon wedges, fried pine nuts, minced parsley, and/or sumac

Muhammara

UMM SAAD, Simlin

3 large red bell peppers

1 **round** khubz or pita bread, enough for **½ cup (80 g)** crumbs

1¼ **cups (275 g)** whole walnuts

3 tbsp (45 ml) pomegranate molasses

4 **cloves** garlic, minced

2 **tbsp** lemon juice

½ **tsp** paprika

½ **tsp** salt

½ **tsp** ground cumin

½ **tsp** cayenne

½ **tsp** Aleppo or black pepper

¼ **cup (60 ml)** olive oil

olive oil for drizzling

Garnish: whole walnuts, fresh mint leaves

Roast the peppers over a gas flame or in a 400°F (204°C) oven for 30-40 minutes or until charred on all sides. Discard the charred skin.

In a food processor, make fine breadcrumbs and set aside. Add the peppers and walnuts and grind until fine. Add the breadcrumbs and all the other ingredients except the olive oil. Then add the oil and pulse. If the mixture is too thick, add more oil and 2 tbsp (30 ml) of water.

Transfer to a plate, drizzle with olive oil, and garnish.

Muhammara is a smoky-sweet-spicy dip starring roasted red bell peppers, pomegranate molasses, and walnuts. Use whole walnuts for their oils. Incredible for ftoor or mezze, muhammara is superb in warm khubz as a sandwich.

Mutabbal

UMM HASSAN, Sayda

Betinjan (eggplant) is a regal fruit found in Zaatari's souks, holding court with fresh produce harvested by camp workers from local farms, and is used in many dishes as it is highly valued for its healthy properties. Loaded with fibre and anti-oxidants, baby eggplants are used for the famous makdous houran; large ones are used in mutabbal, soups, mains, and more.

There's nothing quite like the sensory experience of cooking betinjan in a Zaatari kitchen. To capture the same vibe in your kitchen, fire up your gas burner and prepare mutabbal over sweet chai and the songs of Fairuz or Umm Kulthum. You'll be mesmerized as the flames dance, releasing the smokiness of mutabbal into the air, carrying you away.

1 large eggplant (about 1 lb or 2.2 kg)

3 cloves garlic, minced

½ cup (125 ml) tahini

2 cups (500 ml) full-fat yogurt

2 tbsp lemon juice, freshly squeezed

1 tsp salt, or to taste

Garnish: olive oil, Italian parsley, mint, paprika, sumac, pomegranate seeds, chopped tomato, or walnuts

Grill the eggplant over an open flame on a gas grill until soft and charred, using tongs to turn it, or bake at 425°F (218° C) for 30 minutes or until soft. Let cool, then remove and discard the skin.

In a bowl, mash well with a fork. Add the remaining ingredients and mix well.

Place in a serving dish, cover, and chill in the refrigerator.

Before serving, use the back of a spoon to make a hole in the middle, or use fork tines to make a pattern around the edges. Drizzle olive oil over the top and garnish.

Enjoy with khubz and fresh vegetables.

The Artist

My name is Mohammed Amaari and art has always been in my blood. It's how I see the world and communicate, how I visually portray my inner experiences. I believe art is therapy that can heal war trauma and bring peace. I was born in Daraa in 1987 to a family of artists; my uncles are well-known graphic artists and calligraphists in Syria. I graduated from the fine arts conservatory in Damascus, specializing in contemporary art. Before the war, I participated in many art exhibitions in Syria. My paintings are often expressionistic in style, sometimes abstract too.

I am the director of Jasmine Necklace (Tawq Al Yasmeen), a group of artists who come together to create art initiatives for children living in Zaatari. I wanted to pass my artistic expertise on to the next generation. I envisioned cultivating educational and artistic skills to begin their healing from the trauma of war violence, displacement, early marriage, and child trafficking. Jasmine Necklace was inspired by what art means to me in life: that art is a message and art is for everyone.

Art can be made from anything; everything is a canvas. As a graphic artist, in camp I often paint on tent canvas or discarded cardboard, which are part of the art piece itself, using oils and sometimes mixed media of newspaper pages and pictures. My art tells stories, from ancient Syria to the current war, mixing people with symbolism, inspired by the beauty of Daraa, Damascus, and all of Syria; loss and hope as experienced by the people of camp, young and old. A great joy was illustrating the hundreds of handwritten recipes for this book. Using watercolours, I painted atop each page, rendering a graphic interpretation of the recipe, its ingredients, and the author's story.

My work has been shown in exhibitions in Jordan, the United Kingdom, the United States, and Switzerland, with some proceeds benefiting homeless children or those who are ill or burdened by life's traumas. To follow an exhibition, go to facebook.com/StampsOfHopeSyrianRefugeeArtists/ ❖

Jazmaz

UMM SANNA, Elmah

You may know it as Palestinian shakshuka, but in Zaatari, as in much of Syria, jazmaz, the morning essential of eggs poached in *tamatim* (tomatoes) and onion with spice is as pleasing to make as it is to eat. No wonder variations of jazmaz spread from Tunisia and the Magreb across the Ottoman Empire. Sometimes made with spinach, Zaatari purists prepare jazmaz as their fore-mothers did, on two-unit portable gas grills as they multi-task their mornings. Their secret is slowly simmering the tomatoes, preferably cherry tomatoes. Spices vary from chef to chef, with cheese such as feta sometimes crumbled on top of the poaching eggs, and hot sauces like *shattah* (p. 247) often served alongside. Bread is the only utensil needed. If you're short on time, scramble the eggs in the tomato mixture instead of waiting for them to bake.

For **SABANIKH (SPINACH) JAZMAZ**, substitute 1 lb (450 g) spinach (rinsed and squeezed until dry) for the tomatoes. Cook 3 chopped garlic cloves and ½ tsp each of ground coriander and salt with the onion (omitting other spices), add spinach, stir well, and cook for 5-7 minutes until wilted. Make wells for eggs and cook as below. To serve, drizzle with olive oil, and garnish with black pepper and chopped cilantro.

2.2 lb (1 kg) tomatoes

1 large onion

2 tbsp olive oil

3 tbsp (25 g) pine nuts

1 tsp each salt, ground cumin, sweet paprika, dried basil, dried mint

1 tbsp pomegranate molasses

¼ cup (60 ml) water

½ tsp black pepper

5 eggs

Garnish: cilantro, fresh mint

Chop the tomatoes into small pieces and mince the onion.

In a large pan, heat the oil over medium heat and sauté the onion until golden. Add the pine nuts and fry for 2–3 minutes until golden. Add the tomatoes, seasonings, pomegranate molasses, and water. Lower the heat and cook for 20–25 minutes, stirring occasionally until the mixture has thickened.

Make 5 wells in the mixture and drop an egg into each. Lower the heat, cover with lid and bake until eggs are cooked as desired. Alternatively, mix the eggs well in a bowl and add them to the tomato mixture, stirring until thickened and cooked through.

Garnish and serve.

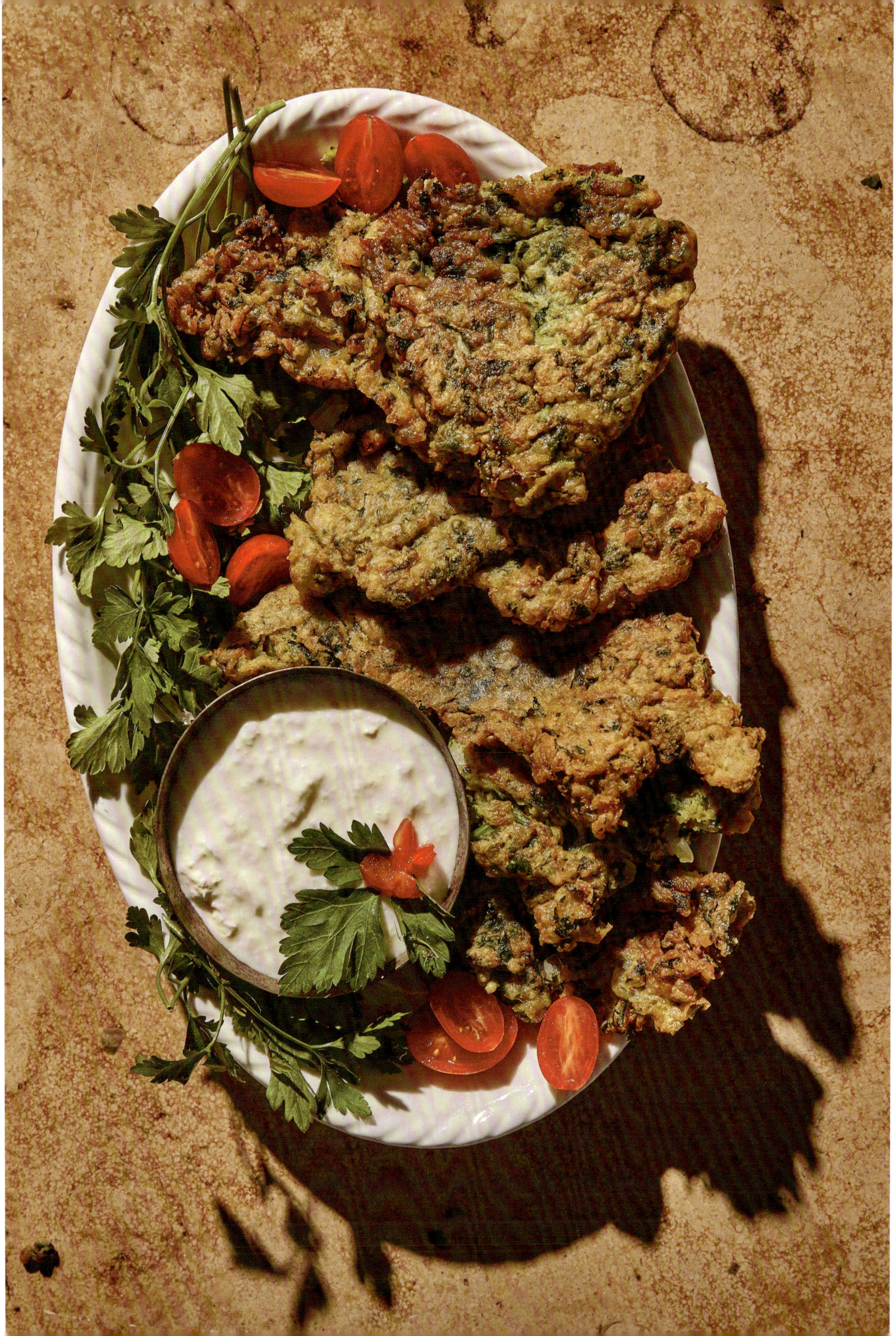

Ejjeh

UMM HAMEED, Busra

"Fall is when olive harvesting starts in the Houran," Umm Hameed explained. "Known in Syria as 'Mother of Orphans,' our Houran lands are one of the most beautiful places in the world, famous for its bountiful agriculture and ancient ruins. The olive tree is among the most important trees, and Hourani olive oil is viewed as more than just food, but as medicine for any sickness and for general wellness. We like to drink a spoonful of olive oil every morning.

"At the start of winter, people prepare fields for planting, spreading seeds like wheat, and lentils—the most famous pulse in Houran—and other grains like barley," she says. "With fresh air and pure, clean water, it's God's paradise on his earth. I wish that my kids, husband, and I return to Houran as soon as possible. My husband is in another Arab country. I believe Syria will gather us, as my kids need both me and him."

Umm Hameed had fresh eggs all year from her own chickens, as many people have chickens in Zaatari. Unlike in North America, where eggs are washed (which removes a protective membrane), according to Hameed, "Here eggs are best stored at room temperature. These eggy fritters with parsley are a favourite—simplicity at its best."

In a large bowl, combine the flour and water.

Mince the parsley and onion and mix it into the eggs, adding salt and pepper. Add the egg mixture to the flour and water, stirring well.

In a large frying pan, warm the oil over medium heat. Drop ⅓ cup (80 ml) of the batter, spacing 3 inches (7.5 cm) apart, and fry for 2-3 minutes, or until golden, on each side. The oil should reach half-way up the sides of the fritters. Remove to plate and repeat with remaining batter.

Enjoy with laban, tomatoes, cucumbers, and olives.

1.1 lb (500 g) flour

1 cup (250 ml) water

2 bunches parsley, rinsed and patted dry with paper towel or clean kitchen towel

1 large onion

5 eggs, beaten

½ tsp salt

¼ tsp black pepper

⅓ cup (80 ml) olive oil, or more as required for frying

Mfarakeh

UMM MOHAMMAD and UMM AHMAD,
as-Sanamyn and Jasim

3 tbsp (45 ml) olive oil

1 large onion, minced

2.2 lb (1 kg) potatoes, peeled, washed and dried, and diced to ¼–½" (6-12 cm)

½ tsp black pepper

½ tsp salt

½ tsp ground cumin

1 tsp Maggi powder

5 eggs, beaten

Garnish: olive oil, chopped cilantro, paprika

In a large frying pan over medium heat, fry the onion in the olive oil until slightly golden.

Add the potato and seasoning, mix well, and cook for 12-15 minutes or until the potatoes are soft inside and crispy outside.

Add the eggs and cook, stirring frequently for 3-5 minutes, until the eggs are set. Turn onto a serving platter and garnish.

At Zaatari, we sometimes add meat with onion, reducing the oil. For **Mfarakeh with zucchini**, a healthy variation in summer, substitute 4 diced zucchini for the potato. Lower the heat, cover, and cook for 15 minutes, until tender. Proceed with adding eggs and enjoy.

Variations of Mfarakeh are found in ninth- and twelfth-century Baghdadi-Damascene cookbooks. Mfarakeh means to crumble or scramble, and although usually it refers to eggs, this version uses potatoes, which were introduced to Greater Syria (also known as Balad al-Sham, comprising Syria, Jordan, Palestine, Lebanon and parts of Turkey) in the early twentieth century. The original Mfarakeh recipe differs, but its legend endures. For a more luxurious version, saffron can be used in place of cumin.

Fatayer with Kishk

UMM ALA'A, Nawa

"When I came to the camp," Umm Ala'a explained as we worked the *saj* cooker, "I had no job and was living on coupons. When I felt hungry, in my mind I smelled my mother's and grandmother's bread, especially fatayer with kishk, which we always made together. Food reminds everyone of life in Syria and the people we miss. I thought of making fatayer with kishk and this was my first attempt to cook it by myself. Then someone asked me to make it for him and gave me money. Inspired, I started selling it, creating a source of income for my children, which put me over the moon. Alhumdillah."

Fatayer filled with kishk and savoury tomatoes is a beloved Bedouin snack, a double-crust flatbread that takes much practice when baking on a saj (large disk-shaped pan—sometimes dome-shaped depending on the dish being cooked—heated over a gas flame) but can be easily made open-faced using an oven. Women and camp bakers use *karaa*, large, round canvas pillows often made from repurposed UNHCR tents, to flip the large, round fatayer onto the saj without burning one's hands or marring the shape of the finished product. For an easier open-faced version, use a cookie sheet in an oven, making either two large fatayer or 12-14 smaller ones. Leftover dough, wrapped well in plastic, can be refrigerated for several days or frozen.

Historically in Syria, fatayer was baked in a partially underground village taboon oven. Fold pieces of open-faced fatayer in half to mimic the authentic saj-baked version, and enjoy hot fatayer with laban and sweet chai with mint. This recipe will warm the hearts of eight or more.

Mana'eesh

UMM HUSSEIN, UMM ADHAM, and UMM NAWAL,
Tasil, Buser al-Harir, and al-Mansoura

Mana'eesh are hand-size savoury pastries or flatbreads sold in souks throughout the Arab world. At Zaatari they are made to order in small batches by hand and topped with all sorts of fillings. Traditionally baked using dough scraps in the village communal taboon oven, mana'eesh are prepared for children's school lunches in the WFP camp kitchen. Girls riff on the usual fillings by making small pizzas topped with tomato sauce, vegetables, and cheese. According to 12-year-old Sewar, the Italians learned about pizza from the Ottomans, who had spread delicious Syrian mana'eesh throughout the empire.

Mana'eesh dough is softer and thinner than the dough used to make fatayer with kishk due to the addition of fat in the form of olive oil, and a higher ratio of water to flour. Umm Hussein learned how to prepare mana'eesh in Tasil from her mother and husband, both pastry chefs: "While the dough is rising, we prepare oil and zaatar, jibneh, muhammara (p. 32), spinach, meat, and other fillings. After 1 hour the dough is ready to prepare the pies. As they bake, we make chai (sweet black tea)." Nodding, Umm Adham and Umm Nawal added: "We are Hourani people. In winter we like to eat them around the heater. Come join us any time!"

DOUGH

2 cups (500 ml) warm water

1 tbsp sugar

1 tbsp dry yeast

1 tbsp salt

6 tbsp (90 ml) olive oil

5 cups (625 g) flour

In a large bowl, dissolve the sugar in the water and add the yeast. Leave it for 10 minutes or until the yeast bubbles. Add the salt, olive oil, and add the flour gradually, mixing well to form a soft, smooth dough, adding more water if needed. Turn onto a lightly floured board and knead for 15 minutes. Cover and let rise for 1 hour or until doubled in bulk. Prepare shapes, add the toppings (below), and let rest for 5 minutes. Bake at 450°F (232°C) on cookie sheet for about 10-12 minutes, until golden.

ZAATAR TOPPING

½ cup (70 g) zaatar

⅔ cup (160 ml) olive oil

Mix zaatar with olive oil. Shape the dough into 2-inch (5 cm) balls and roll each ball until it is ⅛ inch (3 mm) thick. Dimple the dough using your fingers.

Place on a baking sheet. Dimple the dough using your fingers and top with 2 tbsp (30 ml) of the mixture. To prevent the zaatar from burning, spritz with water. If desired, top with pomegranate seeds.

MUHAMMARA TOPPING

Shape the dough into 2-inch (5 cm) balls and roll each ball until it is ¼ inch (1 cm) thick. Place on a baking sheet.

Dimple the dough using your fingers and top each circle with 2-3 tbsp (30-45 ml) of muhammara using the back of a spoon to spread the muhammara to dough edges.

JIBNEH TOPPING

2.2 lb (1 kg) chopped Akkawi or Nabulsi cheese

1 bunch parsley, chopped

2 tsp (10 ml) ghee

Mix chopped Akkawi or Nabulsi cheese (types of Syrian and Palestinian cheese; goat cheese and mozzarella can be substituted), with parsley, chopped, and ghee. Shape the dough into 3-inch (8 cm) balls and press into oblong boat shapes. Divide the filling evenly.

SABANIKH FILLING

2.2 lb (1 kg) spinach

1 lb (450 g) onion

1 lb (450 g) ground lamb

1 tsp salt

olive oil

Rinse spinach and pat dry with paper towel so the spinach isn't soggy when baking. Chop and place in a large bowl.

Mince onion and fry it with ground lamb until the meat is no longer pink. When cool, add it to the spinach along with the salt.

Shape the dough into 3-inch (8 cm) balls, add 2 tbsp (30 ml) to centres, and fold in 3 sides, overlapping to create triangles with small center openings. Drizzle with olive oil.

Coach Najma

I am Coach Najma, "Coach Star," twenty-five years old, from a family of four sisters and five younger brothers. I was living at home in Daraa when the war started, ripping life apart, changing everything. I loved high school, where I played football, but left because of the war. In March 2013 I came to Zaatari Camp with my mother and siblings; my father was detained in Syria and is still missing. Life was very difficult: traumatized by war, living in a tent amidst the heat and dust, no breadwinner to support us. I decided to look for work. An organization required a beauty salon supervisor: my first job. I felt happy and my psychological condition improved. I married and had two beautiful little girls who also love football. I continued working because I enjoyed it so much.

Life changed completely in 2019 when I participated in table tennis training with Peace and Sport, a visiting international organization at the Blumont Center. I was hired as a coach in June 2020 and table tennis became my favourite sport. I trained in more sports and coaching, every day feeling deeper renewed hope. As a coach, I meet new people inside and outside camp, building strong relationships with children and parents. I help change society, conveying values of love, cooperation, and teamwork, repairing the damage caused by war.

Every year, over three hundred and fifty people participate in our Peace and Sport programs, including children with disabilities. Many compete nationally and internationally, winning titles and trophies, including from the International Table Tennis Federation (ITTF). Girls especially love table tennis, and their smiles and laughter from learning new skills together is my energy. All our players do better at school and negotiating life; sports build self-esteem and social skills and increase one's focus and ability to set and achieve goals. Peace and Sport pays for the coaches, uniforms, and equipment, and supports competitions. During COVID-19, we used WhatsApp and social media to deliver our programs. Players sent videos of their practice for the coach's advice in addition to synchronous engagement. Mothers said this was vital to their children's mental and physical health during the lockdowns when everyone had to stay inside the small caravans and do school online too. Our coaches and players promoted safety by delivering masks, sanitizer, and health messages.

From an early age, I felt daunting responsibility to support my family, without the benefit of finishing school, consumed by war trauma and life's difficulties, exasperated by cultural traditions that prevent women from working. Peace and Sport changed my life. My dream is to return to Syria and complete my studies, help children, and apply my experiences to rebuilding Syria. I wish to continue in sports, reach a global level through my work. I thank Peace and Sport and the ITTF for supporting me and our Zaatari community. ✦✕✦

Taking a Jawleh with Mohammed

"Yallah, let's go—we're ready." Mohammed and friends beam shyly, funnily, from bicycles adorned Arabi-style with fringes and tassels, back seats reserved for ferrying goods and passengers. Bicycles are the primary transport here, and this is a treat—a 5.3-kilometre square *jawleh* (tour) around camp. We're ready, my visitors and I, excited to explore camp with the speed and freedom of wheels, led by teenage boys.

Long accustomed to walking or driving in UN vehicles, I love the independence and opportunities that bicycles offer. However, only males ride bicycles, with females as passengers; girls and women covet this freedom and potential. Some rode bikes in Syria, others learned pedalling at community centres in the camp.

Before 2020, Mohammed explains, they'd start their mornings at the base-camp fence, using the Wi-Fi and tower strength to post messages for their families to relatives in Syria, Lebanon, Turkey, and everywhere. They'd Google news to share, have fun watching sports videos, and playing

games. Now, connectivity is stronger across camp, so posting messages or going online is possible almost anywhere.

We wrap our shemaghs (Arab headscarves) against the desert sun and speed to the UNHCR Innovation Lab to check out hydroponics—vegetables incubated in mattresses and other ingenuities. Inside, girls are preparing robotics for a national contest. I smile, aware of their ingenuity from years of youth co-design sessions on robotic helpers—robots to assist with housework, homework, transportation. One of my favourites was "peace robots" by a young girl: two robots holding hands for peace. At the Noor Hussein centre for people with disabilities, I chat with the audiologist about the need for hearing-aid batteries and a project we'd like to start to support children with autism and their caregivers. I'm overjoyed to see an old friend working at the centre. Paralyzed by a sniper in Syria, thirty-year-old Younis uses a wheelchair and is waiting for news of his application for asylum abroad. He and his widowed mother will go together. It's my last time seeing Younis: a fatal heart attack, I learn sadly on Facebook.

Access to the water tower in district 4 is guarded, but our visitors' smiles earn camp panoramas, with the sun still setting low. Over selfies, Mohammed points out the landmarks and tells us how camp has grown since 2012, including the road construction, electricity, water, and waste management work by ACTED and Oxfam that employs many people in camp. Mohammed was only twelve when his family left Syria, but he has vivid memories. He and his friends share stories about camp life, supporting their families, and dreams for the future. All want to return to Syria, with ambitions ranging from attending university to running the family business. Sports, especially football, are their passion; everyone wants to play professionally. Their hero, Cristiano Ronaldo, inspires the most popular haircut for boys in camp. They reminisce about the time Ronaldo and other famous players visited. Then attention turns to the visitors, with questions about their thoughts on football and the world. Eyeing me, they ask why I'm not wearing hijab.

It's a short hop over bumpy paths, between caravans, Shami goats, and boys shooting marbles, to Questscope—an NGO dedicated to supporting livelihoods and culture. Amidst

Mural by Mohammed Jokhader.

Mural by Mohammed Jokhader

Sabah al-Khair, As-Salamu Alaykum, and *Marhaba*, coffee is brewing and there are olives, majdoulah and shelal (Syrian braided string cheeses), and saman from Daraa.

We catch up on news with the librarians and trainers while the boys play football, admire each other's sneakers, and listen to live music. As eleven a.m. approaches, our path is Market Street. Along the way, we chat with more librarians and trainers at Relief International, Lutheran World, and Blumont. The librarians give us the pulse of camp, recommend books for purchase, and encourage the boys to attend the library. They highlight the Jane Eyre book club at Relief International and the al-Hakawati club at Norwegian Refugee Council.

Islam, fifteen, greets the librarians with hand slaps and recites his latest poem. In the background, the adhan resounds across Zaatari's mosques. The boys stop to pray.

On Market Street, over falafel and people-watching—them watching and being amused by us—Mohammed points to the ring road and the desert. Here, caravans are spaced further apart and doves circle from rooftops, trained to return home. As in other districts, camp artists have painted the caravans by theme—education, water, and so forth—as well as extraordinary wall murals on NGO buildings. We weave through districts 8 and 9, the Bedouin community. Boys leave us for school and others join in, excited to have guests. Near the Mercy Corps playground, we stop for chai and laughter with families I've known for years. As lunchtime nears and one boy peels off to bring bread to his mother, Abu Hussein insists we join them for *oozy*—spiced chicken over rice with fried nuts.

Bellies full, we cycle the desert road, past families barbecuing, and take photos of the massive solar panels that power camp. The entire Ring Road is a football pitch, with pickup games dotting the route. At the Norwegian Refugee Council (NRC), which provides essential services at three centres, including tailoring and upcycling, over chai we watch librarians wearing the Syrian storyteller's red tarboosh build passion for reading with young girls. Next is district 2, to visit the imam and learn that his school needs more books. We weave to a Blumont Service Center, an old pink communal kitchen from 2012 repurposed to support everyday needs. I love how the pure, unadulterated heart of the camp beats in these places, where life is simple and neighbours connect. Over heartfelt greetings we discuss needs and family news.

We jump on our bikes, but quickly stop: Mohammed signals Ahmed, driving his father's donkey cart with boys kicking a football alongside. With the day's vegetables sold,

Ahmed is enjoying a favourite pastime and our visitors climb on board and pass caravans with lush gardens and fountains. They're amazed by Syrians' ability to grow olive and loofah trees, fragrant Damask roses, jasmine, sunflowers, herbs, and vegetables in the desert. Outside Blumont, young girls play dress-up—all princesses. Inside, a European delegation has just left: we can still feel the energy of girls' singing and a karate demonstration; everyone is here. Shown the art galleries, our visitors buy paintings, jewellery, and tote bags made from upcycled UNHCR canvas tents.

With the sun getting low, we leave the bikes and walk along the Shams Élysées, admiring the wedding dress shops, purchasing spices and hot mana'eesh. The work week is winding down. I know it's Thursday by the number of boys leading sheep for henna party feasts and donkey carts ferrying large red velvet wedding chairs, light towers, and sound systems. I wish we could stay for dancing and celebration, but our guests must depart. At base camp we thank Mohammed and friends for a beautiful day and hope to see them soon.

Art in Tandem

Love brings people together, but so does art. My name is Riham al-Zamel and I came to Zaatari from Inkhil at age fourteen in March 2013. Drawing was my pastime, along with sewing, beauty, and Arabic font (calligraphy): an escape from daily life, my dreams for the future. In 2017 I married Iyad Sabbagh, an artist and calligrapher from as-Sanamyn, who opened my creativity, teaching me oil painting and acrylics.

Iyad began painting at age seven, self-taught in oils and watercolours. His fame in Arabic font—a highly specialized art for writing Quranic verse—began at age thirteen; people say his gift is from Allah. Iyad came to camp in April 2013, painting on tent canvas inside his family's tent using colouring pens brought from Syria, then at NGOs and painting murals outside. He taught calligraphy and drawing to youth inside his tent, enabling them to sell their art and support their families. Iyad's canvases and murals of our people and the effects of war have been shown on CNN and in the *Guardian* and the *New York Times* as well as in galleries in Europe and the United States.

As artists we are more than husband and wife. We paint, creating energy together, and hold exhibitions to sell our work. I love my husband because he taught me painting, encouraging my own expression and style. For me, art is therapy: I connect the past, present, and future through my gaze as a young woman, now blessed by Allah with three children. I love painting so much. Income from my art is mine to buy whatever I want. We wish to travel and open our own studio. ❖

TIGER Girls and Zaatari Camp Libraries

I have many soft spots at Zaatari. Two gems are TIGER (These Inspiring Girls Enjoy Reading) and the international, award-winning Zaatari Camp Libraries—the world's first refugee-run library system. TIGER, for girls twelve to seventeen, began in 2015 as a UNHCR initiative with Blumont, UNHCR's implementation partner. Information and fabulous videos are available online, but we share stories from TIGER and their trainers (due to TIGER's overwhelming success, there are now Inspiring Guys as well).

Wearing dark blue vests with a fiery orange tiger emblazoned on the back, TIGER Girls radiate energy. I recognize them anywhere by how they carry themselves, with pride and purpose, their internal glow, their *je ne sais quoi*.

One of my earliest TIGER memories, from spring 2016, is of enjoying ftoor after a workshop on designing technology for camp. As we ate outdoors, the girls introduced me to *makdous houran* (stuffed, pickled baby eggplants) and the dishes they made. Their mothers' sous chefs, they were proficient at making fattoush and other salads, potato, pizza, *bamya* (okra), rice with green beans, and sweets, including "cake"—the basic sweet every Syrian girl first learns to make. I knew from being in their homes how well they had mastered knife skills, and about their attention to detail, such as washing rice three times, making dough, using spices, measuring ingredients, and garnishing plates. In their hands, a simple fruit salad was a tapestry of colour, shape, and taste.

As we scooped and ate, teacher Umm Alaa explained that TIGER was a social initiative to support girls' education and to deal with early marriage, a complex and interconnected problem. The girls jumped in, explaining that many were absent from school not because families didn't value girls' education or disliked the curriculum, but because girls had to help at home with siblings, cooking, and cleaning (without modern conveniences), and also because of peer bullying and harassment by boys outside the school; road conditions, distance, and weather; and early marriage. Some families marry their daughters before the legal age of eighteen for reasons of financial security, tradition and more. Marriage means quitting school, assuming household responsibilities in your young husband's family home, and likely becoming a young mother. The community sought a solution with UNHCR, and TIGER was born.

Their holistic approach includes the girls' families. Hundreds of girls have participated, with graduates returning as teachers. The program focuses on Arabic-English fluency and integrates girls into society through social projects that enable them to speak their minds and creatively use technology and design-thinking techniques. Because they are innately curious and sports-loving, their many projects include writing, weaving, supporting people with disabilities, recycling, cultural preservation, hydroponics, coding, robotics, and COVID-19 support—including the Mask House at Blumont, where over twelve hundred masks were made daily in 2019-2021. The 2016 "Love Coats" project led by Professor Helen Storey left an indelible memory. Storey noted that the girls didn't have warm coats for winter, so they repurposed UNHCR blankets as gorgeous coats for each other, sewn with fancy trims, then modelled them exuberantly for their families in a fashion show.

The organization empowers girls to step into and live their dreams. They are young activists, leaders of tomorrow. Like their mascot, the tiger, they are fearless. This comes across especially when they are chatting about daily life; however, their stories are private due to cultural norms and UNHCR's protection mandate. Few outsiders hear Ghazal and Najah recount gathering their friends together to walk in unity for the start of school at eight a.m. and then home at twelve-thirty p.m. "No one will separate us. With unity there's power. If we were just individuals, we would be weak. After school, we help each other with house chores and then study together."

TIGER Girls nod as Latifa speaks about their friend who left TIGER and school for two years because she got married, believing her future was in marriage. "After many problems led to divorce, we all talked and she returned to TIGER, back to school, and is a strong student. We are very happy she returned to us—this is a wonderful success story." Amidst wide smiles, clapping and *zaghrouta* (trilling), the girls added that getting married is every little girl's dream, a fairy tale where you are the princess, with a giant party, gold, and a beautiful dress. But not every marriage story ends happily ever after, and girls today have different dreams: of education and careers.

In 2023, many TIGER Girls are among the 300 Zaatari young people attending local universities on scholarship or through private funding, studying nursing, medicine, engineering, and computer science. More Zaatari youth qualify for university but cannot attend due to financial hardship. Students struggle with purchasing textbooks, while fluctuating, weak Internet and electricity rationing make it difficult to attend online lectures, work on projects, and charge devices.

Zaatari Camp Libraries (ZCL) plays a vital role in supporting students and all of Zaatari. Like TIGER Girls, who are major users of ZCL, the librarians are fearless. They had no exposure to public libraries in Syria and are untrained in librarianship, yet they viscerally understand the value of knowledge, literacy, and reading. Their mission, *Iqra'a* (read), is the first word of the Holy Quran.

In 2015 I came across a library caravan opening at a Blumont community centre. Sleuthing revealed eleven more across camp; the librarians connected, and ZCL began, run from six NGOs: Norwegian Refugee Council, Blumont, Lutheran World Foundation, Questscope, Nour Al Hussein Foundation, and Relief International.

Winner of the 2021 International Joy of Reading Award, ZCL is unique because it is run by camp residents who work as librarians—not NGO staff or external visitors. With a limited budget and resources, the librarians draw on their Syrian heritage to design innovative programs and services that rival those of public libraries. ZCL offers book clubs, writing clubs, cultural preservation, story time, literacy initiatives, a readers' advisory, Internet access, and community outreach. Being a Zaatari librarian calls for much creativity: sourcing books outside camp is challenging, requiring legwork. Titles may not be available in Arabic; high-quality books are expensive, particularly translations and literacy workbooks for children; and the library budget is severely limited. As is the norm in Arab and other countries, all books and magazines must have political, religious, and cultural content approved by national authorities, so some titles are prohibited. There is not a single bookshop.

The libraries have different hours, facilities, resources, and strengths. Blumont's libraries offer weekend and evening hours to support university students and daytime workers, and have strong early education and children's programs thanks to materials donated by the Kalimat Foundation. Questscope supports marginalized youth and Arab culture by collaborating with experts in different fields; its librarians run book, poetry, and writing clubs. In winter 2020, thanks to an anonymous donation, Questscope piloted the camp's first Kindle/e-book club

Relief International has three libraries and leads ZCL's effort to develop a shared, cloud-hosted catalogue and circulation system while protecting people's personally identifiable information (PII). While PII protection is of universal concern, it is vitally important for war refugees and is governed by UN regulations. The system will support collection development, build staff technical competency, and help users locate books across camp. Relief International also offers teen book clubs—to avert chronic book shortages, stapled copies are made.

The NRC library focuses on early literacy and education. The librarians adapt al-Hakawati, traditional oral Syrian storytelling, using stories by Syrian children, illustrated and published by NRC. They place the storyteller's *tarboosh* (red hat) on a child who wishes to read, to ensure individualized attention. LWF and Nour Al Hussein, the newest ZCL members, have small collections of books and plans for growth.

The librarians use Society Boxes to further serve people. Akin to a little free library, it is a wooden box with a Plexiglas door from which people take and donate needed items. Placed strategically across camp, the boxes contain books, games for early literacy, drawing pens, reading glasses, toys, playing cards, *msbahah* (prayer beads), finjeen cups, fabric and trims, stands for mobile phones, small tools, and so on. To help people understand the concept, a camp artist painted a mural (above right) with "Iqra'a" ("read") and Surah 92 (al-Layl 92 "The Night") from the Holy Quran: "Never will you attain the good [reward] until you spend [in the way of Allah] from that which you love. And whatever you spend—indeed, Allah is knowing of it."

Librarians partner with beauty salons—where women with children spend hours preparing for events—providing books and magazines about beauty, fashion, food, health, and parenting as well as materials for children. Also targeted are barber shops, coffee shops, and the maternity hospital.

The Internet safety project protects at-risk groups, especially women and girls who are less experienced with mobile phones and social media and are vulnerable to harassment by predators. Existing media and information literacy programs are Western-based; ZCL's program uses the Quran and Arab culture to guide privacy protection, information sharing, and fact checking. Many Syrians are targeted by online scammers who proffer fake employment, immigration, and other opportunities, as well as disinformation about amnesties, return of property, and military conscription in Syria.

Zaatari librarians dream of creating a central branch, Syrian-style: with a fountain; madafa (salon), with Arabic cushions for playing *Tawilat al-Zahr* (backgammon) and reading over Turkish coffee and drinks; a children's area; a student study area; a computer learning and homework centre; tool-lending collections; and sewing machines, fabric, and apparel. For these aspirations to become reality, financial support is needed—and books by the thousands.

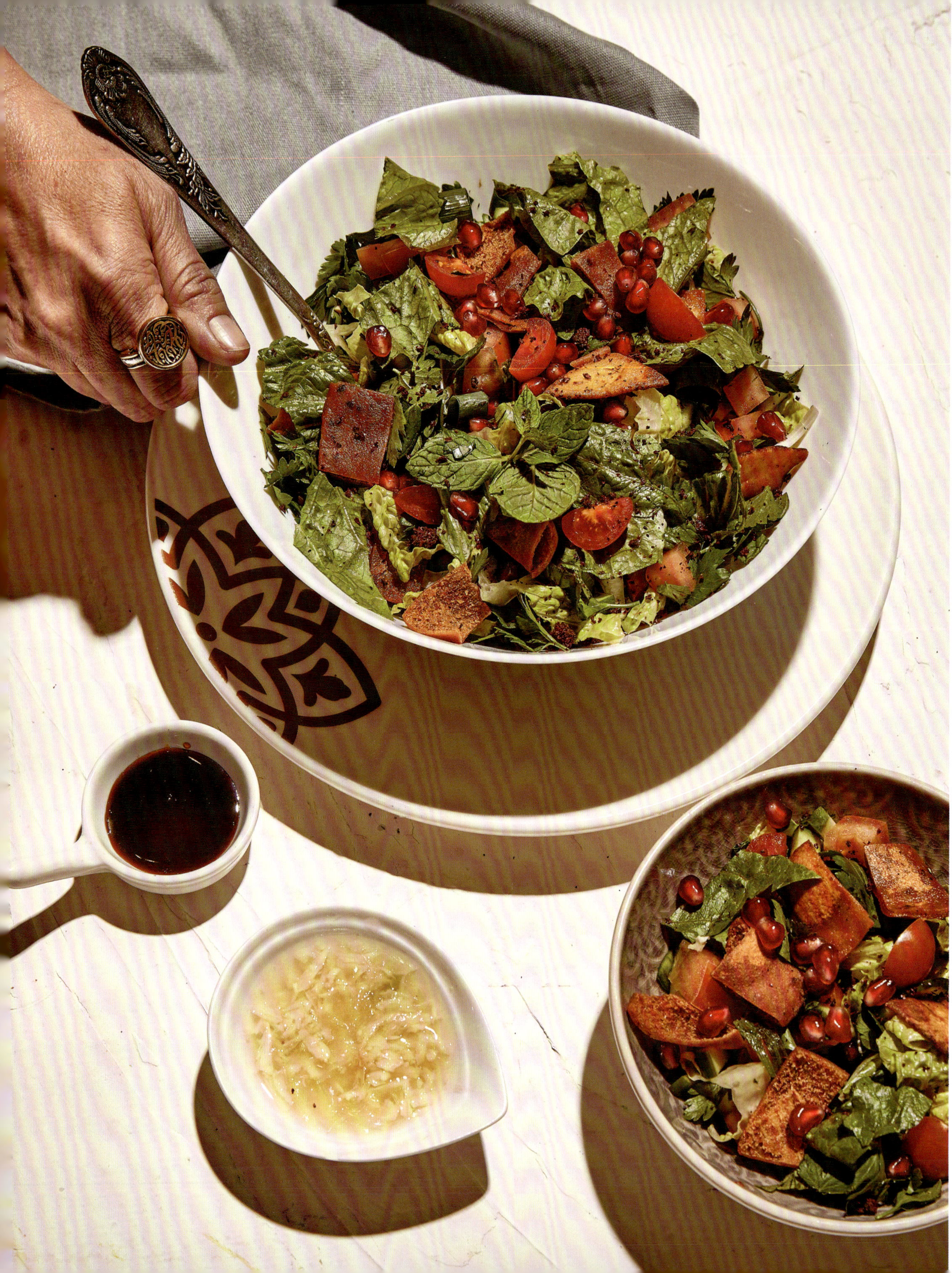

Fattoush

SADIRA (age 14), Busra

Fattoush is a farmer's *sulta* (salad), a gorgeous medley of vegetables and herbs topped with fried bread. Mint, pomegranate, parsley, and sumac star in fattoush. Like most salads, fattoush can vary from household to household. For example, some home cooks add purslane (a type of succulent, slightly acidic) for its textural and flavour components, while others may omit the coriander altogether.

❖

Tear the bread into small pieces and fry in hot oil, turning to brown both sides. Remove from the oil, drain, and sprinkle with a little salt.

Place the vegetables, herbs, sumac, and pomegranate seeds in a large bowl.

In a large glass, whisk the lemon juice with the salt, garlic, and molasses. Add the oil and mix well. Adjust to taste. Add to the salad and toss. Arrange in a large dish, garnish with fried bread, sumac, more pomegranate seeds and lemon wedges, and enjoy.

BETINJAN VARIATION

3 eggplants

1 tsp salt

oil

To make eggplant fattoush, peel and chop eggplants into 2" (5 cm) pieces, sprinkle with salt, let sit for 1 hour, and pat dry.

Fry until golden, drain, mash, and add to salad.

2 khubz (or pita bread)

olive oil for frying

salt

2 cucumbers, halved and cut into ½-inch (1.3-cm) slices

1 cup (200 g) chopped cherry tomatoes, or 2 tomatoes, chopped

1 red or green pepper, seeded and chopped

½ head romaine lettuce, chopped

1 cup (25 g) chopped cilantro

1 cup (25 g) chopped mint

1 cup (25 g) chopped parsley

3 green onions, sliced

2 tbsp sumac

1 cup (150 g) pomegranate seeds

⅓ cup (80 ml) fresh lemon juice

1 tsp salt

3 cloves garlic, minced

2 tbsp pomegranate molasses

⅓ cup (80 ml) olive oil

Garnish: sumac, lemon wedges

Jarjeer Sulta

RAGHAD (age 14), Khirbet Ghazaleh

3 cups (75 g) arugula

1 cup (25 g) fresh mint leaves

1 cup (150 g) pomegranate seeds

2 bell peppers or tomatoes, thinly sliced

3 tbsp (45 ml) lemon juice

½ tsp salt

½ tsp dried mint

¼ cup (60 ml) olive oil

Garnish: sliced carrot rounds and lemon

In a large dish, combine the arugula, fresh mint, pomegranate seeds, and bell pepper or tomato.

In a small bowl, whisk together the lemon juice, salt, dried mint, and olive oil. Pour the dressing over the salad and toss gently. Serve in a large bowl on a platter with the sides garnished.

This beautiful salad starring *jarjeer* (arugula, a.k.a. rocket) takes minutes to prepare and is the accompaniment for most dishes. Dried mint in the dressing is the secret to this refreshing salad.

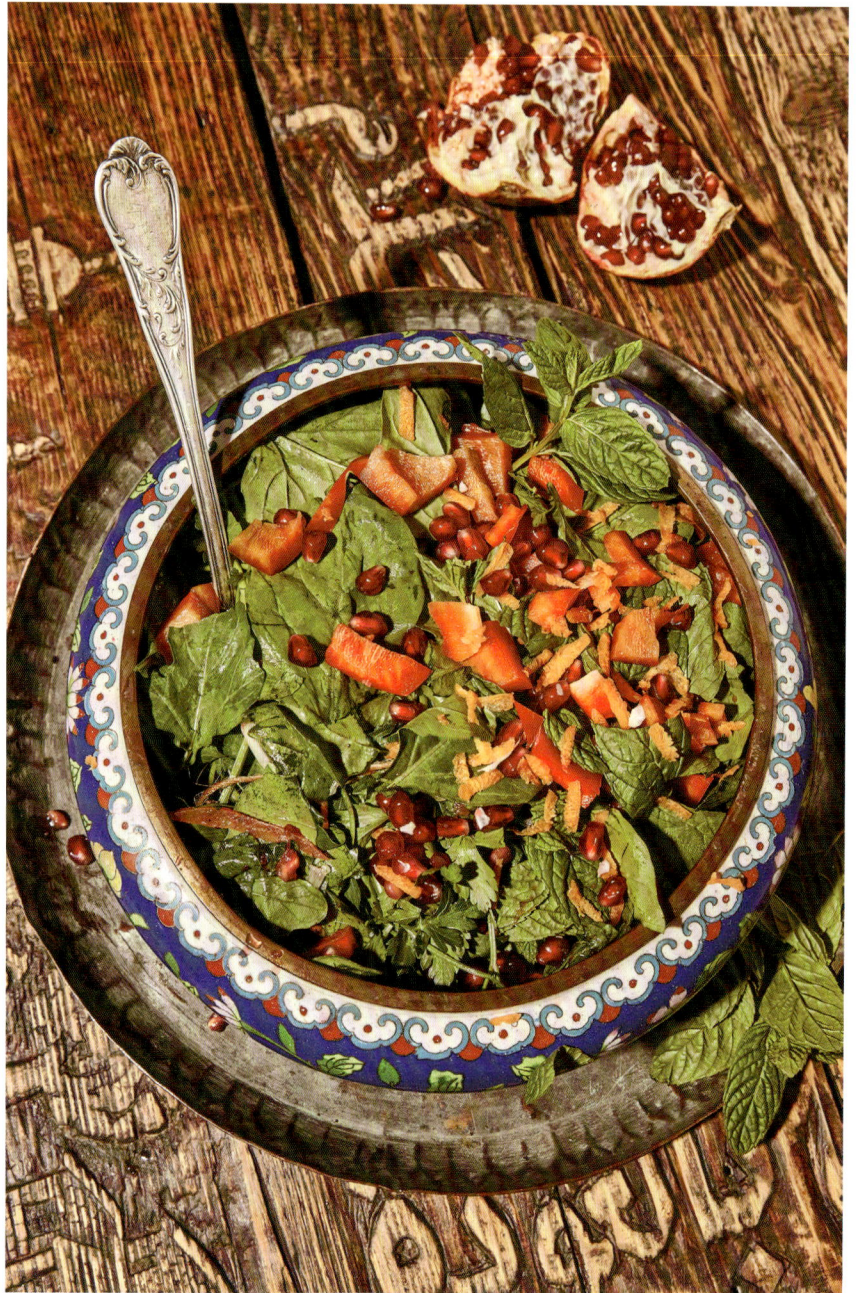

Laban Sulta

MAIS (age 15), al-Hrak

This simple sulta of yogurt and cucumber, like green salads, is a fresh side accompaniment. We serve laban salad during summer and it is wonderful with warm bread, lamb, and hot dishes.

2 cloves garlic

1½ tsp salt

1 tbsp fresh mint, or **2 tsp** dried mint

2 cups (250 g) sliced and quartered cucumber (peeled and drained)

3 cups (750 ml) full-fat yogurt

Garnish: olive oil, mint, grated cucumber

Mash the garlic with the salt with a mortar and pestle, and combine it with the mint and cucumber. Add the yogurt and adjust the seasoning—it should be a good balance of mint, salt, and garlic.

Serve chilled, drizzled with olive oil and garnished with mint and grated cucumber.

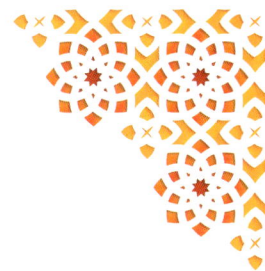

My Dreams

I am Sadira, a TIGER Girl. I live with my parents, two brothers, and sister. My youngest brother was born in Zaatari when we arrived in 2013; I was seven years old.

We used to live in peace, go to school, and to the market with my mother. Then the events started. I became afraid to go to school and to go shopping for fear of our lives.

I heard my father say to my mother that Jordan is a calm and beautiful country. I liked the words and told my father, "Take us to Jordan, because I fear that if we stay here, I will lose our family or myself." We left in the morning and travelled six days to reach the Jordanian border and camp on March 6, 2013. I heard from my father that, due to war conditions and lack of water, electricity, and gas in Syria, our people were leaving in large numbers. One night we saw two to three thousand refugees enter Zaatari.

At the reception tent we received blankets and slept there. On the second day we went to our new home (tent). I felt frustrated. My father said, "Be patient, my daughter, because the future is ahead of you," and this is how life began. Every day I went with my father to get bread from the distribution centre; every fifteen days we went to get our food rations.

I used to ask my father, "When will this suffering end?" Life was difficult and educational opportunities were few. My father and I went to the school, where it took six days to register because of the large number of refugees. Now I attend TIGER Girls after school, and it has changed everything for me. I dream of becoming a doctor, of my brother becoming an engineer, of my sister becoming an aerospace engineer. These are our days in the Zaatari Camp; hope is here. ❖

Dove of Hope
SAFA

Destiny sent me the dove of hope
To pull me from my shell
I wonder how it will fly me up
With all the feelings I have.
But it doesn't matter
O dove, just keep trying
And I will remain like an idiot
Staring absurdly at emptiness.

بعثَ إليَّ القدرُ حمامةَ الأملِ
حتى تنتشلني من قوقعتي
تُرى كيفَ ستحملني
وأنا الممتلئةُ بكلِّ هَذهِ المشاعرِ ؟؟!!
لايهم حاولي أيتها الحمامة
وأنا سأبقى كالحمقاءِ
أنظرُ ببلاهةٍ للفراغِ .
أنظرُ ببلاهةٍ

Batata

RANEEM (age 14), al-Musayfira

"I make batata for our breakfast. Sometimes I add a little onion. It is very easy, but you must watch the pot and keep young children away."

4.4 lb (2 kg) potatoes

2 tbsp olive or vegetable oil

1 tsp salt

Garnish: parsley or cilantro

Wash and dry the potatoes using a cloth or paper towels. Peel the potatoes and chop into ½-inch (1.3-cm) pieces.

Heat the oil in a large skillet or Dutch oven. Add the potatoes and salt and fry until golden.

Transfer to a serving dish and garnish with love.

Bamya

KHADIJEH (age 13), Jabab

1 lb (450 g) okra

olive oil, for frying

1 large onion, chopped

1 green pepper, chopped

5 cloves garlic, chopped

1 lb (450 g) lamb or beef, cut into bite-size pieces (optional)

4 tomatoes, chopped

1 tbsp baharat (seven-spice mix)

1 tbsp pomegranate molasses

salt and pepper, to taste

Garnish: cilantro or parsley

Wash the whole okra, then dry with a cloth or paper towels. Chop into

"I love *bamya* (okra) because it is delicious and healthy. This is one of the first meals I learned to cook by myself. You can omit the meat. We serve bamya with rice for ghada'."

1½-inch (3.8-cm) pieces. In a large pot over medium heat, fry in olive oil for 5 minutes, remove them from the oil and set aside.

Add more oil to the pot, if needed, and fry the onion and green pepper until fragrant and softened (3-4 minutes).

Add the garlic and fry for 1 minute. If using meat, add the pieces and brown for 3-5 minutes. Add the tomatoes, 1½ cups (375 ml) of water, and the spice. Bring to a boil, then lower the heat and simmer until reduced—about 1 hour. Add the okra and simmer until hot. Season with salt and pepper.

Garnish and serve with plain rice.

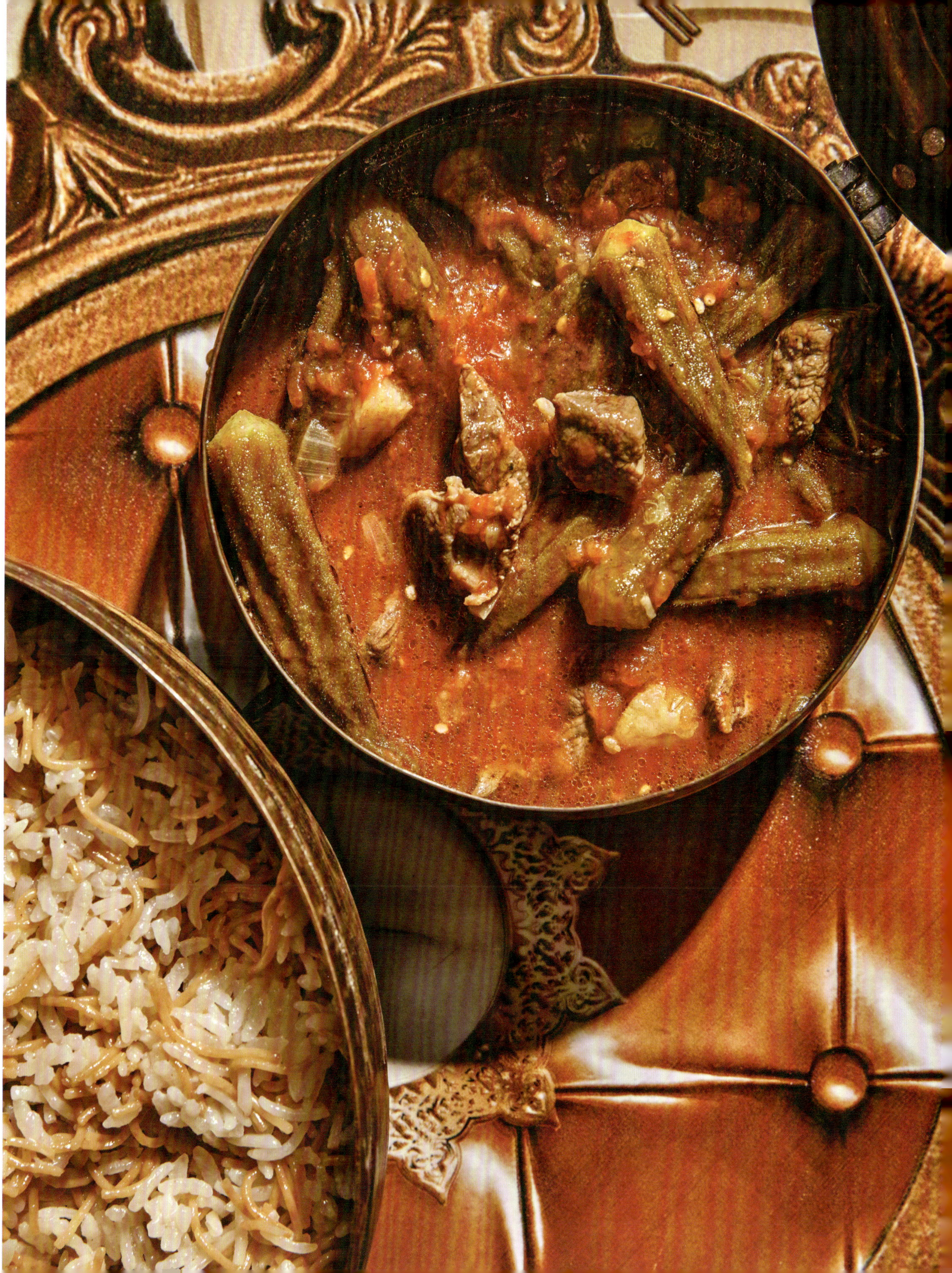

Fasula khadra wa bandura

HALA (age 14), al-Muzairib

2.2 lb (1 kg) green beans, washed and trimmed

1 tsp Maggi powder

2.2 lb (1 kg) tomatoes

1 small onion, finely chopped

¼ cup (60 ml) olive oil

9 oz (¼ kg) ground beef or lamb

½ tsp Aleppo pepper

1 tsp salt

¾ tsp dried mint

Chop the green beans into ¾-inch (1.9-cm) pieces.

Remove the skins from the tomatoes by blanching them in boiling water for 45-60 seconds. Plunge the tomatoes into ice water (to stop the cooking) and slip off the skins. Peel, and finely chop the tomatoes.

Put the green beans in a large pot, add enough water to cover. Add Maggi, and bring to a boil, then simmer for 5-6 minutes over low heat. Remove from heat and drain.

In a large pot over medium heat, fry the onion in the oil until soft. Add the meat (if using) and brown it. Cover, lower the heat, and simmer for 10 minutes.

Stir in the tomato, then add the green beans, pepper, salt, and mint, stirring for 2 minutes. Cover and simmer for 10 minutes before serving with rice or rice-vermicelli (from Sheikh el-Mahshi recipe p. 105).

Fasula khadra wa bandura features green beans with tomatoes and ground meat. Hala, who loves to cook, says "This is the first dish I learned to make from my mother and in Daraa we used green beans grown on our farm. With meat optional, it is a healthy dish to serve with fragrant rice."

Camp of Hope

We are the girls betrayed by time, our childhoods stolen by war, driven to a desert forsaken of all creatures—humans and animals alike. As little girls we felt the suffering and understood the bad situations around us. People called us "refugees." The word hurt a lot. We were just people inhabiting an empty desert, looking for safety. It was a difficult life.

We've lived half of our young lives in Zaatari. Much has improved since the beginning, especially livelihoods, schools, and centres for education and social engagement. But for us there are difficulties that only girls and women understand.

Our safety is in TIGER. We are TIGER Girls. Our TIGER trainers live in Zaatari and empower us by building our education and personality. From them and from each other we learn how to face problems in the camp and the world. We learn how to find and use our voices, manage stress, deal with harassment, take part in meaningful initiatives for our community, and, most importantly, how to follow our dreams and ambitions.

TIGER teaches us not to let anyone destroy girls' dreams—if families and society don't accept girls' dreams, then their dreams have no value. Family is important in the life of a girl. If families understand our situations, then they can help us achieve our dreams as TIGER Girls, our innocent dreams on behalf of every Syrian girl.

We say to ourselves, "Allah won't forget anyone among his creation." We thank almighty Allah that made us for all the blessings we have, and we ask Allah to return us home to Syria. Thanks to King Abdullah II, son of Hussein, and thanks to Jordan. ✦

Our Cultural Heritage

For a TIGER Girls project, we learned about and shared Syria's ancient ruins and traditions. We studied educational videos on our digital tablets and visited the Blumont Art Gallery in district 2 where camp artists described their models and paintings of important heritage sites. Delegations visit the gallery, and the outside walls are beautifully painted Damascus, Shami-style.

Syria's cities and archaeological remains are among the oldest in the world and six are UNESCO-protected; however, many were heavily damaged or destroyed by the war. We wrote about many sites and then burnt the page edges to symbolize our lost heritage. This was visceral; it activated a strong need to share and preserve our heritage.

The fourteenth-century Hama Norias—water wheels —in Houran supplied water from an aqueduct to the city and farms along the Orontes River. Only seventeen remain today, and these are heavily damaged due to mortar shelling. The sounds of the wheels are the heartbeat in the beautiful nights of Hama city.

Aleppo, Halab, is four thousand years old. Famous for trade, textiles, and manufacturing, it was ruled by the Hittites, Assyrians, Akkadians, Greeks, Romans, Umayyads, Ayyubids, Mamluks, and Ottomans. Its treasures are the Citadel, a twelfth-century Great Mosque, many sixteenth- and seventeenth-century *madrasas* (schools), *hammams* (baths), souks, and houses, and especially its people. Aleppo was under siege from 2012 to 2016 and suffered greatly. The al-Madina Souq, the world's largest covered market, was destroyed and burnt; the grand minaret of the Great Mosque was destroyed.

Busra, dating from 106 CE, is in Houran, Daraa; people have been living there for twenty-five hundred years. Busra is famous for its second-century Roman Theatre, but also for the al-Omari Mosque—one of the oldest surviving Islamic mosques—and for Madrasah Mabrak al-Naqua and the Cathedral of Busra. Alhumdillah, the Roman Theatre survived the war, but other ruins were heavily damaged. The famous singer Fairuz once sang at Busra's theatre.

Damascus, Sham, City of Jasmine, has been inhabited since 10,000–8000 BCE, making it one of the oldest cities in the world. This trade capital is renowned for its craft industry and its architecture, which includes Roman city walls, the Great Umayyad Mosque, and the Citadel, outside of which stands a statue of Salah Aldin. Nearby is the famous Souq al-Hamidiyya. The Damascene Sword stained-glass monument sits in Umayyad Square, where people gather. During the war, parts of the Old City, the Umayyad Mosque, the Citadel, and the Madrasa al-Adiliye were heavily damaged.

The Forgotten or Dead Cities in Idlib, Northern Syria, are first- to seventh-century limestone villages—houses, pagan temples, churches, bathhouses, public buildings, and monuments that were abandoned in the tenth century but around which other settlements and agriculture grew. Throughout the war, people took sanctuary in the Forgotten Cities; the site has been damaged by shelling and relics have been stolen.

Qal'at Salah Aldin's tenth-century castle is the finest in Syria. The castle, near Latakia, built into the cliff face—with towers, drawbridge, dungeon, and stables—is as majestic as was the ruler himself. Salah Aldin, whose celebrated statue can be found in Damascus, was a Sunni Kurd and founder of the Ayyubid dynasty, which drove the Christian crusaders from Muslim lands.

Crac des Chevaliers is one of the world's finest castles, strategically situated on a high ridge. Near Homs, it was built by Christian crusaders—the Order of Saint John of Jerusalem (1142–1271) but refined by the conquering Mamluks, who succeeded Salah Aldin. Both castles were used strategically in the war and Crac des Chevaliers sustained heavy damage.

Palmyra, "the Pearl of the Desert," is an oasis near Homs with first- to second-century ruins from its days as a cultural trading centre, including Greco-Roman colonnaded streets, temples, and a theatre, but also reveals Persian-Islamic influences. Palmyra suffered greatly during its occupation by Daesh, who destroyed the Temple of Bel, the Temple of Baal Shamin, the Arch of Triumph, and columns in the Valley of the Tombs and also looted artifacts.

Syria, our beautiful country, home of jasmine. We would like to learn more and to visit Aleppo, Homs, Hrak, and Damascus. We dream of living in its houses, smelling its perfume, and helping it live again. ❖

al-Qari "The Reader"

I wish to be a librarian. How beautiful is this phrase when said by a child who does not know how to read and write! Our centre's librarian, I first laughed a lot to myself, but my laughter faded at his repeated insistence of this sentence.

Thus, the wondrous story of a ten-year-old child who visits the library often, sits at a table, sometimes in a corner, or in the stacks, turning pages to view their pictures.

Aref lives with a large family. His father is married to three women, and Aref's mother is in Syria. Aref's family forbade him from readings or writing and I mused that these circumstances would prevent him from realizing his dream. But Aref's words, "I wish I could become a librarian like you," were stronger than everything.

He was learning many library skills from me verbally: book arrangement, classification, circulation. One day he said, "I want to read what is inside it." This affected me deeply, and I decided to teach him to read, even just one book or story. I taught him the alphabet and how to pronounce "alif" and the twenty-eight letters: alif, baa, taa, thaa, jeem, haa, khaa, dhal, thaal, raa...

As he learned, he grew happier, eager to recite his new knowledge, read aloud to me from books that his persistence had unlocked. Aref's love for reading increased with each conquered book. He read many books—stories and nonfiction—and became more dedicated to becoming a librarian. Aref also returned to school, proud that he could read. His story had a great impact on my life. I felt the spirit of books calling, saying, "We hope to be read by Aref."

After three years, Aref left the library, left books, to find a job to help his family and his mother in Syria. He said he should be helping them. He sends something regularly to his mother, even if only a book. ❖

Kuraat al-Tamr

MAIS (age 13), Mhajjah

Crunchy *kuraat al-tamr* (date balls) are easy to make and are healthy. If using Oreos, include the cream centres in the date mixture. Sometimes I add a pinch of cinnamon, sugar, or rosewater, depending on their taste and my mood.

2.2 lb (1 kg) pitted dates

1 cup (220 g) saman, butter, or vegetable oil

1 cup (120 g) finely crushed biscuits (Nilla, Graham, or Oreo)

Coating: toasted sesame seeds, finely chopped pistachios, coconut, dried rose petals

Put the dates and the saman in a pot and cook over low heat until the dates are soft. Add the crushed biscuits and mix well. If sticky, add more crushed biscuit.

Remove from heat and roll into small balls, using saman (or butter) on your hands to prevent sticking. Roll the balls in the desired coating(s) and share with loved ones.

Harissah

FATIMAH (age 11), Simlin

3 cups (540 g) coarse semolina

1 tsp baking powder

1 cup (200 g) sugar

2 tbsp milk powder

peel of **1** orange, grated

2 cups (175 g) unsweetened coconut (any texture)

2 eggs

2 cups (500 ml) full-fat yogurt

2 tbsp vanilla extract

¾ cup (165 g) saman or melted butter

1 cup (150 g) whole blanched almonds or chopped mixed nuts

Every Syrian girl learns how to make *harissah*, a rich cake made with yogurt, coconut, nuts, and semolina (a coarse, nutty-sweet, high-gluten flour ground from hard durum wheat). The cake is drenched in our basic syrup (not to be confused with the North African hot pepper sauce *harissa*) which is used in many Syrian recipes, sometimes altering the flavours. For special occasions such as weddings, we add a cream centre to harissah; this fancy version is called basbousa (p. 189) and I hope you try it. A simpler version when eggs are unavailable is called *nammorah* (p. 222); it's also nice but is denser; I hope you always have eggs.

In a large bowl, mix together the semolina, baking powder, sugar, milk powder, orange zest, and coconut. In another bowl, mix together the eggs, yogurt, vanilla, and saman.

Add the liquid ingredients to the dry ingredients and mix by hand. Let rest 30 minutes for the semolina to soften.

Prepare syrup by boiling the sugar and water, then let simmer for a few minutes. Remove from heat and add the flavourings. Cool to room temperature.

Grease a large baking dish with saman or vegetable oil. Turn the harissah into the dish and press flat with a moistened hand. Use a wet knife to score a diamond pattern and place a whole almond in the centre of each diamond. Alternatively, sprinkle with chopped nuts.

Bake at 350°F (175°C) for 30 minutes or until golden, then brown under the broiler for a few seconds to make the top crispier. Remove from heat and let cool for 5 minutes. Use a sharp knife to re-score the diamonds, drench with cold syrup, and garnish.

SYRUP

1 cup (200 g) sugar

1 cup (250 ml) water

1 tsp rosewater

1 tsp lemon juice

Garnish: 1 cup (150 g) chopped pistachios or almonds

Awameh, p. 81

Shawarma, p. 72

Meet You at the Shams Élysées

Zaatari has over three thousand microbusinesses, but we lost count in 2013. The original Market Street, nicknamed the "Shams Élysées" by camp residents after the famous Champs-Élysées street for shopping and cafes in Paris, is now the site of just one of several markets. At night the souks light up, tarab music (famed from Aleppo) pulses, and everyone is out. Narghile, flavoured tobacco smoked using tubes and large water pipes, wafts through the air, mingling with barbecue-skewered shish tawook, shoqaf, and kababs, spicy rotisserie-grilled shawarma (p. 72), served on hot flatbreads like *shraak* (p. 212) or *taboon* (p. 211) from the bakeries. People crowd around falafel stands as golden orbs of chickpea batter in blistering oil are smashed onto bread, smeared with tahini, pickles and spice, and served up.

You can rent or buy almost anything, from morning to late at night. Kaleidoscopic stalls of artfully arranged local fruit and vegetables draw customers early in the day. Spice shops and coffee shops redolent of Aleppo entice with bins of exotic dried herbs, spices, flowers, while more beckon with secrets of home cooking and Arab medicine. At the many barber shops, men share local news over coffee before getting their celebrity haircuts and spa shaves. One barber shop doubles as an art gallery, kitty-corner to Zaatari's best bakery.

Bridal shops with window mannequins in the latest fashions for brides and partygoers are for women only, their backrooms beauty spas for hair, nails, makeup, sugaring, and henna. Nearby, a shop sells gold and silver jewellery. You'll also find halal meat, housewares, fashion, furniture, bicycles, mobile phones, electronics, and sundries. Prices are low, aligned with people's incomes. No one pays the sticker price. Indeed, there's never a sticker, as haggling is ancient tradition and Syrians are expert in reaching a price that is good for both buyer and seller.

The street food is fantastic—try it all! In winter, vendors sell *awameh* and *asabe' zaineb* (deep-fried pastries in syrup, pp. 81 and 84). All year, pastry shops sell savoury mana'eesh and fatayer; beloved sweet shops sell varieties of baqlawah with nuts, syrup, and qishta, along with *knafeh* (p. 86). Not to mention *booza* (p. 79), a Damascene-style ice cream made using mastic (a hard resin from the mastic tree with a bitter taste that changes to pine as you chew) and *sahlab* (a floral-tasting powdered flour made from orchid tubers), a unique, almost stretchy texture.

When Zaatari Camp opened in 2012, so did the souks. Vendors would come to replace their dirt floors and sheet metal walls with caravans, ceramic floors, Plexiglas windows, and signage. Syrians are renowned for trade and entrepreneurship, for craftsmanship in metal and woodwork, textiles and embroidery, and especially culinary and fine arts. Zaatari preserves these skills and knowledge. The war disrupted everyone's livelihood and educational pursuits; in need of income, people re-invented themselves, drawing on their heritage. Hallmark industriousness and resilience paired with the tradition of running enterprises together and apprenticing sons to learn and support family businesses. Female entrepreneurship is also strong: beauty salon and gown rental, sewing and embroidery, catering, textiles, mosaica, jewellery, perfumery, soap making, and childcare—employing other women. Shopping at Zaatari supports families, builds futures, and preserves culture. No haggling over that.

Abu Mahmoud's Falafel Shop

I am Abu Mahmoud. In Daraa, I worked in restaurants all my life; it was my passion, but it stopped with the war. When I arrived at the camp in 2013 and needed to find income for my family, I decided to continue my love for excellent falafel and foods Daraa-style. I bought a caravan, hired two people, and opened a restaurant. I later added a kitchen with storage and space for customers to sit and eat. In the future, I hope to add more employees and locations so it will be easier for people to enjoy our food.

Our days are very long, from seven a.m. until midnight, and our busiest days are Thursdays, Fridays, and holidays. We deliver to organizations and schools. We are famous for our falafel, *ful*, and *hummus msabbaha* (Syrian hummus with chickpeas left whole). Everyone comes here: camp residents and employees. Most people order their food for takeaway or eat it outside. Falafel is part of our Syrian heritage—delicious, healthy, and cheap. Everyone can afford falafel, but it is very difficult to make exceptional falafel and everyone is a critic. The secret is the spices and the method. We sell large quantities of falafel on our busy days; I have never had time to sit and calculate. I love to cook, but the restaurant keeps me too busy to help at home—there, my wife and daughters are the chefs.

Falafel

ABU MAHMOUD, Daraa

Deep-fried balls of ground and spiced chickpeas dipped in sumac—yum! At Zaatari, as in much of the Arab world, people are as picky about falafel as they are about hummus. Though easy to make at home, falafel is so ubiquitous at ftoor or as a sandwich throughout the day that it's simpler to grab it at a shop. But which shop? Everyone has a favourite and Abu Mahmoud's is the best according to all in the camp. Experts judge falafel by the spice and flavour, the moistness and texture of the interior, and the crispiness of the shell; then there's bread type, tahini sauce, spices, pickles, and the chef's secret. Best to be perfectly clear when ordering, as I asked for ten pieces and left with ten sandwiches, to everyone's great amusement as I shared them around base camp.

Falafel can be frozen and thawed before frying (or baked as a healthier option, though not as authentic or popular) and is delicious in salad. We love ours simply dipped in sumac. For sandwiches, split a round of khubz, smash 3–4 falafel, and smear with Abu Mahmoud's tahini sauce, adjusting the flavouring as he does: "Individual preferences vary greatly—many people taste test tahini sauce during its preparation and adjustments are made as needed." Finish with cucumber pickles and it's a wrap!

❖

In a large bowl, cover the chickpeas with water and soak for 10 hours. Drain.

Using a blender, combine the chickpeas with all the other ingredients and blend until minced. Transfer to a bowl and refrigerate for at least one hour.

Shape into 1-inch (2.5-cm) discs using a falafel press or spoon. Heat the oil in a large pot and test temperature by frying one falafel ball—the oil should bubble once the falafel hits the oil. Add falafel balls, careful not to overcrowd the pot, and fry until golden on both sides. Dip in sumac and serve.

1 cup (165 g) dried chickpeas

1 medium onion

1 cup (25 g) parsley

1 cup (25 g) cilantro

6 cloves garlic

1 tsp ground cumin

1½ tsp ground coriander

½ tsp dried mint

1 tsp Aleppo pepper or **½ tsp** hot pepper

1 tsp salt

½ tsp black pepper

2 tbsp flour

1 tbsp baking soda

sunflower oil for frying

Garnish: sumac

TAHINI SAUCE

½ cup (125 ml) tahini

¼ cup (60 ml) full-fat yogurt

½ tsp salt

2 tbsp lemon juice

3 cloves garlic

½ cup (125 ml) ice water

Blend together everything except the ice water. Adjust to taste, then add the water gradually until very creamy.

Shawarma

UMM AHMAD, Dael

1 onion, sliced

4.4 lb (2 kg) lamb shoulder/leg cut into pieces, **or** chicken breast and thighs, skin on

MARINADE

1 tsp ground cardamom

1 tsp paprika

10 cloves garlic, crushed and minced

1 tsp curry

1 tsp ground cumin

1 tsp ground ginger

¼ tsp nutmeg

1 tsp coriander

2 tsp salt

1 tsp Aleppo pepper

1 tsp orange zest

1 tsp lemon zest

2 tbsp orange juice

2 tbsp lemon juice

½ cup (125 ml) full-fat yogurt

½ cup (125 ml) water

½ cup (125 ml) olive oil

¼ cup (60 ml) vinegar

2 tbsp tomato paste

All people forget the weather and daily life when they queue for Syria's famous sandwich when it is made by a shawarma master. In Amman, families eat it on curbs or in cars. In Zaatari, the aroma of marinated meat being shaved as it grills on vertical spinners will lure you like a siren's call, omnivore or not. The shawarma master marries meat with tahini, while shredded chicken dances with *toum* (a garlicky and creamy sauce, similar to aioli); both are wrapped in shraak or khubz (pp. 211 and 210) with tomatoes, *mouneh* (pickled turnip, p. 256), cucumbers, and a few hot french fries, then fried and pressed and passed into grateful hands.

Place the onion in a large dish. Combine the marinade ingredients in a food processor and blend well. Place the meat or chicken on top of the onion and cover with the marinade, turning to coat. Refrigerate for 10-12 hours, turning occasionally.

Remove the meat/chicken from the marinade and bring to room temperature. Skewer and grill over heated coals until cooked through. Alternatively, bake the meat at 325°F (160°C) in a dark pan with 3 tbsp (45 ml) olive oil for 1 hour, turning as needed; bake the chicken at 375°F (190°C) for 45 minutes.

Remove from heat and discard the skin. Cover for 5 minutes, then shred with a fork.

To assemble, place a heaping amount of meat or chicken in the bread and top with tahini or toum (depending on whether you are using meat or chicken), pickles and a few french fries. Fold in the sides and roll up.

For an added (and street-authentic) touch, flatten the sandwich and fry in 2 tbsp (30 ml) vegetable oil until golden on both sides.

TOUM (GARLIC CREAM) FOR CHICKEN

1 cup (135 g) whole garlic cloves

1 tsp salt

¼ cup (60 ml) lemon juice

¼ cup (60 ml) ice water

3 cups (750 ml) canola oil

In a food processor or using a mortar and pestle, combine the garlic and salt well. Add 1 tbsp (15 ml) lemon juice, ½ cup (125 ml) oil, and 1 tbsp (15 ml) ice water, blending after each addition. Repeat until all the ingredients are used up, ending with the oil. The mixture should be thick, like mayonnaise. Adjust the seasoning. Refrigerate for at least 3 hours before using. Keeps in the refrigerator for several weeks.

Abu Muhanned's Bakery

Welcome to our family-run bakery on Market Street. You were probably led by your nose, as our taboon bread can be smelled for blocks. I arrived with my wife and children at Zaatari in March 2013. In Daraa I worked in a chicken slaughter-house; I knew I would have to find new work in Zaatari.

When I bought the bakery, I didn't know how to make bread. The owner was very skilled; he stayed on, teaching me and my sons until we were proficient, and then left. My sons, three employees, and I work from six a.m. to six p.m. We are always busy; it changes with movement in the market. Our customers are from the camp and its organizations—schools, the hospital, the police, and delegations visiting from all over the world.

Many people say our shraak and taboon breads remind them of Daraa. Each piece is handmade and baked in our special ovens. Making excellent bread takes skill and focus; nothing can distract you. Shraak bread is paper thin and used to wrap shawarma sandwiches and in *msakhan* (a dish of shredded chicken and sumac, wrapped in the shraak) and other dishes. Taboon bread is heavier, with dimples. Everyone misses taboon bread baked in the wood-fired underground ovens in their villages. Syrians eat fresh bread, made daily, and they are tough critics. Everyone knows excellent bread by the smell, sight, and, of course, taste.

We don't deliver and we don't sell outside the camp. We have difficulties with our bakery space being too small, lack of electricity, and the price of materials and access to them. The bakery has been very good to me and my family. I hope to get a chance to travel, to see the world again, and find a place for the education and future of my children. I invite you to try our bread! ❖

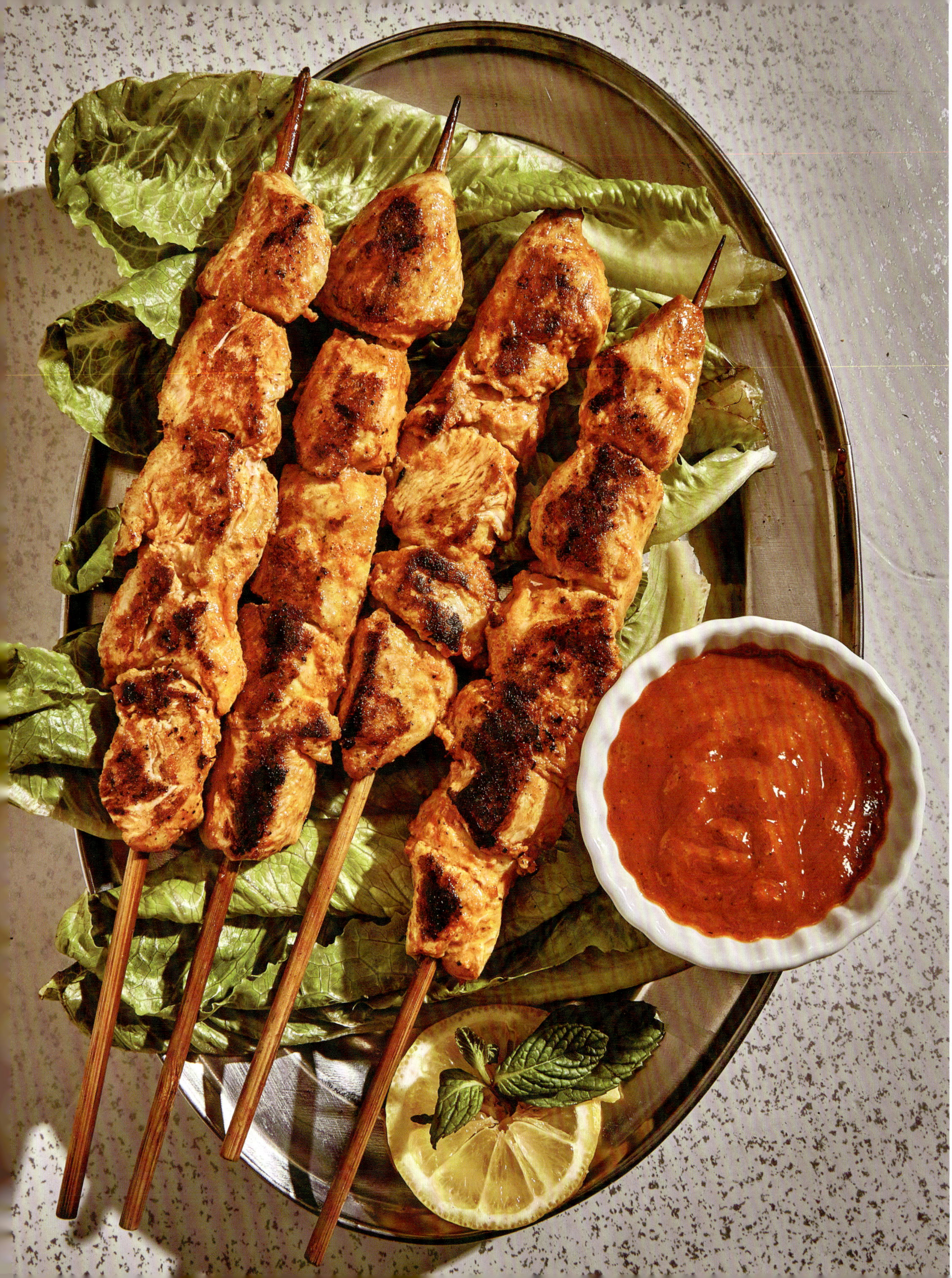

Shish Tawook

ABU OMAR, Al-Yadouda

Shish Tawook is simpler than shawarma, with cubed chicken marinated in subtly spiced yogurt. Serve with (or wrap in) bread, lettuce, grilled onions, tomatoes, pickles, and toum (p. 72)—or use in salad. Metal skewers conduct heat better than wooden ones. If you use wooden skewers, soak them for at least 30 minutes to prevent burning. You can also bake skewers suspended on a tray rim at 400°F (204°C) for 25-30 minutes, turning occasionally.

Zest half of the lemon. Cut the lemon in half, discard the seeds, and blend both halves together with the zest, yogurt, tomato paste, mustard, oil, garlic, and seasonings in a blender or food processor.

Turn the mixture into a large bowl or plastic bag and add the chicken, coating on all sides. Cover and marinate in the refrigerator for 3-24 hours.

Thread the chicken cubes closely together on metal skewers and grill for 10-12 minutes or until cooked, turning often. Thread the onion and tomato separately and grill until charred and the onion is tender.

1 lemon

1 cup (250 ml) full-fat yogurt

3 tbsp (45 ml) tomato paste

1½ tbsp mustard

3 tbsp (45 ml) olive oil

4-5 cloves garlic, peeled

½-inch (1.3-cm) piece ginger, peeled and quartered, or **1 tsp** ground ginger

½ tsp cinnamon

1 tsp paprika

1 tsp ground cumin

1 tsp salt

½ tsp Aleppo pepper, or dried chili flakes

½ tsp Maggi powder

2 lb (900 g) chicken breast, cut into 1-inch (2.5 cm) cubes

4 small onions, unpeeled

4 whole tomatoes

al-Majd Barbershop

I am Abu al-Majd from Daraa. Before the outbreak of war and the worsening of living conditions, I was studying physical education at university and learning barbering from my father's friend. I had to leave Syria and arrived in Zaatari Camp in March 2013.

To help my father, I opened a barbershop on the Shams Élysées. I prepared the salon with metal sheets as walls above the dirt floor, a plastic chair with four stones under the feet to make it higher, and a small broken mirror. I provided full grooming services: hair cutting, beard shaving, and sanding—use of a rubbing cream to remove black sunspots.

As the camp changed, so did my salon—to a caravan with a ceramic floor and Plexiglas front windows. I obtained more equipment, expanded services, added chairs for waiting and drinking coffee, and hired a barber and a trainee. Our customers are from all camp districts and relatives and friends. Hours are ten a.m. to ten p.m. We are busiest after five p.m., when people finish work and come for shaving, and all of Thursday. The busiest times of the year are the days before Eid al-Fitr and Eid al-Adha—our most important Muslim occasions.

Men ask for shaving; some ask for cutting or colouring, face care; some buy hair cream. They like short styles, and everyone shaves fashionably. How long they stay depends on the wait or just the person—some customers like to stay and talk with others. The hairstyle or beard model depends on age. Modern styles, like Cristiano Ronaldo's haircut, are very popular with young men. School haircuts for students, classic cuts for older people, banky (an Arabic name for a haircut that's short on the sides and long on top) and spiky cuts for boys, and US Marine-style cuts for young men and boys are all in demand too. But the Shafi shave, after Hassan al-Shafi, the Egyptian musician, is the most requested style of all.

I love this profession. I know all my customers, hear their stories—good and sad—and prepare them for their jobs, weddings, Eids, graduations, and birthdays. I face many difficulties with the location, continuous power cuts, and lack of modern equipment. I think often of making modifications, such as buying a solar-energy system and expanding the salon so I can train more young people to help their families.

Mahal Halaweat Sweets Shop

I am Abu Ahmed, from a family of sweet makers. I left Syria because of the war and arrived in Jordan in December 2012. After I registered in Zaatari, I wanted to continue sweet making but needed money. I worked outside and then returned and purchased a caravan with my little savings. I replaced the décor with sweet shop colours and started working with my three brothers from eight a.m. to midnight. Our busiest times are after seven p.m., Thursdays and the day before holidays and weddings. Everyone comes here. We make: baqlawah, soft and coarse knafeh, harissah, ghraybeh (p. 78), barazek (p. 223), maamoul, and more. Our *warbat*, large triangle-shaped baqlawah, is filled with nuts—peanuts, pistachios, cashews, and walnuts—house-made qishta or Akkawi or Nabulsi cheese. *Mabroumah* has these same fillings but is made from knafeh dough and rolled into logs. Our baqlawah syrup is flavoured with lemon and a hint of rosewater. Since I was a boy, my favourite baqlawah has been walnut. On our busy days, we sell out of walnut and all of our baqlawah, as well as soft knafeh and harissah.

In 2013, I opened Zaatari's tenth sweet shop. How much we love our sweets—these reminders of home that we serve on many occasions. Some sweets are not easily made at home, so sweet shops are vital to our way of life, whether buying by the kilo or just a few pieces. Sweets are also important for nutrition, for calories. I face challenges with electricity and the high price of ingredients, especially nuts. During the COVID-19 crisis, when our hours were limited, we began home delivery. I hope to expand the shop, open other branches, and hire more employees. Syria is famous for sweets because we sweet makers know our work, we are passionate about sweet making, and, most importantly, do it with love for our customers. ❖

Ghraybeh

ABU AHMED, Daraa

1 cup (220 g) cold saman or butter

1 cup (125 g) icing sugar

4 cups (500 g) flour

1 tsp vanilla extract, or ½ tsp rose or orange blossom water

1 cup (125 g) pistachios

Ghraybeh is the tastiest, most quintessential cookie of Syria and other Arab countries. Saman, sugar, flour, and flavouring—what could go wrong? Just like its cousin, shortbread, so many things! Technique is key; at Zaatari, two-year-olds are experts and will call you out on taste and crumble. Camp bakeries make these cookies by the thousands daily, they scale the saman-sugar-flour mixture in kilograms. The clack-clack rhythm of oven trays, hand-adjusted every five minutes, is entrusted only to the most seasoned nose and eye. This recipe is from Abu Ahmed, the owner of the Mahal Halaweat sweets shop.

In a large, chilled metal bowl, mix the saman with the sugar. Add the flour and flavouring, mixing well. Refrigerate for 30-45 minutes.

Remove ¼ of the dough, keeping the remainder in the refrigerator. Shape into uniform 1-inch (2.5-cm) balls or into rings and place 1 inch (2.5 cm) apart on an ungreased cookie sheet. Slightly flatten each cookie and place a pistachio on the seam. Chill for 20 minutes.

Bake at 325°F (160°C) for 12-15 minutes or until the bottom of each cookie is light brown and the top is slightly golden. Place on a cooling rack for 15-20 minutes. Do not remove the ghraybeh until cooled as they are fragile.

Repeat with the remaining dough.

Booza

UMM FIRAS, Damascus

"I grew up in Sham (Damascus), and when I think of my city of jasmine, my fondest memories are of shopping at the al-Hamidiyah Souq inside the old city walls. When my daughter got engaged, all her female relatives, including my grandmother, gathered for shopping in the souk. As per tradition, we stopped for lunch and at Bakdash, the famous shop established in 1895, for booza flavoured with sahlab, mastic, and pistachios. We loved watching them stretch the booza with paddles."

Sahlab and mastic are the magic ingredients in Booza: sahlab is a floral-tasting powdered flour made from orchid tubers; mastic is hard resin from mastic trees—known as the world's first chewing gum—it initially tastes bitter and then changes to pine flavour.

"Our shop is much like Bakdash. It's easy to make booza at home—you can substitute cornstarch for sahlab—but it won't be as stretchy or taste quite the same. When stretching, close your eyes and imagine Damascus."

1½ cups (375 ml) heavy cream

2½ cups (625 ml) full-fat (whole) milk

1 cup (200 g) sugar

1 tsp ground mastic

1 tbsp powdered sahlab, or **¼ cup (30 g)** cornstarch

1 tsp flower blossom water

1 tsp vanilla extract

handful of chopped pistachios

In a large pot over medium heat, bring the cream, milk, sugar, and mastic to a boil and cook until thickened. While it is heating, remove ½ cup (125 ml) of the milk and stir the sahlab, flower blossom water, and vanilla into it; mix well and return to the pot until thickened again (1-2 minutes).

Turn the mixture into a bowl, stir, and let cool. Whisk well and place in the freezer. Every 30-45 minutes, remove from the freezer and stretch and fold it using 2 spatulas or paddles.

Prepare a loaf pan by lining it with parchment paper and spreading chopped pistachios over the bottom. When the booza is very thick, stretch it again and spread it over the pistachios. Freeze for 3-4 hours.

To serve, invert the pan and press additional pistachios into the top and sides of the booza, or scoop the booza into a cone or dish.

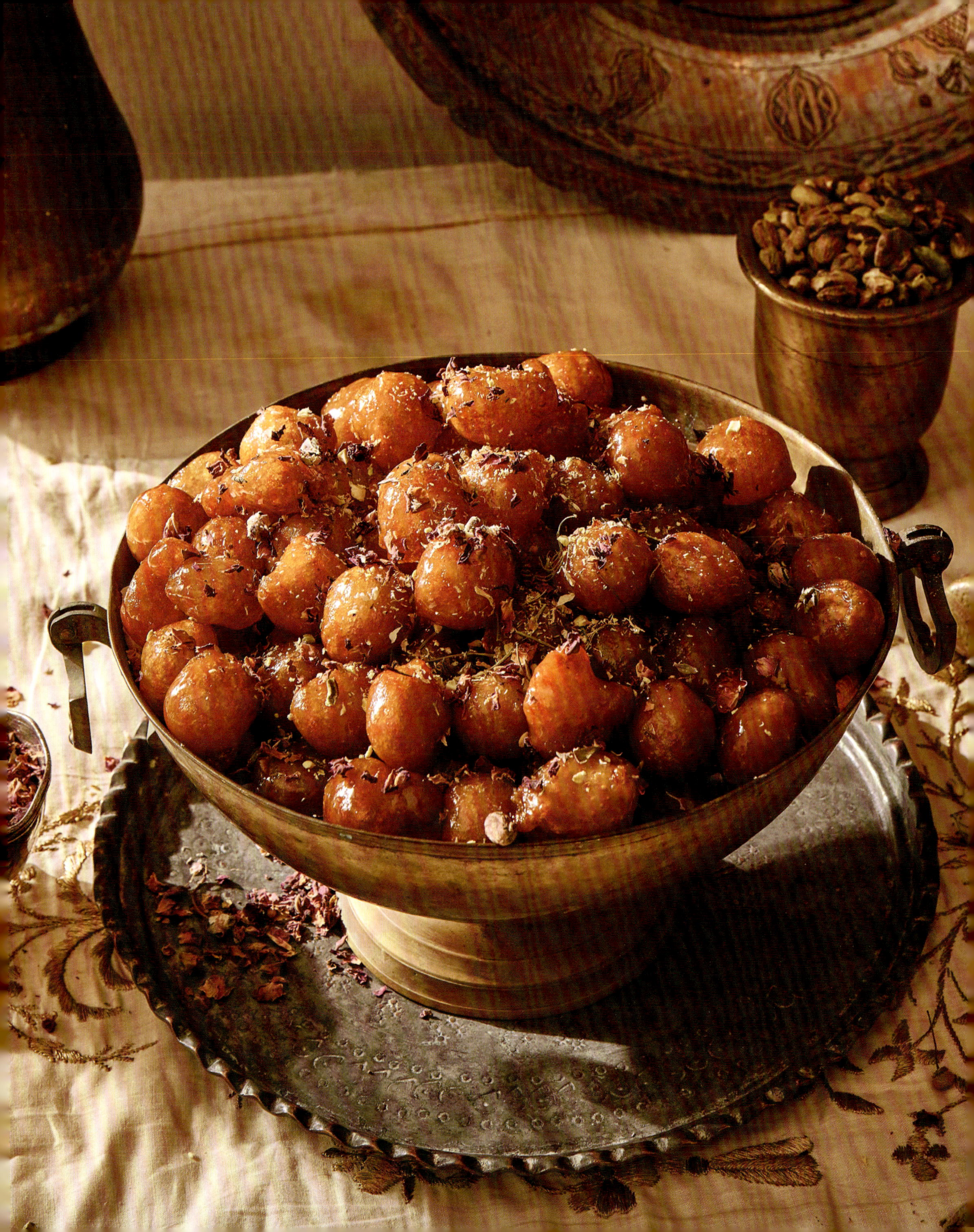

Awameh

ABU FIRAS, Mhajjah

These little, deep-fried balls of yeasted dough disappear fast! They are beloved throughout the Arab world and are iconic of Syria, dating to the ninth century. Made at home and in the souks, Zaatari affectionately calls this signature sweet "fried apricots" because of their appearance. The syrup is perfumed with rose-water and lemon and is used in many recipes with variations. Try infusing the syrup with cinnamon sticks or cardamom pods, and pair with Turkish coffee.

❖

For the dough, mix together the water, yeast, and sugar and let the mixture foam and bubble.

Mix together the flour, salt, cornstarch, and baking soda. Add the yeast mixture and stir for 2-3 minutes. Cover and put aside in a warm area for 2 hours or until doubled.

Prepare syrup by boiling the sugar and water, then let simmer for a few minutes. Remove from heat and add the flavourings. Cool to room temperature.

Snip off the corner of a plastic bag—or use a traditional piping bag—and fill the bag with dough. Squeeze small amounts of dough into hot oil. Rotate and stir the balls to prevent sticking. Remove when golden. While hot, dip them in syrup.

DOUGH

1 cup (250 ml) water

1 tsp yeast

1 tsp sugar

1 cup (125 g) flour

pinch of salt

1 cup (120 g) cornstarch

1 tsp baking soda

oil for frying

SYRUP

1 cup (200 g) sugar

1 cup (250 ml) water

1 tsp rosewater

1 tsp lemon juice

Asabe' Zainab

UMM ALI, al-Karak

1 cup (125 g) flour

2 cups (360 g) fine semolina

1 tbsp baking powder

2 tsp ground anise seeds

1 tsp nigella seeds

1 tsp ground mahlab (optional)

1 tsp instant yeast

1 tbsp sugar

¼ tsp salt

2 tbsp olive oil

½ cup (125 ml) warm water

vegetable oil for deep frying

SYRUP

1 cup (200 g) sugar

1 cup (250 ml) water

1 tsp lemon juice

Asabe' Zainab, a.k.a. Zainab's Fingers, found in the souks, are fragrant golden pastries dotted with nigella seeds, crunchy on the outside, soft on the inside, and soaked in syrup. Their distinctive shape is achieved by pressing one side of the dough against a cheese grater.

Mix the dry ingredients together in a large bowl. Add the olive oil and mix with fingertips until crumbly. Gradually add the water, kneading until the dough is soft and smooth. Cover and leave for 15 minutes.

Divide the dough into two balls. Roll each into a log ½-inch (1.3-cm) thick. Cut each log into 1½-inch (3.8-cm) pieces. Roll each piece into a ball and roll one side against a cheese grater to create Asabe' Zainab's special texture. Place on wax paper or a baking sheet. Repeat with the remaining dough.

Deep-fry in hot oil, stirring, for a few minutes or until golden. Remove from the oil and soak in cold syrup for 2-3 minutes. Serve warm or cold with chai.

To make the syrup, bring the sugar and water to a boil, then simmer for 10 minutes. Remove from heat and stir in the lemon juice. Let cool and serve.

Knafeh Nabulseyeh (Soft)

ABU AHMED, Daraa

1.1 lb (500 g) plain Akkawi or Nabulsi cheese

1.1 lb (500 g) knafeh pastry

½ cup (110 g) saman or butter, melted

saman, for cooking

Garnish: ground pistachios

SYRUP

1 cup (125 ml) water

2 cups (400 g) sugar

1 lemon, juiced

2 tsp orange blossom water or **1 tsp** rosewater

Abu Ahmed and his brothers sell out of knafeh every day at their al-Baghati Sweets Shop. Knafeh, made from shredded filo dough with cheese and sweet syrup and served warm, is famous throughout the Levant, especially styles made in Syria and Palestine. Al-Baghati Sweets Shop makes two types of knafeh: coarse and soft. Preparation of the pastry and the cooking method differ, as coarse is baked, has a dry crust, and uses less syrup, while soft is cooked on the stovetop and requires flipping.

The key to great knafeh is the right cheese. Named after villages in Palestine, Akkawi cheese is made from cow's milk, while Nabulsi cheese is from sheep or goats—yet both are preserved in brine and require soaking to desalinate before using in knafeh. They are superb for cooking because of their taste and how well they melt—stringy and gooey. Mozzarella, cut with a little feta or ricotta, can be substituted. Prepare the cheese and the syrup the night before.

❖

Cut the cheese into squares. Cover with water for 5 hours, then change the water every 2 hours until the cheese is mostly de-brined (should retain pleasant salty taste). Strain and crumble, or cut into small pieces.

In a food processor, coarsely grind the pastry in batches. Transfer to a large bowl and knead with the melted saman.

For the syrup, bring the water, sugar, and lemon juice to a boil. Reduce the heat and simmer for 8-10 minutes or until thick. Remove from heat and add the flavouring. Let cool.

Brush a large round skillet pan with 2-3" high sides with saman. Cover with the knafeh dough, then distribute the cheese over the top. Cook over medium-high heat for 10 minutes. When the edges have browned, reduce the heat to the lowest setting and flip the knafeh so the cheese is underneath and the golden pastry on top. Douse with syrup, garnish, and serve.

Knafeh is also tasty filled and baked with homemade qishta—the same cream used in qatayef, served during Ramadan. Pack half the shredded, saman-rubbed knafeh into a greased cake pan. Spread 2 cups (500 ml) qishta to within 1 inch (2.5 cm) of the sides, top with the remaining knafeh shreds, and drizzle with ¼ cup (60 ml) saman. Bake at 350°F (175°C) for 40-45 minutes or until golden. Remove from heat, douse with syrup, and garnish with ground pistachios.

Miniatures by Tarek Hamdan

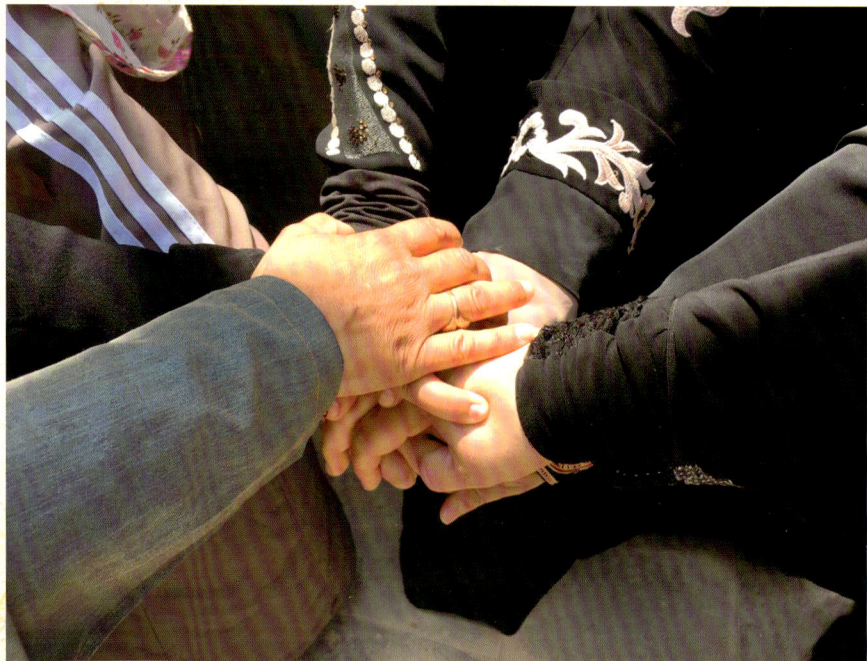

Made in Zaatari

❋

"Who has food photos on their mobile?" Ninety hands, women's and men's, raise their mobiles and excitedly start sliding photos of dishes and feasts they have prepared at home. Total foodies.

I knew I'd be OK when the director of the UN Women's Oasis was called away, leaving me with my *shwey shwey* (little) Arabic, and ninety people with whom to discuss the Zaatari cookbook. They had all enrolled in a cooking class to support the school kitchens and other venues. It's often said that food transcends language, and here, especially, cooking is about love for family and guests.

It was unusual for men to be at the Oasis; unlike other community centers that are frequented by women and men (albeit usually for gender-specific activities), the Oasis is a women's-only center. Here, the focus is women's empowerment, providing multi-district services around prevention, protection, awareness-raising (especially about gender-based violence), remedial education, leadership, civic engagement initiatives, and securing livelihoods. The Oasis always bubbles with laughter and singing, energy from women hooking wall-size rugs depicting camp scenes and messages about women's rights, sewing blankets and clothing, and making mosaics and jewellery as lunch simmers in the kitchen and children play in daycare.

Across camp at Made in Zaatari, similar scenes unfold. Inaugurated on International Women's Day in March 2019, the business is dedicated to women's creativity and economic empowerment. Co-created by the women of Zaatari, UNHCR, Blumont, and Zaatari's "Designer in Residence" Professor Helen Storey from the London College of Fashion, and with support from the Givaudan Foundation, Made in Zaatari initially focused on soap making and catering but expanded quickly to include jewellery and fine arts. A community of twenty-eight women, who self-manage under the centre's supervisor, Made in Zaatari is divided into five departments: the soap and perfume lab; the beauty salon; the crèche (daycare); the production kitchen, which provides catering, including to families isolating during the COVID-19 crisis; and a shop. The women work every day

from nine to three, making products for sale in the shop and outside Zaatari, receiving visitors, and, with UNHCR, organizing bazaars inside and outside camp. The women of Made in Zaatari, like the Women's Committee, which engages hundreds of women, are involved in other NGO initiatives across camp dedicated to female empowerment and activism.

What do Zaatari Syrian women want? They have a list—the same universal human rights that people everywhere want:

- Equal gender rights and protections
- Participation—and power—of women in society and politics
- Literacy and education
- Mobile phone ownership and knowledge about electronics, computing, and social media
- Freedom to ride bicycles and to drive donkey carts and cars
- Roles and opportunities in the labour market and business ownership

The Blumont Center in district 2 has art galleries exhibiting oil paintings and watercolours by over one hundred artists. Many of the works have been shown on CNN and in the *Guardian*, the *New York Times*, and travelling exhibitions worldwide. Other items include handmade wooden toys and reproductions of heritage tools and Syrian landmarks —many of which were destroyed or badly damaged in the war—along with hand-crafted jewellery, soaps, and textiles. The work found here, as elsewhere in camp, is outstanding: jewellery made from date seeds with ground coffee and Yemeni spice, intricate carvings, beadwork, mosaics, rugs, and handbags made from UNHCR tents. Come and meet the artists and watch them work—and bring your Jordanian dinars for their artisanal gems.

Houran Soap

1 lb (500 g) sodium hydroxide

4 cups (1.25 l) cold water

8 cups (2.5 l) olive oil

8 tsp (40 ml) fragrance oils: rose, jasmine, bay leaf, orange, almond, lavender, oud, amber, coffee

Decoration: ground coffee or beans, rose petals, dried herbs

Add the sodium hydroxide to the water, stirring until completely dissolved. Leave overnight, then slowly stir in the olive oil and your preferred fragrance oils until the mixture holds together.

Pour into plastic moulds, adding decoration. (You can also pour into one large mould and cut into blocks after set.) Cover with wax cloth, and leave for 1 week in the shade.

This recipe makes 4 litres of soap.

Houran soap

The Beginnings of Made in Zaatari

My name is Auntie Ahlam and I used to live in Syria in our beautiful quiet village. When the war started and life worsened, my brother, his sons, and I left for Jordan; we arrived at Zaatari in January 2013. I had nothing in the camp, only sitting in the tent.

I began volunteering with Save the Children. My niece was a participant. I led fun activities—games, songs, and face painting—to help alleviate the children's bad psychological state. In those early days, the children had much war trauma, and you could hear the shelling, see the flashes from camp. Volunteering gave me new life.

Life for women was very bad. They had much stress from the war—trauma and worrying about family and their homes in Syria. Life was difficult in camp too: getting water, cooking, and cleaning; bringing children to school while dealing with domestic violence, psychological pressures, and the general condition of life in the camp. Every day thousands arrived from all over Syria, escalating stress levels despite the amazing efforts of all organizations working in the camp. No one knew the future—if we would ever return home and what would become of us.

A camp-wide women's committee was suggested to UNHCR and was organized by Blumont. I was named leader of fifty women. We discussed women's problems, taking suggestions and solutions from women. Next, we exchanged knowledge and experiences, receiving training in embroidery, sewing, and knitting, which we in turn taught to women at Blumont and at home. I gained experience in leadership and hands-on skills in textile-making. I started making perfumes and soaps, perfecting our Houran cold soap-making. Here is our classic recipe for Houran Soap, with variations. We use local olive oil, but coconut oil is good too.

In 2015 I befriended Professor Helen Storey and participated in sessions to help women. On International Women's Day in March 2019, we opened Made in Zaatari. I am the centre's supervisor and a member of the soap and perfume department. We are fortunate that the Givaudan Foundation supports our soap-making efforts since 2017. Our speciality Surprise Soaps contain a toy to encourage children to wash their hands;

Surprise Soaps

Surprise Soaps grew from an initiative by Givaudan with the London School of Hygiene and Tropical Medicine. In 2020 I trained women in Mafraq and nearby villages. I have many challenges, but I am stronger than the difficulties. The Givaudan Foundation is training us in producing new items like candles made from local beeswax and in expanding women's skills. We hope to transform our centre to a factory with secure job opportunities and a future for many women.

The Artist

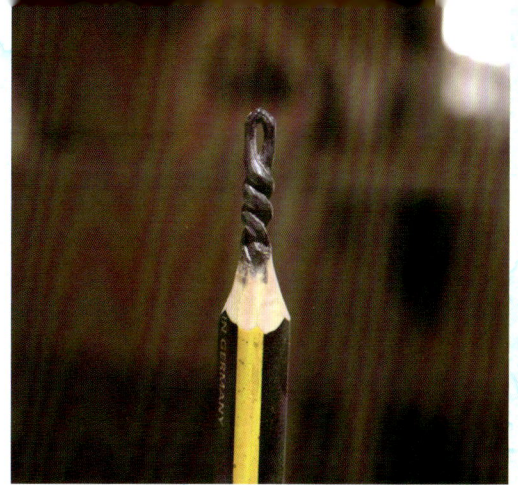

I am Tarek Hamdan and miniature sculpting of everyday objects with motifs from Syrian heritage is my joy. Pencils, stones, broomsticks, cutting boards—everything has a story waiting to be carved. From Muzayrib, Daraa, I worked in construction, and since childhood my hobby was drawing and sculpting. When the war began, I brought my family to Jordan. We arrived at Zaatari Camp in October 2013 and for four years I worked in construction before returning to drawing and sculpting. I watched videos on YouTube and thought of carving lead on pencils. It was a unique art form in camp and I loved it very much, despite my poor eyesight, worsened from the strain of carving.

I joined the camp artist committee—fellow artists who work in different media—and started sculpting and painting intensively. Professor Helen Storey bought some of my pieces. I moved my work to Made in Zaatari, where we sell heritage art from local resources. I am very grateful to Professor Helen for her support.

I fashioned my miniature sculptures as earrings, rings, necklaces, and more, in addition to stand-alone pieces from wood and stone. Most are sold to visiting delegations from around the world and through SouqFann.com. My work has been shown in galleries in France, Italy, and the United Kingdom and was selected for the Venice Design Biennale 2021. Helen introduced to me to British jewellery designer Bleue Burnham, and he has cast my most well-known pieces into silver and gold, now selling in Paris and London.

It gave me a lot of joy to carve the wooden boards and spoons used in this book's food photography. The carvings are based on our refugee experience, our Houran culture, and Islam. The largest board is an old wooden door on which I carved our story before the war, then our lives as refugees and living in Zaatari, and our hopes for the future. The smaller boards depict the many names for Allah, a wedding story, and more. The spoons have faces of people from camp and key ingredients in our Houran cooking. I want to expand my business and participate in exhibitions more widely. I would love to travel and teach people how to sculpt miniatures. ❖

Kabseh, p. 127

Join Us for Ghada'

At Zaatari, lunch is *al-shaghaf*, a love-infused feast, with Daraa (Houran) specialties of *shish barak* (meat-filled dumplings poached in yogurt, p. 131), stuffed vegetables called *mahshi* (meaning stuffed in Arabic), lamb dishes like *shakriyeh* (p. 109), and lentil dishes like *mujaddara* (p. 118). If you're lucky, maybe mleihi with steamed and fried kibbeh (p. 176)—usually reserved for weddings—will be served, or everyone's favourite, *rgagah*: thin layers of pastry and spiced chicken (p. 136). We sit on the floor around main dishes for sharing communally with bread as cutlery, accompanied by salads and sides, always laban, maybe pickles, and lots of chai. After, we'll enjoy Turkish coffee and perhaps puff on narghile. Bring a gift from home for your hostess, or pickup some pine nuts, pistachios, or olive oil en route.

While stuffing and shaping dough its famous crescent-shape for shish barak, Umm Hussein explains that ghada' is the most important meal because it gathers all the family together to partake in hefty dishes comprising protein and fat to fuel them through the day—unlike ftoor mezze, which has light dishes, or evening dinner with guests. Every time I'm with Zaatari women, I'm humbled, impressed by their adroitness, not just culinarily but socially. These are women who prepare dishes, where everyone knows their roles and tasks, the signature exactitude of chopping or flavouring to bring a balance of savouriness, sweet, bitter, salty, and sour to the table all at once. Equally impressive is the cooks' timing, their ability to serve everything together optimally prepared. Perfect garnishing completes the tastes, textures, and aesthetics, expressing the personality of the cook.

There are so many ways to describe ghada' cooking. Grape leaves stuffed as yabraq and yalanji (pp. 154 and 157); mahshi such as cabbage leaves, eggplant, or zucchini, poached in tomato or yogurt sauce (pp. 100, 103, and 105). Lentil-based or vegetarian, like *horaa osba'o* (Burnt Fingers, p. 112), or *mloukhieh* (tender young leaves of the jute plant, p. 94). One-pot dishes of meats and grains are favourites, such as Yemeni-style smoky *kabseh* (p. 127) or *jaj mandi* (p. 124). Many dishes feature pleasingly sour components, with pomegranate seeds and molasses, and ground sumac, in dishes such as *kabid al-jaj* (chicken livers, p. 129) or

msakhan (a thin flatbread topped or rolled with shredded chicken seasoned liberally with sumac, p. 117).

Each dish is a story coloured through time, often told through the flavour of stories. The cook weaves her narrative with Baharat seven-spice blend, Aleppo pepper, sumac, cumin, curry, balanced with lemon and *lumi* (dried limes) punched with holes, pomegranate molasses, and chilies. More subtle communication occurs through salting—the cook's way of expressing her feelings to her husband, as over- or under-salting signals she is unhappy. In Zaatari, the use of whole grains such as bulgur (cracked wheat) and freekah (wheat that has had the outer hull burned off) prevail over rice, which was brought to the Arab world from India by the British during colonial times, greatly affecting food preparation and changing people's diets.

In cities and villages, if the husband and family were working outside the home, the woman would fill safertas, etched brass or aluminum stacking containers with a carrying handle for lunch delivery, each container filled with a different hot dish. A delivery boy would hang the safertas —heavier than today's plastic containers and now rare collectibles—from a wooden pole across his shoulders.

Dishes weave millennia of infusion from the Silk Road with creations from Syria's hubs of Daraa, Damascus, Aleppo, and Homs. The most important ingredient is always love. Sahtain! Enjoy your food with double health and prosperity!

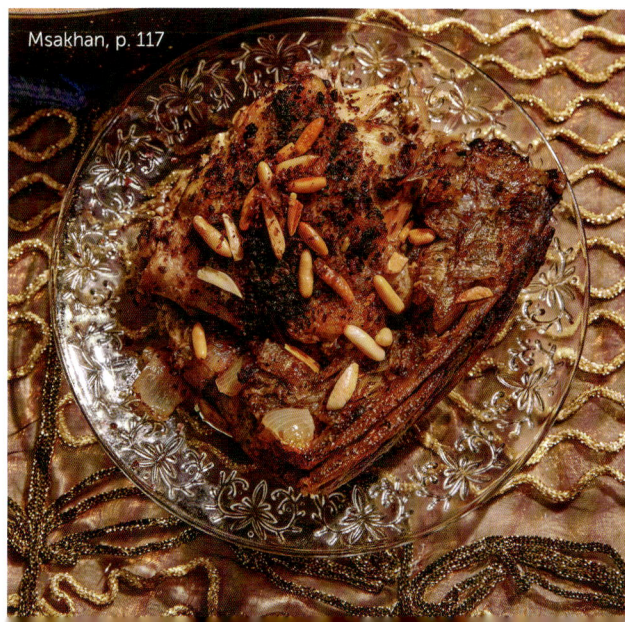
Msakhan, p. 117

Mloukhieh

UMM JOUMAH, Nawa

10 cups (300 g) fresh jute mallow leaves, picked through and stems trimmed

3 tbsp (45 ml) olive or canola oil

1 head garlic, unpeeled, with cloves separated

1 onion, chopped

¼ cup (55 g) saman

1 cup (25 g) chopped coriander leaves

1 tsp salt

½ tsp Aleppo pepper

½ cup (125 ml) lemon juice

Garnish: lemon wedges, chopped cilantro

Deep green and loaded with vitamin A, iron, and antioxidants, mloukhieh (also known as jute mallow) grows abundantly in Syria. The plant is traditionally used for both its fibres when mature, and its leaves for cooking when young. Often cooked with saman with roasted garlic, salt, and lots of lemon, which cuts its bitterness. (Hint: You can dry-roast garlic on the stove or douse it in olive oil and bake, uncovered or wrapped in foil, for 50-60 minutes.)

Zaatari women buy large bags of fresh jute leaves to make mloukhieh as a fast, inexpensive way to feed families. The leaves are often cooked with meat or chicken, making it a more substantial dish, and served with rice. Puréed soup is another easy version. Spinach or collard greens can be substituted, the latter needing more cooking time. Arab groceries sell dry mloukhieh—follow the package directions for soaking.

⁘

Wash the mallow leaves well, squeeze to remove excess water, and pat dry using a kitchen towel.

In a large pan over medium heat, fry the garlic until fragrant and softened with brown spots, about 7-8 minutes. Remove from heat, let cool, and peel.

In a large pan, fry the onion in the saman until golden, then add the mallow leaves, coriander, half the roasted garlic, salt, and pepper. Cook, stirring often, until reduced. Remove from heat, season to taste, and drizzle with lemon juice. Garnish with lemon wedges, cilantro, and the remaining roasted garlic. Serve with rice.

For mloukhieh with chicken or meat, sauté ½ lb (225 g) chicken or meat until browned on all sides. Prepare the onion as above, adding 1 chopped green or red sweet pepper. Add the mallow, coriander, roasted garlic, chicken/meat, and 2 tsp baharat (seven spice) and cook for 3-5 minutes. Add water or broth to cover and simmer for 20 minutes or until the meat and mallow are cooked. If using bone-in chicken, remove the skin and bones, shred, and return to the pot. Season to taste and garnish.

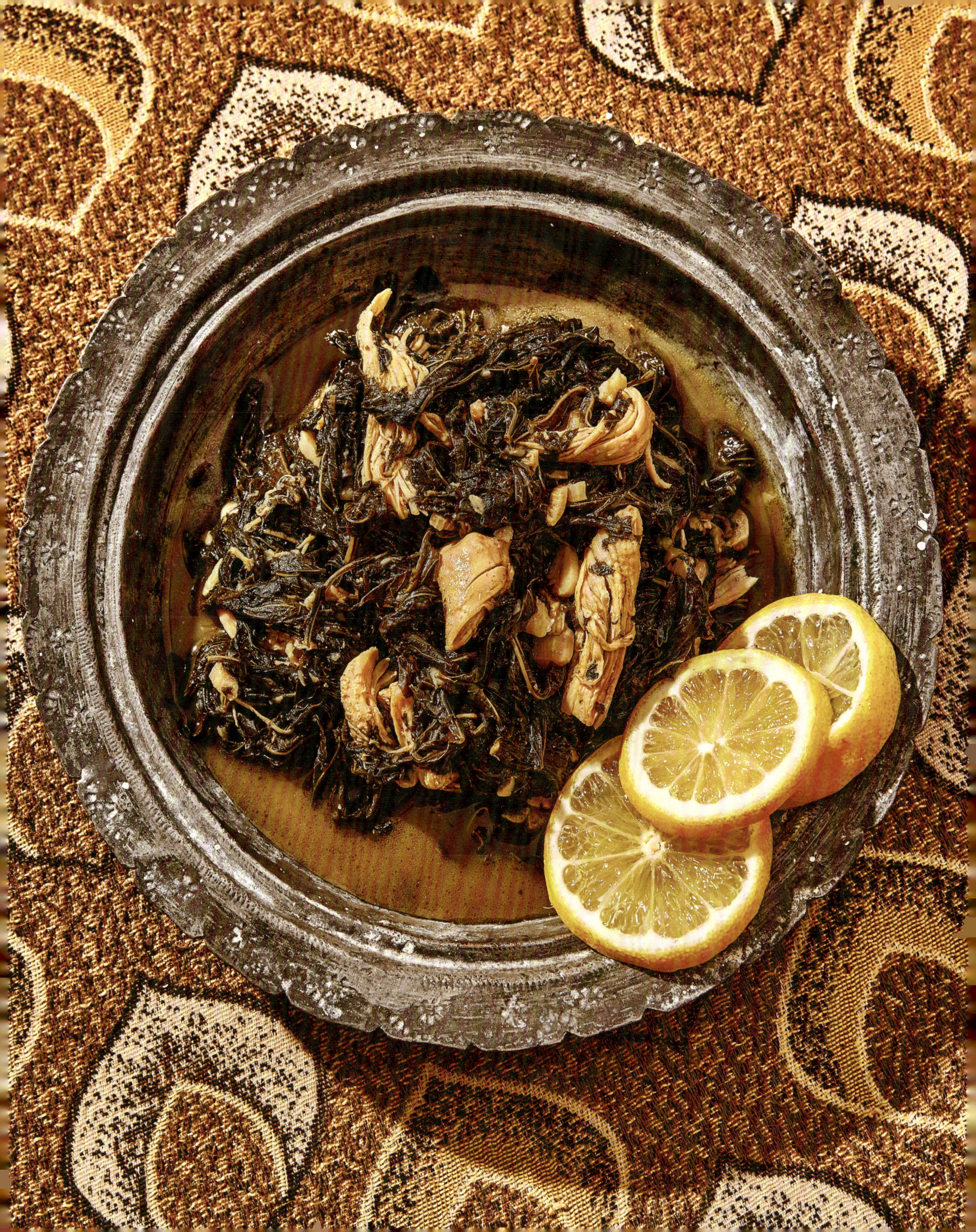

Abu Suleiman's Donkey Cart

I am Abu Suleiman from Al-Nueayma. In Syria, I worked in construction and supported my family well. We arrived in Zaatari in August 2012. Construction wasn't possible so I worked on farms outside camp that grow fruits and vegetables for the country. Every morning I left with others. Then COVID-19. We could not work on the farms and there were few jobs inside camp.

I rented a strong *himar* (donkey) and cart to start a taxi business. This is the primary means of transportation in Zaatari and thus the himar is vital. The owner and I agreed to split the profits equally. A good himar costs 50-250 dinars (USD 70-350), depending on its age and strength, so many drivers rent.

My son and I dressed my donkey, named Saber, "The Patient One," with red and blue tassels, made the cart nice, and started taxiing people between districts—to the hospital or food markets, to henna parties and weddings.

Other people soon got the same idea and donkey taxis increased, so I switched to selling vegetables.

My day starts at eight a.m. I feed Saber fodder and barley, pack water for us both, as the sun will be very hot, and we head to the vegetable centre on Market Street, where the trucks have arrived with the morning's produce. Loaded up, we go to the districts and have many customers. I call out, "Fresh vegetables" and what we have today: lettuce, spinach, cucumbers, tomatoes, watermelons, lemons, potatoes...I know fifty percent of my customers; they like to chat, sometimes have coffee or juice, tell me what they need tomorrow if they're cooking a special dish. Many people, women and the elderly, don't leave their homes often, and during COVID-19 I was their regular visitor.

My day ends when the vegetables are sold, sometimes at five p.m., sometimes eleven p.m. My house doesn't have space so I stable Saber at my friend's house. I clean him and his space daily, but my friend's neighbour gets upset with his smell and presence—sometimes Saber brays to say hello if donkeys or dogs are nearby. He is very kind and strong and works hard. I feed Saber again, adding vegetables, as he loves carrots, cucumbers, watermelon, and apples. He doesn't get tomato or eggplant; those are bad for donkeys.

Alhumdillah, my family, we are happy with the himar because he is our livelihood. I wish to buy Saber and add stable space to my house so I may care for him better. Inshallah.

al-Bazala al-Khadra

UMM FAREED, Dael

"We prepared *al-Bazala al-Khadra* with green peas from the small garden at my grandfather's home, which is filled with coriander and green peas—they are so delicious," says Umm Fareed. You can substitute frozen peas.

2.2 lb (1 kg) sweet green peas, shelled

½ cup (125 ml) olive oil

1 cup (250 ml) water

1 cup (25 g) minced coriander

3 cloves garlic, minced

salt to taste

Garnish: fried pine nuts

Stir the peas, oil, and water together in a large pot. Cook, covered, over medium heat, shaking periodically, until the peas are softened. Add the remaining ingredients. Stir and shake for about 5 minutes until garlic is softened and flavours melded. Remove from heat, transfer to a serving dish, and garnish.

Mnazzaleh

ABU MAHMOUD, Keswa

2.2 lb (1 kg) baby eggplant

olive oil, for frying

2 medium onions, diced

3 cloves garlic, minced

1.1 lb (500 g) ground meat

1 tsp salt

1 tsp Aleppo pepper

1 tsp cinnamon

½ tsp ground coriander

4 cups (800 g) tomatoes, chopped

¼ cup (6.5 g) chopped parsley

Garnish: sliced green pepper, fried pine nuts

Peel and hollow out the eggplants. Fry in olive oil on all sides until golden. Remove from heat and drain.

In the same pan, fry the onion until soft. Add the garlic, meat, and seasonings and cook until the meat is no longer pink. Remove from heat.

Heat the oven to 350°F (190°C). Place the tomatoes in a large baking dish, drizzle with oil and sprinkle with salt, pepper, and parsley.

Stuff the eggplants with the meat mixture and place on top of the tomatoes. Bake for 25 minutes, garnish and serve.

Mnazzaleh is baby eggplant stuffed with seasoned meat and baked. It is a favourite year-round dish, served hot with green pepper, pine nuts, and bread. Abu Mahmoud says it is "a very delicious and nutritious dish that supplies the body with energy. It reminds me of happy family gatherings in Syria."

al-Batal, "The Hero"

Sorry for running late to share my story—thanks for waiting. I just returned from completing my al-Tawjihi (high school) exam. My name is Ibrahim but people call me al-Batal, "The Hero," because my passion, my love, is sports.

I hardly remember Daraa and Syria, except feeling we were happy and safe. I was seven when the war started, when my father brought us to Jordan in November 2012. Now I am seventeen and live with my parents, two brothers, and five sisters. When we arrived in Zaatari we lived, or "sat," as we say, with my uncle's family in one tent. There was no room for us and the situation was very bad. Then we received our own tent and our new lives began. I registered at school, entering fourth grade. I went daily to the mosque to memorize the Quran and I played football in front of the tent. Sometimes I went with my father to sell vegetables by a Blumont centre, where I met coaches, practised football, and fell in love with sports. I played all morning, leaving at noon for lunch and school.

I saw a new sport played on a curved table with a large ball and no arms or hands, a fusion of table tennis and football. My friends said, "This is teqball." I went to coach Ahmed and registered to learn. I thought anyone who played football could easily play teqball—I would be a master. Truth is, it needs a lot of training, focus, and desire to learn its rules. Our daily training included playing skills and activities about the values of cooperation, acceptance of others, team spirit, teamwork, and non-violent communication.

All these exercises helped me change for the better, physically and psychologically. I became calmer, self-confident, less violent. I learned that sport is about morals. I noticed how peace prevails among the players, and this is what I wish for the whole world. All this is due to the coach's interest, his unwavering support, and our desire to learn. With the coach, mutual respect and trust prevail. He sits with us, listens, and helps solve our problems with each other and in life. Sports is an essential part of my being. It is health and life and brings us together. After six months of training, I participated in camp competitions and won second place.

My biggest difficulty is the place and environment in which I live. The hot summers, cold winters, seasons of rain and sandstorms hinder my training. I dream of continuing training, playing professionally, and becoming a coach to educate children, like I benefited. Now I go practise... I hope you try teqball yourself. Thank you to my coaches and the Peace and Sport organization for their support of the camp children.

Malfouf Mahshi

UMM HUSSEIN, Jasim

2 large heads red cabbage or **1 large bunch** Swiss chard

1 cup (190 g) coarse bulgur

2 cups (500 ml) water

1 medium onion, finely chopped

1 cup (25 g) finely chopped parsley

½ cup (12.5 g) finely chopped mint

½ cup (35 g) sliced green onion

1 tsp cinnamon

1 tsp black pepper

½ tsp chili powder

1 tsp baharat (seven spice)

½ cup (125 ml) olive oil

¼ cup (60 ml) pomegranate molasses or **½ cup (125 ml)** tomato paste

½ cup (125 ml) lemon juice

6-7 cloves garlic, minced

1 tsp salt

1 tsp dried mint

Garnish: a little black pepper, dried mint, lemon wedges

This *Malfouf Mahshi* recipe calls for red cabbage, one of the healthiest of the cabbage family, and easy to roll. A beautiful wintertime favourite, it's perfect alongside roast meat and potatoes. Our recipe has bulgur, but rice and ground meat can be used.

❖✕❖

Core the cabbage and separate the leaves. In a large pot over high heat, boil the cabbage leaves in salted water to cover until tender. Drain and set aside. If using Swiss chard, remove the stems and ribs, rinse the leaves, and boil in salted water for about 1 minute. Plunge the leaves in cold water, rinse well and pat dry with a cloth or paper towel, and set aside.

Bring the water to a boil, remove from heat, add the bulgur and let sit, covered, for 45-60 minutes, covered; then drain. In a bowl, combine the bulgur with the onion, parsley, mint, and green onion. Add the seasonings and mix well.

Place 2 tbsp (30 ml) of the filling in the centre of each leaf; fold in the sides and roll up tightly. Place the rolls in a large pot and cover with boiling water. Cover, put a heavy rock on top of the lid, and bring to a boil, then reduce the heat, add ¼ cup of the olive oil and pomegranate molasses, and simmer for 1 hour.

In a small bowl, mix the lemon juice, oil, garlic, salt, and mint. Pour this mixture over the cabbage rolls and simmer for 5 minutes.

Garnish and serve.

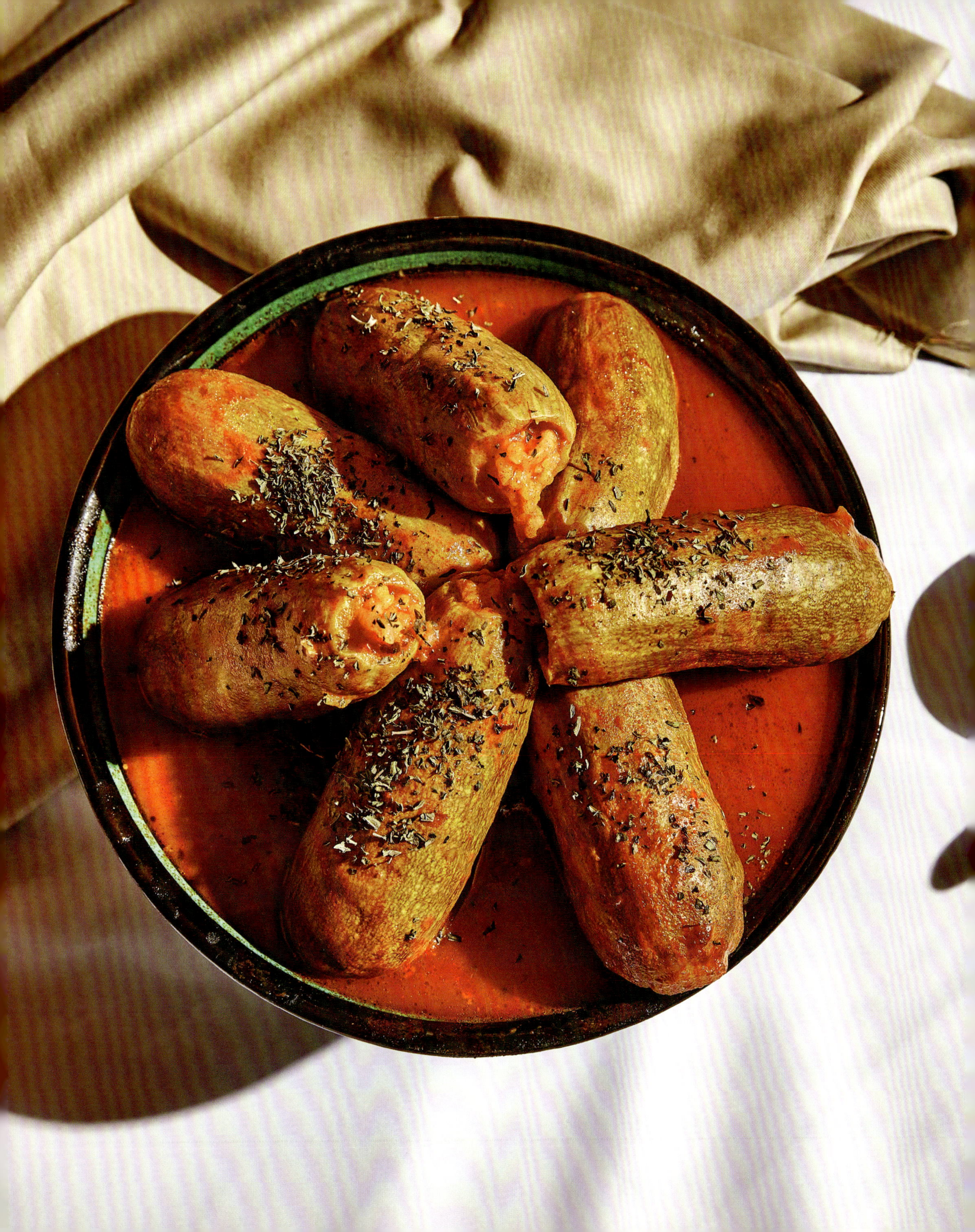

Kousa Mahshi

UMM AYMAN, al-Mansoura

Stuffed with rice and meat then poached in tomato sauce, this is a staple dish at ghada'. Kousa (sometimes spelled cousa) is part of the squash family: similar to zucchini but often paler in colour, sometimes called vegetable marrow. Kousa can sometimes be hard to find outside of specialty grocers or farmers markets, and so this version is made with zucchinis (the dish in the photo opposite is made with kousa however). The zucchinis are hollowed out using a VegiDrill—a ubiquitous Syrian kitchen tool, better than a corer for vegetables and fruit. Replace the meat with cooked chickpeas for a delightful vegetarian version.

✦✕

Rinse the rice by swishing in a bowl with water to cover, drain and repeat 3 times until water runs clear. Soak the rice in warm water for 30 minutes, then rinse and drain well.

In a large pot, heat the oil over medium heat. Add the rice, the herbs and spices, and the meat, stirring well. Cook until the meat is no longer pink.

Hollow out the zucchinis, leaving thin walls. Wash, then soak in a bowl of salted water for 15 minutes. Dry the zucchinis, stuff with the rice and meat mixture, then stack in a large pot.

Combine the saman, tomato paste, and chicken stock. Add to the pot and bring to a boil. Lower the heat and add the lumi, garlic, salt, and mint. Simmer, covered, for 20 minutes. Taste and adjust the seasoning.

Transfer to a serving dish and garnish.

2.2 lb (1 kg) long-grain rice, such as basmati

3 tbsp (45 ml) olive oil

1 tsp ground cumin

1 tsp curry powder

1 tsp coriander

½ tsp black pepper

¼ cup (12.5 g) minced parsley

1 tsp dried mint

3 cloves garlic

½ tsp salt

1.1 lb (500 g) ground meat

4.4 lb (2 kg) zucchini

2 tbsp saman

½ cup (125 ml) tomato paste

3 cups (750 ml) chicken stock

2 lumi with holes punched, or **2 tbsp** lemon juice

1 tbsp minced garlic

salt to taste

1 tsp dried mint

Garnish: lemon slices, chopped parsley

Sheikh el-Mahshi with Rice Vermicelli

ABU NASSER, Inkhil

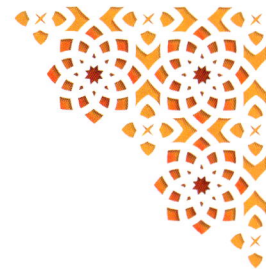

Sheikh el-Mahshi means "king's dish" or, more specifically, "king of stuffed vegetables" because it contains no rice and features meat. Served on special occasions or to honour guests, this heavenly recipe is from Abu Nasser, who spent years as a professional chef in Damascus. Here, zucchinis are stuffed with cardamom-and-lumi-seasoned meat and pine nuts, then browned in oil and poached in yogurt sauce with a hint of garlic.

Rice vermicelli is the classic accompaniment; be careful not to burn it. Use oil and saman, or just oil.

❖

YOGURT SAUCE

4 cups (1 l) full-fat yogurt

1 cup (250 ml) chicken stock

1 tsp salt

1 egg

1 tsp garlic minced

FILLING

1 medium onion, minced

7 oz (200 g) saman

½ lb (225 g) ground meat

¾ cup (100 g) pine nuts

1 tbsp salt

1 tsp black pepper

1 tsp ground cardamom

2 lumi with holes punched or **2 tbsp** lemon juice

1 lb (450 g) small zucchinis

For the yogurt sauce, place the yogurt in a large pot. Add the remaining ingredients, stirring well. Bring to a boil over low heat, stirring constantly so as not to scorch the yogurt. Remove from heat and set aside until ready to use.

In a large pot over medium heat, sauté the onion in the saman until soft. Add the meat and the pine nuts and cook for 5 minutes, stirring well. Add the salt, pepper, cardamom, and lumi. Cook until the meat is no longer pink.

Hollow out the zucchini using a VegiDrill or an apple corer and stuff ¾-full with the meat filling. Simmer in the pot of yogurt sauce set over low heat for 25 minutes.

Place the zucchini in a serving dish. Pour a little of the yogurt sauce over the zucchini, then turn them over and top with the remaining yogurt sauce. Garnish and serve with rice vermicelli.

Rice Vermicelli

2 tbsp olive oil

2 tbsp saman

1 cup (75 g) vermicelli, broken into small pieces

2 cups (450 g) long-grain rice, such as basmati

3½ cups (875 ml) water

1 tsp salt

½ tsp white pepper

Garnish: fried pine nuts

For rice vermicelli, soak the rice in water for 20 minutes, then rinse and drain. In a large pot, heat the olive oil and saman and sauté the vermicelli until golden. Add the rice, coating it in oil, and the water, salt, and pepper. Bring to a boil. Cover (in Zaatari, cooks place a heavy rock on top of the lid) and cook over low heat for 15-18 minutes. Remove from heat, and let it sit, covered, undisturbed, for 20 minutes. Fluff with a fork.

The Imam

Say, "Are those who know equal to those who do not know?"
Only they will remember [who are] people of understanding.
 —The Holy Quran, Az-Zumar "The Groups" 39:9

عن أبي هريرة رَضِيَاللّهُعَنهُ قال: قال رسول الله صلى الله عليه وسلم: « والَّذي نفسي بيدِه لا
تدخلوا الجنَّةَ حتَّى تؤمنوا ولا تؤمنوا حتَّى تحابُّوا أولا أدلَّكم علَى شيءٍ إذا فعلتُموهُ تحاببتُم
أفشوا السَّلامَ بينَكم»

The messenger of God, may God bless and grant him peace, said:
"By Him in whose hand is my soul, you will not enter paradise until
you believe, and you do not believe until you love each other. Shall
I not tell you something that if you do it, you will love one another?
Spread peace between you."
 —Hadith, Abu Hurayra

Bismillah. I am Abu Qusai, imam and teacher in Zaatari. I grew up in a village in
Daraa. My family was semi-poor. A stroke left my father unable to work, so my
mother farmed our plot of land with a few sheep and chickens for income. I
attended the village school and was almost introverted, with a weak personality. According to our culture, this is the personality of a polite person with high
moral character. When I grew up, I found it a disease to be treated.

As a boy, I would close the door to my small room and put a piece of cloth
over my shoulder as an imam's cloak. I'd stand as an imam before the mirror; no
one could see me. At fifteen, during summer vacation I started working in the
vegetable market as a porter, studying the rest of the year. I didn't pass my third
secondary al-Tawjihi exams; I left school and started working, but university was
on the horizon. How do I reach university while working in the aluminum factory every day for eight hours, extremely fatigued? I followed the lessons in the
mosques of Damascus. I was far from the teacher and the school. Alhumdillah,
thanks to God, after eight years I was crowned with success; I achieved my
dream and succeeded in the third secondary al-Tawjihi. I am like an ant from
which a grain of wheat falls dozens of times: it does not give up until it completes its task.

I registered at the al-Fateh Islamic Institute in Damascus and was affiliated
with al-Azhar College. I graduated between the hardship of work and the pleasure of studying. When I began college, I was appointed imam and teacher in the
village mosque.

At the same time, my colleagues and I were gathering students to teach
the Quran and recitation. I had a great presence in my village and its people
were dear to my heart. I was very happy. I worked all day in the plant, spending
evenings at the university or among students at the Holy Quran Institute. At the

beginning of the war, I gave a sermon in Damascus against injustice and murder, asking God to protect the people.

I left with my family for beloved Jordan in 2013. In Zaatari, I had many chances to leave, but I began to teach in the mosques and deliver Friday sermons. Because of the effects of war on children, my colleagues and I built an institute to eradicate illiteracy, to teach the Noble Quran, love, tolerance, and virtuous morals, and provide trips for recreation. Too many children were traumatized by the war and out of school, illiterate, and in danger of not knowing the benefits of knowledge.

Through YouTube and the Internet, I took international seminars and courses for educators, acquiring skills and knowledge about dealing with different types of students: stubborn, soft, and others. By the grace of God, my colleagues and I erased illiteracy in more than five thousand students of all ages, but we are desperately in need of books and school supplies. Too many children share a single copy of a storybook or grammar book for practising writing, causing frustration. Alhumdillah, we have a community box from the camp librarians, which they restock when able and provide learning materials.

My dream is that no one in camp will be unable to read and write; I dream of a virtuous city where love, honesty, and altruism reign. The smiles of the young, the cooperation of adults, and Islam—it produces a love like the sun radiating its rays around the world to light up every heart. ◈

Shakriyeh

UMM SALAM, Busra

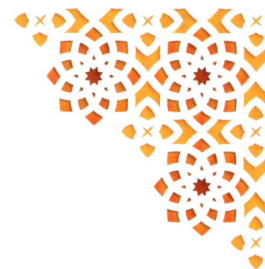

Shakriyeh is fragrant lamb in yogurt, an easy dish to start preparing in the morning and finish just before ghada'. *Shukr* means "to thank"—people are thankful to have meat in order to prepare this substantial dish.

Umm Salam removes the meat from the bone or, for a fancier presentation, leaves the shoulder or shanks whole. Because the meat is slow braised, cuts of meat that contain lots of connective tissue work best, breaking down during cooking, and making the dish taste richer. The yogurt sauce is similar to the one in the Sheikh el-Mahshi recipe, but flavoured with meat stock and dried mint. Like that recipe, serve with rice vermicelli (p. 105).

✦

Cut the meat into 1-inch (2 cm) pieces. In a large pot over medium heat, brown the meat on all sides in 3-4 tbsp (45-60 ml) oil. Add the seasonings, garlic, and onion wedges and cover with 1 inch (2.5 cm) of water. Bring to a boil, then simmer for 2-3 hours, adding water to keep the meat covered. When cooked, remove the meat and keep it warm, reserving the stock for the yogurt sauce.

In a separate pan, sauté the chopped onion in 2 tbsp (30 ml) of oil and the saman until soft.

For the sauce, place the yogurt in a large pot. Add the remaining ingredients, stirring well. Bring to a boil over low heat, stirring constantly until thickened.

Add the meat and the sautéed onion to the yogurt sauce and cook over low heat for 15 minutes. Adjust the seasoning to taste.

Transfer to a large bowl and garnish.

Serve with rice vermicelli, lemon wedges, whole green onions, and radishes.

1 lb (450 g) lamb shoulder or
2 lbs (900 g) shanks

5-6 tbsp (75-90 ml) olive oil

8 cardamom pods

12 black peppercorns

5-6 whole cloves

1 tsp cinnamon

5 cloves garlic, chopped

1 onion, quartered

salt and pepper

1 onion, chopped

1 tbsp saman

YOGURT SAUCE

4 cups (1 l) full-fat yogurt

1 cup (250 ml) meat stock (reserved from above meat preparation)

1 tsp salt

1 egg

2 tsp garlic, minced

1 tsp dried mint

Garnish: fresh mint, chopped parsley, fried pine nuts

Horaa Osba'o

UMM HAMZA, Ataman

¼ cup (60 ml) tamarind pulp

3 cups (375 g) flour

½ tsp baking powder

1½ tsp salt

5 cups (1.1 l) chicken stock

2 cups (400 g) lentils, rinsed

½ cup (125 ml) pomegranate molasses

1 tsp dried mint

2 tsp sumac

1 tsp ground cumin

1 tsp dried coriander (optional)

1 tsp ground cardamom

dash Aleppo pepper

5 tbsp (75 ml) olive oil or saman

1 large onion, sliced lengthwise

8 cloves garlic, minced

1½ cups (37.5 g) fresh coriander

GARNISH

1 cup (250 ml) pomegranate seeds

½ cup (12.5 g) minced parsley

2 tbsp sumac

2 lemons cut into wedges

Horaa osba'o is known as Burnt Fingers because the dish is so flavourful people burn their fingers picking up the homemade dough bits, unable to wait for them to cool. I love this high-protein vegan dish with its Syrian spices and contrasting garnishes. To save time, you can fry khubz in place of making dough.

❖

Soak the tamarind in boiling water for 30 minutes, then mush with fingers or a spoon. Strain to remove the pits.

Mix together the flour, baking powder, and salt. Add 1 cup (250 ml) of water gradually to form a soft dough, then divide it into 3 or 4 balls. Turn the balls onto a floured surface and roll to a thickness of ¼ inch (0.6 cm). Cut the flattened dough into 1-inch (2.5-cm) squares.

Bring the stock to a boil. Add the lentils and simmer for 20 minutes or until tender. Reduce the heat to low and stir in the tamarind, pomegranate molasses, and herbs and spices. Add half of the dough, stirring gently to avoid tearing. Cook for 12-15 minutes, lightly shaking and stirring to avoid sticking.

In a large frying pan, heat 3 tbsp (45 ml) of oil and sauté the onion until golden and set half aside for garnish. Add the lentils to the pan. In a separate pan, fry the garlic and add the fresh coriander, sautéing it until it wilts. Add half of the garlic/coriander to the lentils, reserving the rest for garnish. Fry the remaining dough in the same pan in 2 tbsp (30 ml) of oil; combine with the lentils, reserving some for garnish.

Place the lentils in a serving dish and top with the reserved fried onion, garlic/coriander, fried bread, and garnishes.

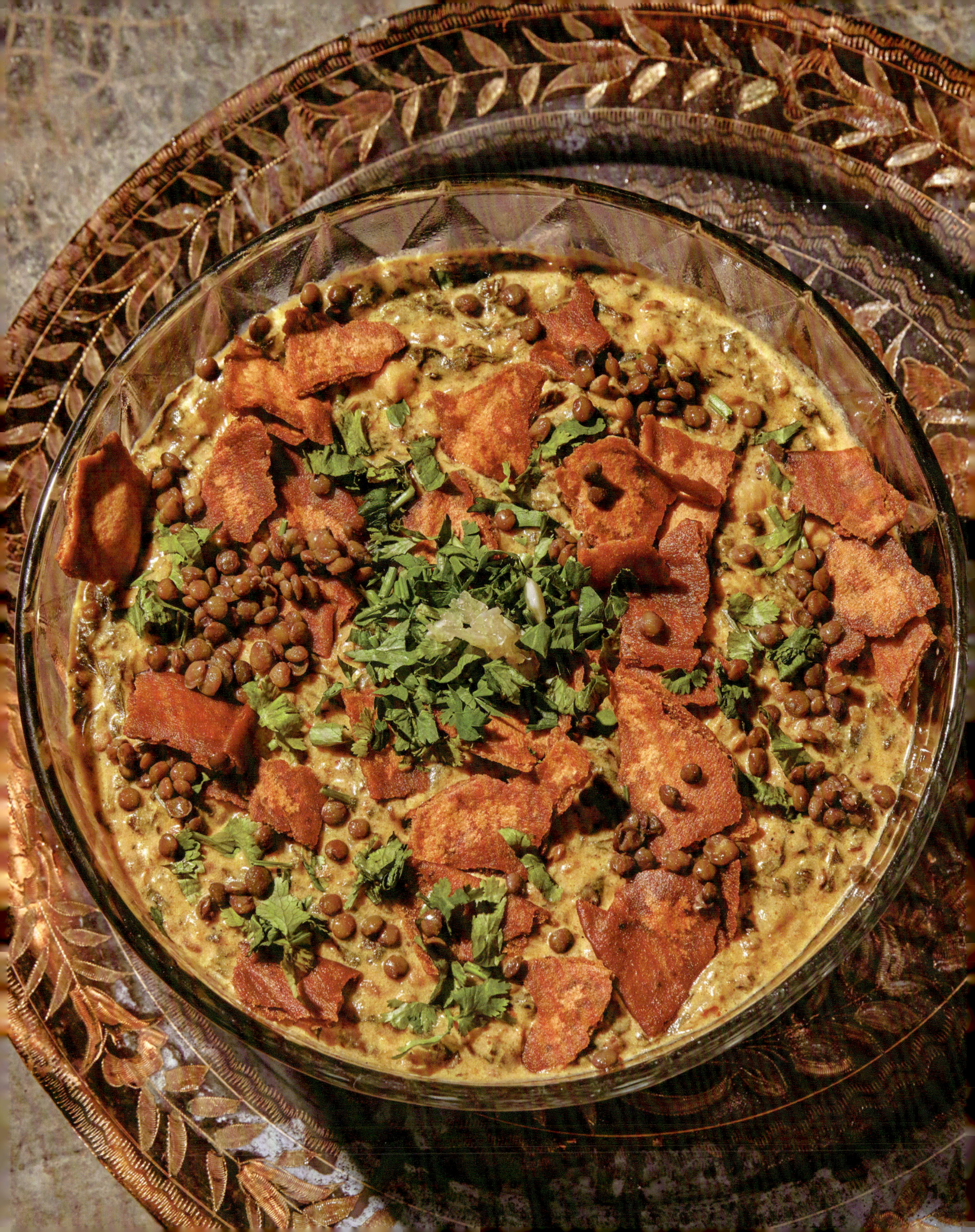

Reshtayah

UMM SALAH, Sayda

Reshtayah is a lovely winter soup consisting of lentils, chickpeas, chard, and yogurt, made hearty by adding potato and bread or bits of pastry or pasta. Khubz can be used in place of making dough.

✦

Mix together the flour, baking powder, and salt. Add water gradually to create a soft dough, then divide it into 3 or 4 balls. Turn the balls onto a floured surface and roll to a thickness of ¼ inch (0.6 cm). Cut the flattened dough into 1-inch (2.5 cm) squares.

In a large pot, bring the lentils and chickpeas to a boil in the stock. Reduce the heat and simmer for 1 hour or until tender, adding water to keep covered. Remove from heat and drain well, reserving the stock.

Fry half the dough in the 5 tbsp of oil and set aside.

In a large pot, heat the oil and sauté the onion, garlic, and potato until softened. Add the seasonings along with the lentils, chickpeas, and chard. Cook for 3-5 minutes or until the chard is wilted. Add the stock and the lumi and bring to a simmer. Add the yogurt and continue to simmer. Add the remaining dough and stir until cooked.

Garnish and serve.

Note: Instead of soaking overnight, the chickpeas can speedily be pre-soaked by bringing them to a boil in plenty of water, removing from heat, and leaving (covered) for 1 hour.

DOUGH

3 cups (375 g) flour

1 cup (250 ml) water

½ tsp baking powder

1 tsp salt

SOUP

1 cup (200 g) brown lentils, rinsed

1 cup (200 g) chickpeas, soaked overnight and drained

9 cups (2.1 l) water or chicken stock

5 tbsp (75 ml) olive oil

1 onion, chopped

4 cloves garlic, minced

1 cup (150 g) diced potato (optional)

1 tbsp ground cumin

½ cup (12.5 g) chopped fresh mint, or **2 tsp** dried

2 tsp allspice

1 tbsp salt

1 tsp Aleppo pepper

3 cups (100 g) Swiss chard or spinach, chopped

1 lumi, punched with holes, or **2 tbsp** lemon juice

2 cups (500 ml) full-fat yogurt

Garnish: olive oil, lemon wedges, chopped fresh mint and cilantro or parsley, fried dough

Msakhan

UMM SAMEER, al-Midan

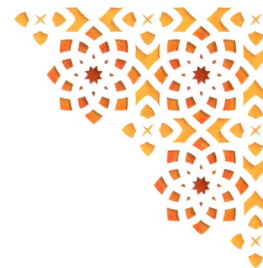

I cannot get enough msakhan. The flavours of skin-on chicken with sumac, onion, and pine nuts, atop taboon bread and baked, create an indelible taste experience. A famous Palestinian and Syrian dish, enjoy for ghada' Zaatari-style, using your hands or aided by a spoon.

For appetizer-size, shraak-wrapped rolls: shred the chicken before mixing with the oil and sumac, then combine with the onion mixture. Spread over shraak cut into 4" (10 cm) squares, turn in the sides and roll up. Brush with oil and bake on trays at 375°F (190°C) until golden, 12-15 minutes.

◈

In a large pot, add the chicken, water, onion, baharat, salt, cardamom, and cloves. Bring to a boil, reduce heat and simmer until chicken is cooked, about 45 minutes. Remove the chicken to a tray and reserve half of the stock. When cooled a little, use your hands to mix the chicken well with 4 tbsp of olive oil and 2 tbsp sumac.

Fry pine nuts in 2 tbsp of olive oil until golden and set side.

In a large frying pan, saute the diced onion in 1 cup of olive oil with Maggi powder, cumin and pepper until it wilts, stirring often. Remove from heat, stir in 4 tbsp sumac and pine nuts.

Brush edges of taboon with olive oil or juice from onions.

In a large round or oblong greased baking dish, place 1 taboon and top with 4 chicken pieces, a quarter of the onion/olive oil mixture and a quarter of reserved stock. Top with another taboon, repeating to make four layers, ending with chicken, stock, and onion.

Bake at 400°F (200°C) for 20 minutes, until golden and then under broiler for 1 minute.

Garnish and serve.

2 chickens, each cut into 8 pieces, skin-on

8 cups (2 l) water

3 onions, each cut into 8 pieces lengthwise

1 tsp baharat (seven spice)

1 tbsp salt

5 cardamom pods

3 whole cloves

1 cup (140 g) pine nuts

1 cup (250 ml) + 6 tbsp (325 ml) olive oil

3 onions, diced

6 tbsp (50 g) sumac

1 tsp Maggi powder

1 tsp ground cumin

½ tsp pepper

4 rounds taboon or kmaj bread

olive oil (for brushing)

Garnish: fried pine nuts

Mujaddara

UMM ABDULQADAR, Inkhil

2 cups (400 g) lentils (green or brown), rinsed

6 cups (1.5 l) chicken stock or water

3 onions, cut in wedges

¼ cup (60 ml) olive oil

1 cup (190 g) bulgur, medium or coarse, rinsed

2 tsp salt

1 tsp Aleppo pepper

1 tbsp ground cumin

Garnish: ½ cup (12.5 g) each chopped green onion, minced parsley or coriander, pomegranate seeds

Umm Abdulqadar left horrible circumstances in Syria. She lost family and friends in rocket and sniper attacks, was widowed, and had her eldest children stranded in Syria. "Alhumdillah, Alhumdillah, I came from Syria to Jordan in 2013 because of the difficult life. Then I got a job at the UN Women's Oasis for women and girls and felt rebuilt. As sisters, they provided support and encouragement, transformed my psychological status so I feel a sense of hope and happiness. Mujaddara reminds me of Fridays when the whole family used to gather—all the people I miss today."

Mujaddara, recorded in the ninth-century *Al Baghadi Cookbook*, is sometimes known as "poor man's food" (due to lentils and grains being inexpensive and filling) or "Christian food" because of its popularity during Lent, when Christians traditionally abstain from meat. Variations include using rice instead of bulgur, but not in Zaatari. Mujaddara is nutritious and cheap; we love it at Zaatari Camp, especially in fall and winter. Serve with mouneh, laban, salad, and bread—our favourite bits are the fried onion garnish.

◆✕◆

Boil the lentils until soft but not mushy, 20-25 minutes. Drain, keeping 3 cups (750 ml) of the liquid in the pot.

In a large frying pan, sauté the onion in oil until softened. Remove half and fry the remainder until golden, then remove from the oil and set aside.

To the lentils, add the bulgur, salt, pepper, and cumin. Cover and simmer over low heat until the bulgur has absorbed the water, about 20 minutes. Add the softened onions and the remaining oil and mix well.

Top with the fried onion and the garnishes.

Maqloubeh

UMM AHMAD, Dael

2 cups (450 g) long-grain rice, such as basmati

1 lb (450 g) stewing meat or chops

1 onion, chopped

2 tsp curry powder

1 tsp salt

½ tsp black pepper

4 eggplants

4 potatoes, peeled

4 tomatoes

5 cloves garlic, minced

3 tbsp (45 g) saman

1 tbsp baharat (seven spice)

1 tsp ground cardamom

1 tsp cinnamon

½ tsp salt

½ tsp black pepper

2 tsp Maggi powder

oil

Garnish: 1 cup (140 g) fried pine nuts or slivered almonds, **1 cup (25 g)** chopped parsley

OPTIONAL TOPPING

½ lb (225 g) ground meat

1 tsp baharat (seven spice)

½ tsp each salt and pepper

For the optional topping, fry the ground meat in oil over medium heat with the seasonings until it is no longer pink. Drain and keep warm.

Maqloubeh means "upside down" and is described in the Ayyubidian thirteenth-century (1226) *Kitâb al-Tabîkh* cookbook by al-Baghdadi. A royal dish for feasts and celebrations, it is rumoured to have been named by Salah Aldin al-Ayyubi, first sultan of Syria and Egypt and founder of the Ayyubid dynasty, when he conquered Jerusalem against the crusaders in 1187. Asked what he would like to eat, Saladin couldn't recall the word betinjan (eggplant) and replied, "upside down dish," proclaiming it the "dish of victory." A different story, however, describes warriors stopping at Palestinian homes, asking to be fed. Frustrated by these soldiers eating their meat, the women hid the meat in the bottom of the pot: if a soldier lifted the lid, he saw only eggplant and rice.

Maqloubeh has changed over time but always includes meat with eggplant (or chicken with blanched cauliflower). A vegetarian version calls for mushrooms and carrots. Any rice is fine, as is baking the eggplant at 400°F (204°C) instead of frying it.

The thrill of maqloubeh is in the flipping of the pot onto a platter: releasing it with its beautiful eggplant sides and then cutting the first piece to reveal its many layers. Be sure to gather your audience to watch this feat—they will be very impressed!

Serve with a simple salad (such as diced lettuce, cucumber, tomato), bread, and laban.

❖

Wash the rice two to three times, until the water runs clear. Cover with cold water and soak for 30 minutes.

In a large pot, heat 2 tbsp (30 ml) oil and fry the meat with the onion, curry, and salt until browned. Remove from heat and add the pepper.

Grease the bottom of a large pot and place the meat mixture in it.

Peel and slice the eggplant to a thickness of ½ inch (1.3 cm). Sprinkle with salt and let sit for 30 minutes, then rinse and pat dry. Fry over medium-high heat on both sides until golden. Layer the eggplant over the meat, extending the eggplant up the sides of the pot.

Slice the potatoes thinly and fry until golden. Layer the potatoes over the eggplant. Slice the tomatoes thinly and layer over the potatoes. Fry the garlic and sprinkle it over the tomatoes. Top with the drained rice. Add the seasonings along with 3 cups (750 ml) of water. Cover and bring to a boil. Reduce the heat to low and simmer, partially covered and shaking regularly, until the rice is cooked, 25-30 minutes.

Remove the maqloubeh from heat and let it rest for 5 minutes. Invert onto a large serving platter, top with the ground meat (if using), and garnish.

Jaj Mandi

UMM MAHMOUD, Nawa

CHICKEN

1 chicken, cut up

½ cup (125 ml) full-fat yogurt

1 tbsp vinegar

zest and juice of **½** lemon

2 tbsp saman

1 tsp ground cumin

1 tsp turmeric

1 tsp salt

1 tsp pepper

RICE

3 tbsp (45 g) saman

2 tsp Maggi powder

1 tsp baharat (seven spice)

1 cinnamon stick

1 tsp ground cardamom

1 tsp salt

1 onion, chopped

2 hot green chilies (such as jalapeno)

2 cups (450 g) long-grain rice, such as basmati

4 cups (1 l) water

2 barbecue coals + **1 tbsp** oil

few saffron threads

juice of **½** lemon

Garnish: 1 cup (25 g) chopped parsley, **1 cup (140 g)** fried cashews or pine nuts, lemon wedges

Zaatari has many ways of preparing meat or chicken with rice. The women showed me how to make mandi, "dewy" smoked rice with chicken using coals. Fascinated, I watched how the rice and chicken were finished by placing a vessel filled with burning coals inside the pot. Mandi is a technique originating in Yemen, where spiced, often yogurt-marinated meat and rice are cooked underground in an oven fitted with a metal cage. The meat's juices enrich the rice suspended underneath, while the steam from the rice cooks the meat—all infused with wood smoke. With its rich flavours, mandi spread across the Gulf to Syria.

Umm Mahmoud shares the below, easy method. Her mother died when she was young and she left school to care for the family. She learned this mandi version from her neighbours in Syria. You can omit the coal-burning stage but the dish won't have the same smoky taste.

◆×◆

In a large bowl, combine the yogurt, vinegar, lemon zest and juice, saman, and seasonings. Use this mixture to marinate the chicken, rubbing it under the skin. Marinate for 3-8 hours, turning occasionally. Remove the chicken from the marinade and roast in a greased pan at 375°F (190°C) until golden, about 1 hour, turning the pieces midway.

Wash the rice 2-3 times and soak it in cold water for 1 hour.

In a large pot, heat the saman and add the seasonings, stirring for 30 seconds. Add the onion and chilies, frying until the onion is soft, 2-3 minutes. Add the rice, stirring to coat well, then the water. Cover and bring to a boil, then lower the heat and simmer until the water has evaporated, about 30 minutes.

Light 2 coals and when whitened place inside a ramekin with 1 tbsp of oil. Place the ramekin in the middle of the rice, cover, and smoke until all the steam has evaporated. Meanwhile, soak the saffron threads in 2 tbsp of warm water. Remove ramekin and fluff the rice with a fork, adding the saffron water.

Arrange the fluffed rice on a large platter, top with chicken, drizzle with the lemon juice, and garnish. Serve with laban.

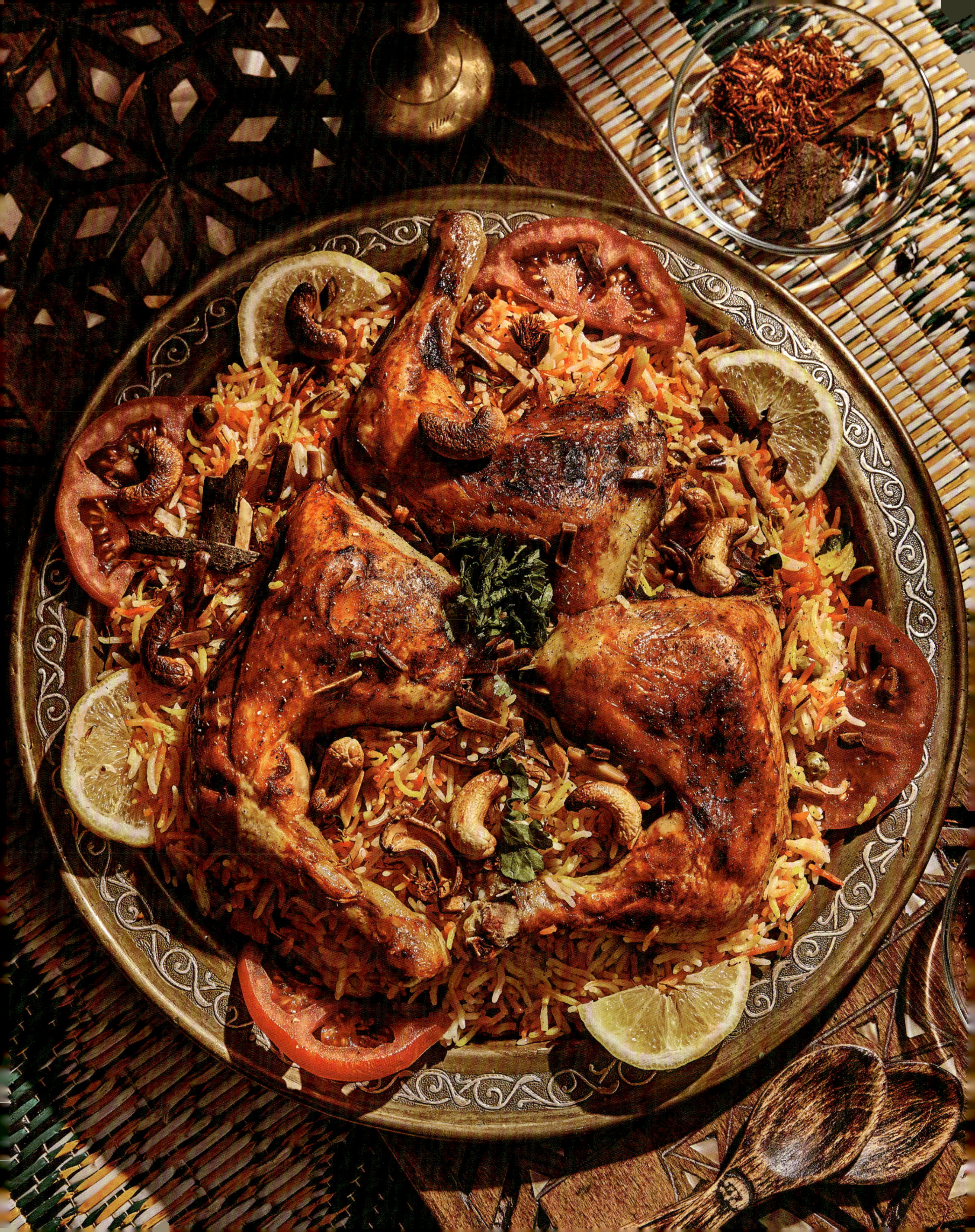

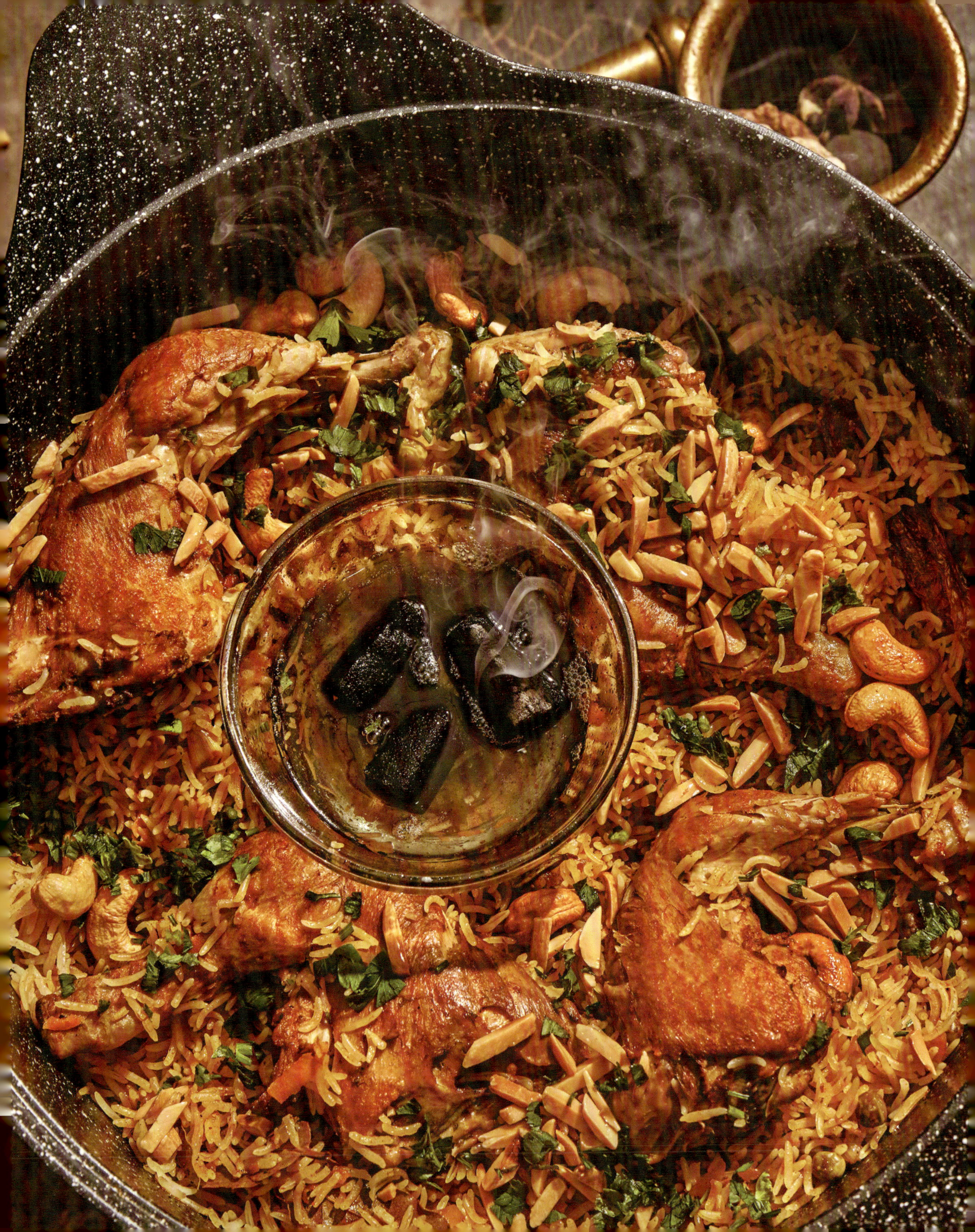

Kabseh

UMM MOAYAD, Jabab

Kabseh means to press or squeeze, hence the name of this dish, in which all the ingredients are prepared in one pot. Like mandi, kabseh is from Yemen, later becoming the national dish of Saudi Arabia. The many versions use meat, including goat and camel, as well as fish, shrimp, chicken, and vegetables, with aromatics and smoked using coals (like mandi). Some cooks use pre-blended kabseh spice, usually comprising cloves, cardamom, cinnamon, lumi, bay leaves, nutmeg, and pepper. Kabseh is eaten using hands and spoons, accompanied by laban and salad.

Wash the rice two to three times, until the water runs clear, and soak it in cold water for 1 hour.

In a large pot, heat the saman and add the seasonings and chilies, stirring for 30 seconds. Add the onion, garlic, carrots, and peas, stirring for 2-3 minutes. Add the chicken and cook for 5 minutes, browning all sides. Add the tomato, tomato paste, lumi, salt, and rice, combining well. Add 4 cups (1 l) of water and bring to a boil, then reduce the heat and simmer, covered, for 30-40 minutes, until chicken is cooked. Remove from heat and stir, fluffing the rice.

Light the coals, burn until whitened, and place in a ramekin with 1 tbsp (15 ml) of oil. Place the ramekin in the pot and leave for 15 minutes with the lid ajar.

Transfer to a serving platter and add the garnishes.

2 cups (450 g) long-grain rice, such as basmati

4 tbsp (60 ml) saman or vegetable oil

1 tsp paprika

½ tsp turmeric

3½ tsp whole peppercorns

1 tsp ground cloves

1½ tsp coriander

½ tsp cinnamon

1 cinnamon stick

5 cardamom pods

2 bay leaves

3 medium hot chilies (such as jalapeno)

1 onion, minced

8 cloves garlic, minced

1 cup (120 g) carrots, chopped

1 cup (175 g) green peas

2 lbs (900 g) chicken thighs and legs

2 tomatoes, chopped

2 tbsp tomato paste

1 lumi, punched with holes, or **2 tbsp** lemon juice

1 tsp salt

2 barbecue coals, a ramekin, and **1 tbsp** oil

Garnish: 1 cup (140 g) fried cashews or almonds, **¾ cup (150 g)** plumped raisins, sliced lemon, tomato, cucumber

Quran Recitation

Did you know that the Holy Quran is recited melodically? Its first word, Iqra'a ("Read"), also means "to recite," and Quran recitation is very powerful. Across Zaatari Camp and Muslim countries, Quran recitation is omnipresent, heard live in mosques and on radio, television, and social media. Most amazing is the visceral feeling one experiences upon hearing Quran recitation. As Imam Abu Firas from Jasim explained to me, "The Quran is something you feel. Listening is healing for the spirit and body. No understanding of Arabic is necessary. Allah designed the Quran to be experienced."

Videos of non-Muslims hearing the Quran for the first time are striking—looks of awe, tears, happiness. Listening has deepened my understanding of "Islam as a religion of peace": Quran recitation brings inner peace, calm, and oneness with the world.

Quran recitation is a highly revered art with a long history. *Qarra'a* (readers) melodiously recite the Quran according to *tajweed*-rules for how to apply each Arabic letter in different linguistic situations. Tajweed recitation rules preserve the Classical Arabic of the Holy Quran that was taught to the Prophet Mohammed (PBUH) by the angel Jibril from linguistic dilution through time and the global spread of Islam. Qarra'a first learn tajweed in grade school, competing by age and gender. Grand masters have social media channels and millions of followers.

We challenge you to listen to Quran recitation and not be moved. Try listening to grand masters Abdel Basit Abdel Samad and Ali Bin Abdur Rahman Al Huthaify (very different styles); Saad Al Ghamdi; or Kurdish Iraqi rising star, and one of my favourites, Raad Mohammad Al Kurdi—all easily found on social media. ❖

Kabid al-Jaj

ABU YOUSEF, Mhajjah

I have so many memories of meetings about this book over *kabid al-jaj* (chicken livers cooked in garlic and pomegranate molasses). Loaded with iron, liver balances beautifully with pomegranate and the dish comes together in minutes. It's an inexpensive dish that's also enjoyed at ftoor—ask your butcher in advance to save you some chicken livers.

5-6 cloves garlic, minced

3 tbsp (45 ml) olive oil

A little over **1 lb (500 g)** chicken livers, washed, trimmed of sinew, and cut into 1-inch (2.5 cm) chunks

1 tbsp saman

4 tbsp (60 ml) pomegranate molasses

1 tsp sumac

½ tsp ground cumin

1 tsp sugar

salt and pepper to taste

Garnish: pomegranate seeds, minced coriander or parsley, lemon wedges

In a large pan over medium heat, sauté the garlic in oil until fragrant and slightly golden, then set aside.

Increase the heat to medium-high, add a little more oil, and fry the livers for 7-8 minutes, browning all sides and removing excess juice as it accumulates. Add the saman, return the garlic to the pan, and add the molasses, sumac, cumin, and sugar. Stir over low heat, letting it bubble up for 1-2 minutes.

Season, garnish, and serve.

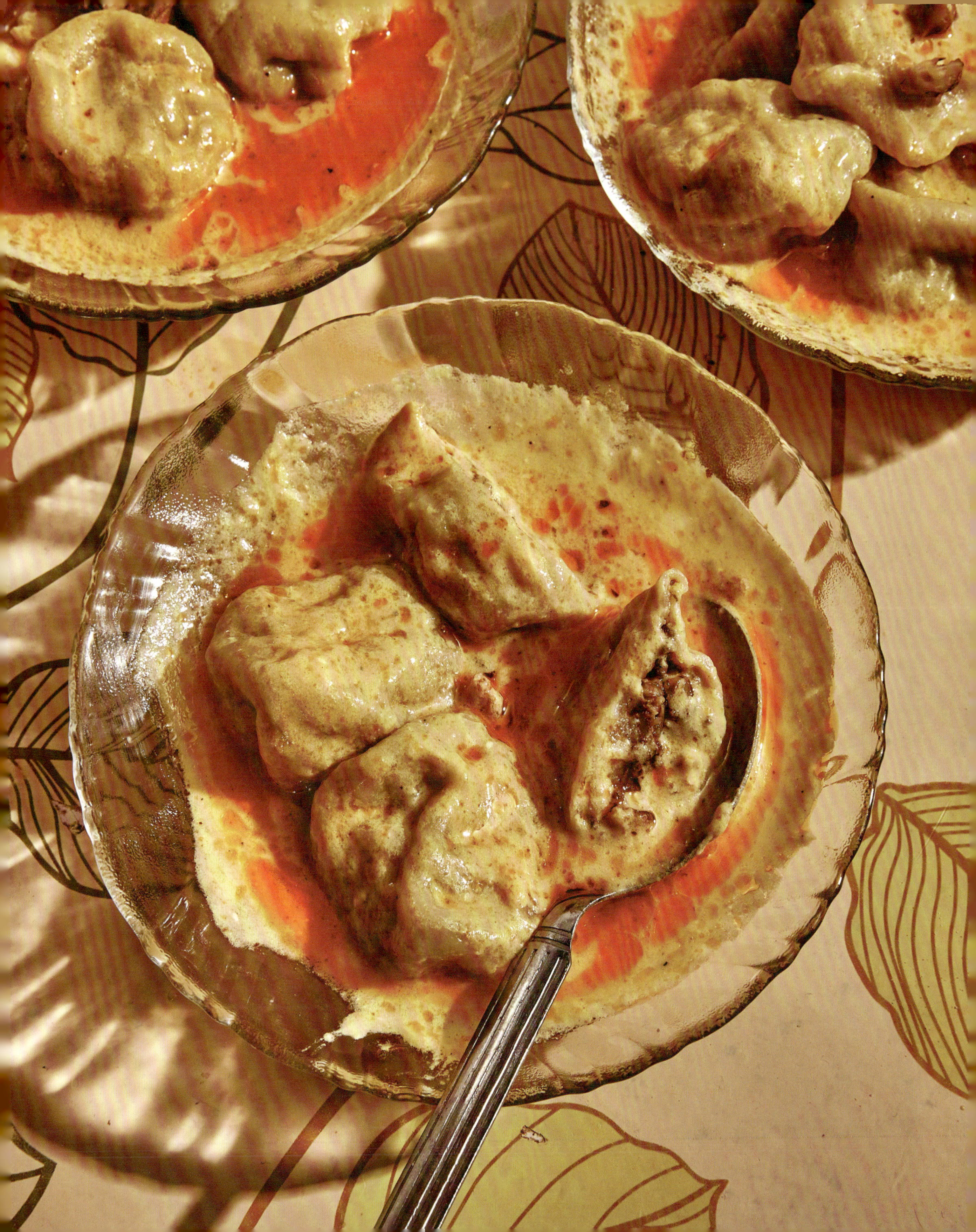

Shish Barak

UMM YOUSEF, al-Musayfira

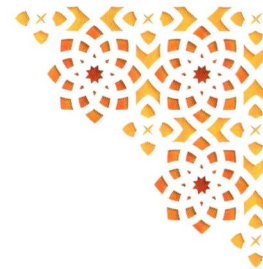

Known fondly as "old man's ear" because of their crescent shape, shish barak are delicate meat-filled dumplings poached in yogurt. On any given day probably half of Zaatari is enjoying shish barak for lunch. Cooks use a finjaan—the little Arab coffee cup without handles—to cut dough circles, but you can use a glass or a cookie cutter. Add pine nuts to the meat for a little sweet crunch, and don't omit the tomato sauce—it adds a lovely taste and creates a nice effect with the oil from the cooked meat. There are two variations of the sauce; the traditional kethi stone version on page 175 (see page 174 for more information on kethi stones) and a simpler version with yogurt, here.

❖

For the filling, brown the pine nuts in oil and remove to small bowl. Add onion to oil and sauté until softened and add the meat, breaking it into pieces. As the meat browns, add the seasonings. Stir in fried pine nuts. Remove from heat and cover.

For the dough, add the oil and salt to the flour and rub well. Add 1½ cups (375 ml) water, and mix well. Add more water as needed to make a soft dough. Let the dough rest for 10 minutes, then shape into 4 balls. On a floured board, roll each ball to a thickness of ⅛ inch (0.3 cm). Cut the dough into circles. Fill each circle with a generous spoonful of the meat mixture, fold, pinch the edges to seal, and bring the tips together, creating a crescent shape. Dust the dumplings with flour to prevent sticking.

For the yogurt sauce, sauté the garlic and coriander and set aside. Over medium heat, bring the laban with the egg and ½ cup (125 ml) of water to a boil, shaking constantly to prevent scorching. Add the garlic, coriander, mint, tomato sauce, and dumplings. Reduce the heat and simmer until the dumplings float to the surface.

Ladle into bowls and enjoy.

FILLING

3 tbsp (45 ml) oil or saman

1 cup (230 g) fried pine nuts

1 onion, minced

½ lb (225 g) ground meat

¼ tsp Aleppo pepper

½ tsp salt

1 tsp cinnamon

DOUGH

8 cups (1 kg) flour

½ cup (125 ml) olive oil

¼ tsp salt

2 cups (500 ml) water

YOGURT SAUCE

4 cloves garlic, minced

½ cup (12.5 g) chopped coriander

6 cups (1.5 l) laban or full-fat yogurt

1 egg

2 tsp dried mint

3 tbsp tomato sauce

The Bedouins

The famed Bedouin tribes of Syria go back millennia, originating in the Arabian Peninsula and are connected to tribes in Saudi Arabia, Iraq, and Balad al-Sham or Greater Syria (now Syria, Jordan, Palestine, Lebanon). *Bedouin* derives from *al-Badiya* (desert) and *al-Badawia* (desert dweller). They are tribal communities led by a sheikh, nomadically eking out a living, reliant on the celebrated Arabian horse, camels, falcons, goats, sheep, and saluki (also known as Persian Greyhound) dogs. For centuries, Bedouin tribes played important roles in Syria's defence, government, and trade, co-existing with farmers through family relationships and trade. In the middle of the twentieth century, many Bedouin settled as farmers, always retaining their passion for desert life and hospitality.

Having inherited their position, sheikhs lead their tribes —large, extended families—in decision making, settling disagreements within and outside the tribe, as well as coordinating with other tribes, farmers, and government. Disagreements and conflicts over lands, property, relationships—all are handled by the sheikh, based on cultural justice norms and Shariah law, with rare government interference. For centuries and still today, Bedouin men use their hand (fingers and thumb) to explain their famous proverb for tracing family lineage and interacting with strangers. As nomads, they would battle over territory, scarce water supply or matters of honour, and so holding out his hand and counting his fingers, a Bedouin will explain: "I against my brothers. I and my brothers against my cousins. I and my brothers and my cousins against strangers and the world."

Thousands of Bedouins live in Zaatari. The Arab desert horse—renowned for its speed, endurance, intelligence, beauty, and fierce loyalty, often sleeping in its owner's goat-hair tent, eating dates mashed in camel's milk for sustenance—is the subject of many paintings by camp artists. These artists also capture the distinctive personalities of camels—the ship of the desert—with their long-lashed eyes and tendency to never forget an abusive owner. Camels are beloved for their vital role as transport, for their milk and meat, for their hides used to make winter coats (*farwa*) lined with sheep's wool, and for their hair woven as garments and scarves. Camel milk does not require boiling or refrigeration, is highly nutritious, and has recently been used by medical scientists as a treatment to inhibit the growth and proliferation of certain types of cancer cells. The artists also portray goats and sheep, which sustain daily life with their milk and meat, hair, wool, and hides; black, water-repellant goat hair is woven for tents that protect against desert heat and serve as insulation in winter. Artists also depict falcons trained to hunt desert prey from their owner's arm on horseback or on the back of a camel. Bedouins consider the saluki hunting dog, one of the world's oldest breeds, to be clean, and the dogs are allowed in the family tent and women's quarters. Bedouins never sell saluki dogs but instead present them as gifts.

The famed Bedouin *saif* (sword) and knives are handed down through families. Often inscribed with a Quranic verse, they hold two distinct edges: *zafiya* or *hafat zafiya* (false edge) and *haqiqia* (true edge), and have served historically in battle, but also in everyday uses, including barbecuing, and for hand-wielding in traditional ardah dance. Many Bedouin cooking techniques and dishes are in evidence every day at Zaatari, with women wearing tribal woven dresses, headscarves, and jewellery, their elderly faces and hands beautifully tattooed (done when they were young, by their mothers). Underground cooking is modified for the modern oven with memories of *arbood* bread baked under ash in open fires. Bedouins welcome anyone who comes to their tent (or house, for many these days) as a friend, serving them choice foods over the playing of drums, oud guitar, and singing, poetry, and dance. ❖

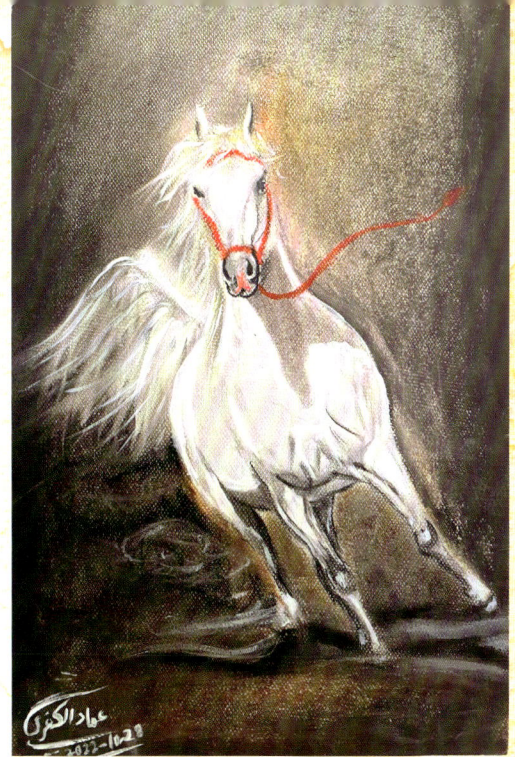

Emad al-Kafri, *Untitled*

Rgagah

UMM IYAD, as-Sanamyn

4 cups (500 g) flour

1 tsp salt

1 cup (250 ml) water

1 cup (250 ml) olive oil

1 lb (450 g) boneless chicken, cut into large cubes

1 tbsp Maggi powder

2 medium onions, chopped

¼ cup (60 ml) olive oil

1 tbsp curry powder

1 tsp ground cardamom

1 tsp ground coriander (optional)

1 tsp Aleppo pepper

1 tsp salt

olive oil for drizzling

A Hourani dish, *rgagah*, "the chip," is also known as *makmoura* in northern Jordan and as *thareed* in Saudi Arabia. Everyone loves these baked layers of pastry woven with chicken (or meat) and caramelized onion, cut into squares or triangles. Simple and delicious! Umm Iyad writes, "I love to prepare this dish because it is my husband's favourite. He is an old man and he loves this kind of food. It makes him think of Syria and home and brings him much happiness." For large celebrations in Daraa, women gather to prepare many tins of rgagah, as it is the perfect party dish. Makmoura, the northern version, typically includes nigella and sesame seeds in the dough and sprinkled over the top before baking.

❖

Mix the flour, salt, and water into a soft dough. Cover and set aside to rest.

Boil the chicken with the Maggi. Drain and shred into bite sized pieces.

In a large frying pan, sauté the onion in the oil with the seasonings until golden. When cool, add the chicken. Mix well and adjust the seasoning.

Preheat the oven to 400°F (204°C).

Grease a large round pan. Divide the dough into 12 pieces. With hands well-greased with olive oil, shape each piece into a ball and stretch using hands (or use rolling pin) into a large, thin circle. Place four circles of dough in the pan and top with a layer of the chicken mixture. Repeat with the dough and chicken mixture, ending with a layer of dough. Drizzle with oil and bake for 45 minutes or until golden.

Ras Kharouf

UMM BASSAM, Khirbet Ghazaleh

5 young sheep heads

oil for frying

2 tbsp salt

1 tbsp Maggi powder

1 tbsp curry powder

2 large onions, peeled and wedged

2 tsp Aleppo pepper

14 cloves garlic, smashed and chopped

2 lemons, juiced

1 cup (25 g) chopped parsley

Garnish: lemon wedges, raw whole vegetables

Ras Kharouf, roasted sheep heads, is a favourite dish for entertaining friends at home and exemplifies head-to-tail slow cooking. Zaatari cooks ask the butcher to start gathering the heads 2-3 days before the event. Five heads feed 4 people, and each costs JD$3-$4 (US$5-$7). The best heads are from sheep 8-9 months old; older ones take longer to cook. The tongue is the preferred part and goes to the most important guest. The brains are fried separately with spices the next day. The broth is pureed with lots of parsley and served as a dipping sauce alongside the heads. The feast is completed with lots of lemon for seasoning, and raw whole vegetables and bread eaten alongside.

Clean the heads, scrape the hair with a knife, and cut in half. Remove the brain and cook next day (by frying in oil with 1 tbsp of salt, ½ tbsp of Maggi, and ½ tbsp of curry for 15 minutes, stirring frequently).

In a large pot, bring the heads, onion, salt, pepper, half the garlic, Maggi and curry to a boil, then simmer for 5 hours (2-3 hours if using a pressure cooker). Remove heads. Strain stock, add parsley, and blend for soup.

To serve, reassemble the heads, or cut into pieces, and place on a large platter. Drizzle with the lemon juice and remaining garlic. Garnish and serve with vegetables, lemon, and bread, with pureed stock in bowls for dipping alongside. Eat by tearing off pieces of the head with one's fingers.

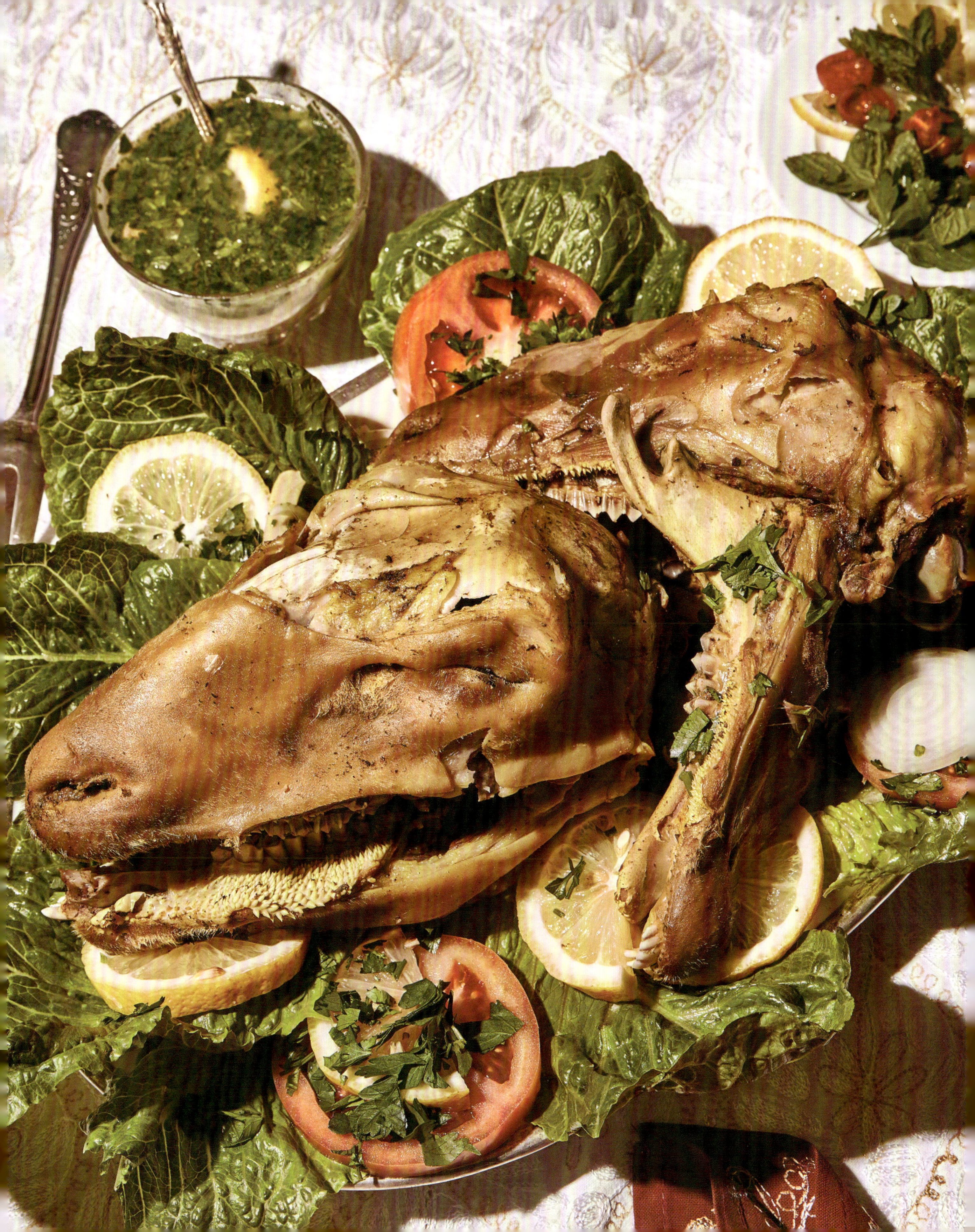

A tamr hindi vendor

Celebrating Ramadan

Ramadan, the ninth month of the lunar calendar, is when people at Zaatari and Muslims everywhere fast all day to grow closer to God. It also involves great foods and social bonding. To understand Ramadan, we journey to the raucous, idol-worshipping desert tribes of 610 CE Mecca, Saudi Arabia, to a cave where an illiterate trader named Mohammed was meditating and the angel Jibril (Gabriel) appeared. Jibril would appear to Mohammed for twenty-three years, teaching the Holy Quran in one hundred and fourteen *surahs* (chapters). Mohammed returned to his family that night with a world-changing message, the Shahada:

أَشْهَدُ أَنْ لاَ إِلَهَ إِلَّا اللَّهُ وَ أَشْهَدُ أَنَّ مُحَمَّدًا رَسُولُ اللَّهِ

Ash-hadu an la ilaha illa Allah, Wa ash-hadu anna Muhammadan Rasulu-Allah.
I bear witness that there is no God but God, and Muhammad is the Messenger of Allah.

Allah had chosen Mohammed as the last of his prophets —after Ibrahim (Abraham), Nuh (Noah), Musa (Moses), Isa (Jesus)—to receive the Holy Quran and spread Islam.

يَـٰٓأَيُّهَا ٱلْمُزَّمِّلُ (١) قُمِ ٱلَّيْلَ إِلَّا قَلِيلًا (٢) نِّصْفَهُۥٓ أَوِ ٱنقُصْ مِنْهُ قَلِيلًا (٣)

O you who covers himself [with a garment],
Arise and warn, And your Lord glorify
—The Holy Quran, al-Muddaththir
"The Enshrouded One" 73: 1-3

Ramadan commemorates the Prophet Mohammed's (PBUH) first meeting with Jibril, receiving the Holy Quran, and the five tenets of Islam: the Shahada, Salat (five daily prayers), Zakat (charity), Sawm (fasting), and Hajj (pilgrimage to Mecca). The excitement of Ramadan approaching is tangible as souks fill with lanterns, boxes of dates, and dried fruit pastes for drinks, and people await the new moon over Mecca. That evening, joyous greetings of "Ramadan Kareem" and "Ramadan Mabrook" echo through camp. Preserving ninth-century tradition, lost in much of Syria, at around three a.m. Musaharati, drummers, in Syrian costume set out, calling, "Wake up sleepers, time for suhoor (breakfast) and fajr prayers. Get up on your sahuras, do not let the reward pass." *Ful mudammas* (a protein-rich bean stew, p. 144); *Tesqieh* (chickpeas in garlicky yogurt) with fried khubz (p. 148); and fragrant Eid bread (p. 161), juices, and coffee are savoured before "the white thread becomes distinct from the black thread."

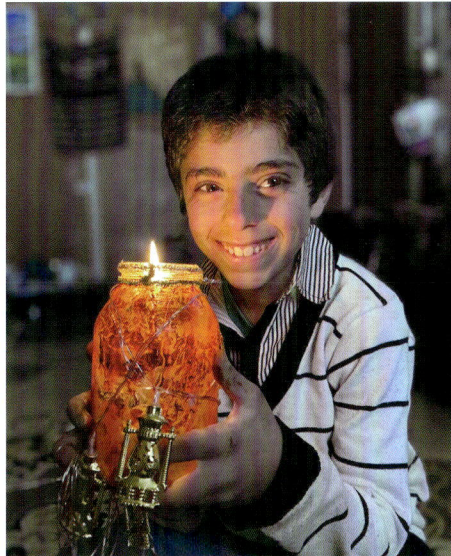

During Ramadan, the gates of heaven open and the gates of hell close, devils enchained. Prayers, kindnesses, and charity are received manifold by Allah, and people's sins are washed away, especially through fasting. Ramadan itself means "scorched heat," and some say it scorches out past sins with good deeds. Fasting brings mindfulness of people less fortunate and heightens one's prayers to Allah; Muslims abstain from bad thoughts and actions—if someone speaks negative words, you withdraw, saying, "I am fasting."

Fasting is broken with water and one date, then coffee, and the Iftar feast. Iftar starts with *adas* (lentil soup, p. 153), followed by salads such as tabbouleh (p. 147), and then mains such as *yabraq* (rice and meat in grape leaves, p. 157) and *fatteh makdous* (crispy fried eggplant with tahini and pomegranate molasses in yogurt and fried bread, p. 151). Drinks—*shaneena* (bubbly salty-yogurt, p. 168), *haleeb wa tamr* (date shakes, p. 169), and juices made from dried fruit pastes such as tamarind, apricot, and licorice—promote healthy fasting. *Qatayef* (fried pastries with nuts and syrup) and rose-infused sweet *qishta* (pp. 164-65), bring smiles to

maamoul, semolina cookies using hand-tooled wooden moulds. Children lay out their best clothes in anticipation of parties and Eid gifts. The powerful communal prayer is held outside with many people wearing white clothing. Next is visiting relatives and calling family in Syria and the diaspora while sharing maamoul as the new year begins.

Ramadan is about Allah, family, and community. The war displaced millions of Syrians; hundreds of thousands are dead or missing. Millions, especially in Syria, suffer from food insecurity and unsafe conditions. As the people of Zaatari celebrate, they reflect on Ramadans past and pass traditions on to their young. But they miss their family, neighbours, friends, the family Quran, grandparents' prayer beads, their houses and lands. Sadly, many have traumatic memories, as Ramadan—the holiest time of peace and good will—was weaponized to target civilians with war atrocity.

وَأَنذِرْ عَشِيرَتَكَ ٱلْأَقْرَبِينَ

And warn, [O Muhammad], your closest kindred.
—The Holy Quran, Ash-Shu'araa "The Poets" 26:214

The drummer by Emad al-Kafri

all. Prayers and Quran reading follow—many people re-read the entire Quran during Ramadan.

Ramadan is a deeply spiritual reset of one's relationship with Allah and the Muslim community. The last ten days of prayers are the most heard by Allah, particularly on Laylat al-Qadr (the Night of Power)—the anniversary of when Jibril first visited Mohammed. Zakat donations on this day receive increased blessings. At camp, Iftar feasts are shared; mosques distribute sweets, echoing the Daraa Hourani tradition of preparing wheat and meat separately in large pots for the poor to bring bowls and fill them.

Ramadan ends with the feast of Eid al-Fitr. Women gather on the eve, as in Syria, and work through the night preparing

Eid bread, p. 161

The Joy of Ramadan

Ramadan comes and people welcome it every year with the same joy. What is the secret of this joy?

Perhaps the secret is that it comes for just thirty days, like a visitor away too long who returns to satiate with love but leaves again.

Perhaps the secret lies in its rituals—stringing up lanterns, crescents, and stars to welcome Ramadan in our homes, when the family gathers for Iftar and the markets fill with juices and foods, especially qatayef.

But the true secret is the joy that Ramadan brings of Allah's mercy and forgiveness. For this, prayers are multiplied, and we read the Noble Quran.

Fasting

Fasting is one of the Five Pillars of Islam and children learn to fast from a young age. Maria, from al-Yadouda, began partial fasting three years ago aged seven.

"I love Ramadan, especially when we start preparing the Iftar breakfast table.

I help my mother bring the dishes to the table. We gather around, waiting for the call to prayer. I love it when we buy new clothes for Eid, and when Eid comes we visit Grandpa, Grandmother, and our relatives."

143

Ful Mudammas

ABU MAHMOUD, al-Nueayma

2 cans (2 x 400 g/14 oz.) fava beans, with liquid

4 cloves garlic, crushed and chopped

1 tsp salt

3 tbsp (45 ml) fresh lemon juice

¼ cup (60 ml) olive oil

1 tbsp ground cumin

1 tsp Aleppo pepper

olive oil for drizzling

Garnish: 1 small tomato, diced; **½** small onion, minced; **½ cup (12.5 g)** minced parsley; lemon wedges

Ful mudammas is a fava (broad) bean stew flavoured with cumin, Aleppo pepper, and lemon, is made at night in large copper pots in Syria's souks, ready for morning ftoor. Ful is especially important for breakfast in much of the Levant and in parts of North Africa, as nourishment for the long day of fasting ahead. Note the ful mudammas in our photo doesn't show much sauce, there should be a lot more!

❖

In a medium saucepan over medium heat, cover the beans with water and 1 tsp of cumin, bring to a boil, then simmer until tender, 8-10 minutes. Remove from heat and use the back of a spoon to mash half of the beans.

Stir in the garlic, salt, lemon juice, oil, remaining cumin, and pepper. Keep warm until ready to serve.

Drizzle with olive oil, garnish, and serve with lemon wedges.

TO USE DRIED BEANS

Abu Mahmoud shares an easy home version of his souk restaurant recipe.

1.5 lbs (680 g) dried fava beans

1 tsp ground cumin

Cover dried fava beans in water overnight. The next morning, drain and rinse the beans, and place in a large pot with cumin and fresh water to cover. Bring to a boil and simmer for 45-60 minutes or until the beans are tender. Mash half of the beans and proceed with recipe.

Tesqieh

UMM FAISAL, Elmah

3 rounds khubz (or pita bread)

¼ cup (60 ml) olive oil or saman

1 can (400 g/14 oz) chickpeas, drained and rinsed

2 cups (500 ml) full-fat yogurt

¼ cup (60 ml) tahini

2 tsp minced garlic

1 tsp ground cumin

1 tsp chili powder

2 tbsp fresh lemon juice

1 tsp salt

½ tsp white or Aleppo pepper

olive oil for drizzling

Garnishes: 1 cup (25 g) chopped parsley, lemon wedges, **1 cup (140 g)** nuts (pine nuts, cashews, slivered almonds) fried in olive oil until golden, chopped tomatoes, pomegranate seeds

Recipes for crumbling day-old bread go back to the thirteenth-century Abbasidian Caliphate cookbook *Kitâb al-Tabîkh* by al-Baghdadi, so no wonder we have many variations from savoury to sweet. *Fatteh* means "to crumble." Most basic is Fatteh Hummus, a Bedouin dish. Umm Faisal, seventy-five years young, taught me to make this dish. She said, "I love this dish because it reminds me of my childhood, when my mother prepared it for our Iftar gatherings, when we break our day-long fast. I like to make it for my grandchildren for its several benefits and delicious taste."

Tear the bread into 1-inch (2.5 cm) pieces. In a large frying pan, heat the oil over medium heat and fry the bread until golden on both sides. Reserve 1 cup (140 g) and spread the remainder over a large serving dish.

In a medium pot, add the chickpeas to 1 cup (250 ml) of water and simmer for 20 minutes. Drain, reserving half of the broth and 3 tbsp (30 g) of the chickpeas for garnish.

In a medium bowl, combine the yogurt, tahini, garlic, and seasonings; taste and adjust.

Pour the chickpea broth over the bread, add the chickpeas, and stir to combine. Top with the yogurt mixture. Garnish quickly with the reserved fried bread and chickpeas and the other garnishes. Drizzle with oil. Serve hot.

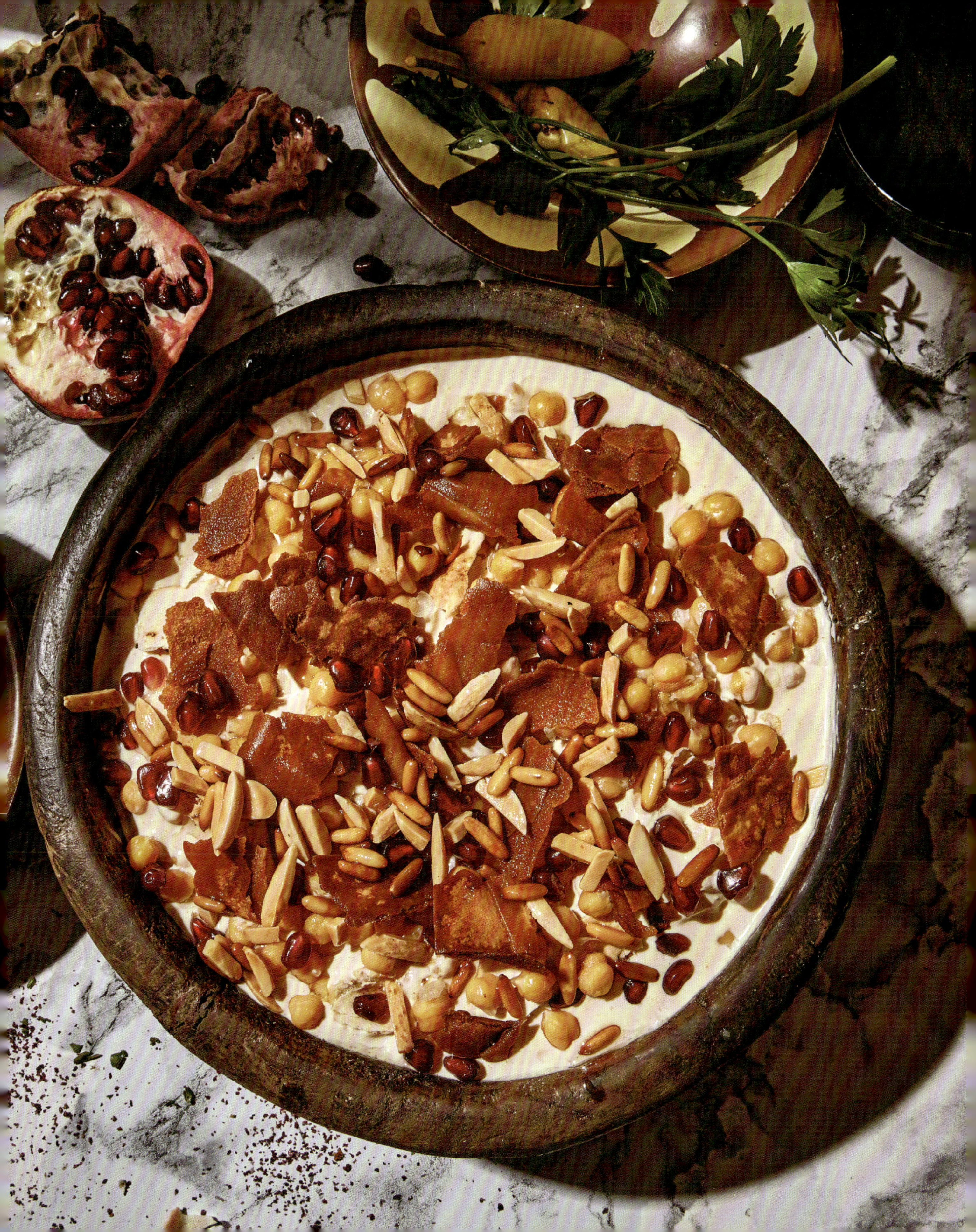

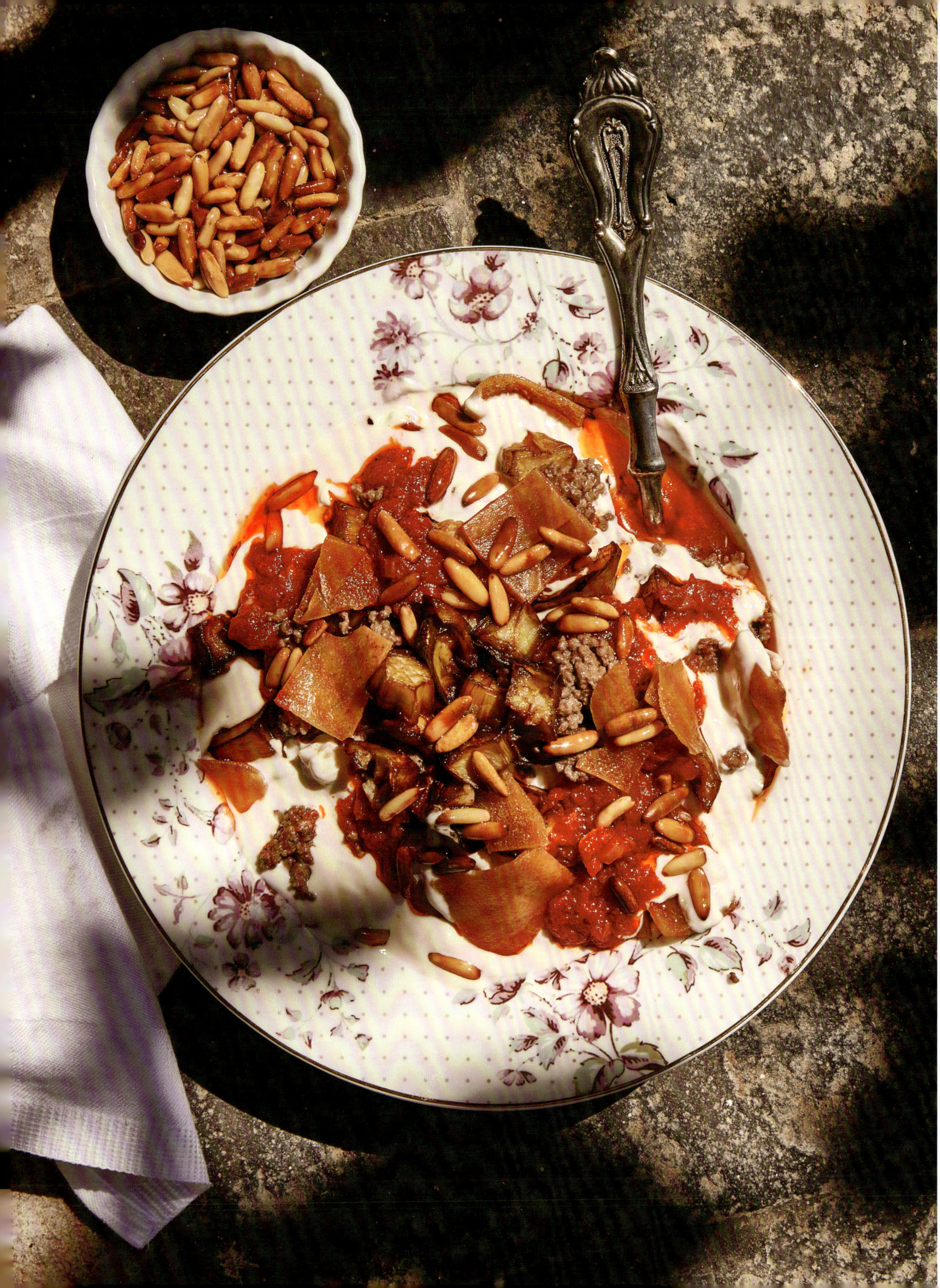

Fatteh Makdous

UMM MAHMOUD, Nasib

Fatteh makdous, tasty served warm or cold, features baby eggplants stuffed with pomegranate molasses-spiced tomatoes, pine nuts, and ground lamb, nestled in fried bread and crowned with garlic- and tahini-infused yogurt, nuts, and parsley. For a time-saving vegetarian version: omit the meat and chop the eggplant into 1″ pieces and fry in oil, adding all the pomegranate syrup and cinnamon with the pine nuts, etc.

Don't try using makdous houran (from the Zaatari Pantry) as a substitute for the eggplant preparation—it's the same name (makdous) but a completely different preparation!

❖

In a large frying pan, fry the pine nuts in the oil until golden, then set aside to drain.

Make croutons by tearing the bread into 1-inch (2.5 cm) pieces. Shallow fry over medium heat until golden. Sprinkle with salt. Reserve ½ cup (70 g) of the bread and arrange the remainder in a large serving dish.

In a bowl, combine the yogurt, tahini, garlic, lemon juice, and a pinch of salt, and stir until smooth.

Slice off the tops of the eggplants and halve them length-wise. Rinse and dry well, then fry in oil over low heat for 20 minutes or until soft. Drain on a paper towel. Scoop out the flesh, reserving the pulp. In the same pan over medium heat, fry half the onion for 3-4 minutes. Add the meat, pomegranate molasses, and cinnamon. Cook until the meat is done. Add half the pine nuts, the eggplant pulp, and salt and pepper; stir well and remove from heat. Adjust the seasonings and fill the eggplant shells.

For the sauce, in a medium saucepan, sauté the remaining onion until golden. Add the tomatoes and cook for 5 minutes. Add the tomato paste and let thicken for 5 minutes. Add the sugar, salt and pepper, and ⅓ cup (80 ml) of water. Simmer for 15 minutes and adjust the seasoning.

Ladle the sauce over the croutons in the serving dish. Top with the filled eggplants. Dollop the yogurt mixture around the eggplants. Drizzle with saman or olive oil and garnish with parsley and the remaining nuts and fried bread.

1 cup (140 g) pine nuts

3 tbsp (45 ml) olive oil

3 rounds khubz or pita bread

6 cups (1.5 l) full-fat yogurt

⅓ cup (80 ml) tahini

6 cloves garlic, minced

2 tbsp lemon juice

10-12 baby eggplants

2 medium onions, finely chopped

½ lb (225 g) ground lamb

2 tbsp pomegranate molasses

1 tsp cinnamon

3 tomatoes, chopped and drained

3 tbsp (45 ml) tomato paste

1 tbsp sugar

3 tbsp (45 ml) saman or olive oil

salt and pepper to taste

Garnish: chopped parsley

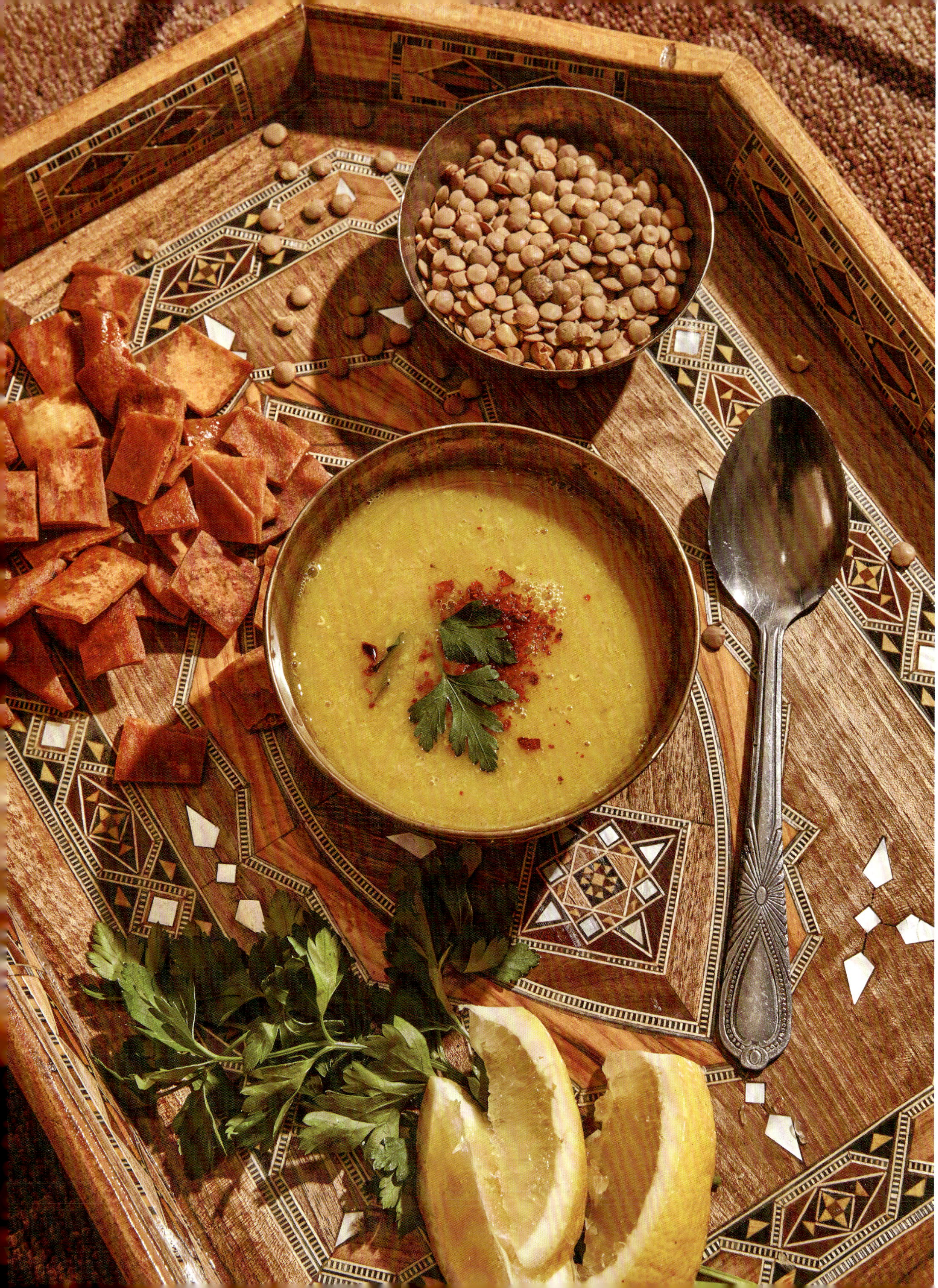

Shorbat Adas

UMM KARAM, Sayda

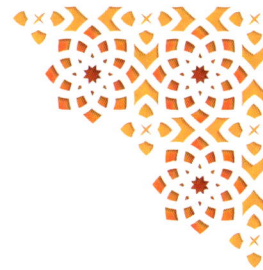

Shorbat Adas, ubiquitously called adas (lentil soup), tastes sublime and is light on the stomach, perfect for restoring liquids and nutrients after fasting all day. Umm Karam's husband loves it so much he asks her to prepare it every day, winter and summer. "I am bored with cooking; every day my husband forces me to cook this same soup," Umm Karam lamented. When asked why he likes it so much, she explained, "When he eats it, he feels he is in his home in Syria—his mother planted lentils in their fields in Houran; she harvested and grated lentils for soup. When we came to Zaatari in 2013, the first foods from WFP were lentils and spaghetti, so my husband never quit this habit of asking for lentil soup."

❖

Rinse and soak the lentils in water for 1 hour. In a large pot, heat the oil over low-medium heat and fry the onion and carrot until soft, 5-7 minutes, stirring often. Add the drained and rinsed lentils, the water, and the seasonings until boiling. Lower the heat and cook, stirring occasionally, until the lentils are tender, about 10-15 minutes. You want them whole but soft. Remove from heat. Purée the soup or serve as is, adjusting the seasoning with lime wedges and croutons.

To make croutons, tear or cut the bread into 1 inch (2.5 cm) pieces. In a large frying pan, heat oil over high heat and shallow fry on both sides. Alternatively, you can brush the pieces with olive oil and bake at 400°F (204°C) for 5 minutes, turning midway through for even browning. Lightly salt the croutons. This is an amazing snack that can be sprinkled with sumac or zaatar and keeps crisp for several days.

1 cup (190 g) red lentils

2 tbsp olive oil

1 medium onion, diced

½ cup (62.5 g) carrot, diced

10 cups (2.5 l) water

1 tsp salt

1 tsp pepper

1 tsp ground coriander (optional)

¼ tsp ground turmeric

1 lime wedge

2 rounds khubz or pita bread

olive oil for frying

Garnish (optional): chopped cilantro

Yalanji

UMM ABDALLAH, Dael

1 lb (450 g) grape leaves (fresh or pickled)

1 lb (450 g) long grain rice, such as basmati

3 ¾ cups (887 ml) water

1 ¼ cup (250 g) chopped tomatoes

2 tbsp minced garlic

1 small onion, minced

½ cup (12.5 g) minced parsley

½ green chili pepper (jalapeno), seeded and minced, or **½ tsp** black pepper

1 tsp ground cumin

1 tsp lemon salt

3 tbsp (45 ml) olive oil

3 potatoes, peeled and thinly sliced

extra olive oil and lemon juice for layering

2 tomatoes, sliced

1 onion, sliced

chicken or meat pieces (optional)

Garnish: lemon wedges, chopped parsley

STOCK

6 cups (1.5 l) water

2 tsp Maggi powder

2 tbsp olive oil

I arrived early morning at Umm Abdallah's house to prepare Yalanji—a quint-essential Ramadan dish. After a strong, quick handshake and many kisses (right cheek—one peck, left side—3 pecks with a pause, then 2 more), she pro-nounced, "Bismillah al-Rahman al-Rahim (in the name of God, the merciful, the compassionate). May God return Ramadan to us with blessings. Yallah, move your hands in Karen, let's get to work!"

One of the most renowned foods of Ramadan, yalanji (rolled grape leaves stuffed with rice) takes many hands to prepare. Umm Abdallah and her daugh-ters, like all women at camp, are experts at tightly rolling the bundles. While most recipes call for layering yalanji, camp women tie them in bundles, making them easier to handle—and place a heavy rock on the lid to aid steaming. The lore is that yalanji is a Turkish word meaning "to cheat" by excluding meat from the rice filling. By topping the stacked rolls of grape leaves with pieces of meat (instead of inside with the rice, as with yabraq), Syrians know that the filling is vegetarian. Enjoy yalanji warm or cold, drizzled with lemon juice, best eaten in one delicious bite. Yalanji keep in the fridge for several days, so no worries about making a big quantity. Trust us—they will disappear fast, enjoyed at any time of day.

❖

Rinse the grape leaves carefully, ensuring not to tear them, and set aside.

In a large bowl, cover the rice with water and swish with your hand. Drain water and repeat 3 times, until water runs clear. Drain the rice, place in a pot, cover with water and bring to a boil. Reduce heat to low, cover and simmer 20 minutes. Remove from heat and let sit covered for 5 minutes. Remove lid, put rice in a large bowl, fluff and add the tomato, garlic, onion, parsley, chili pepper, cumin, salt, and oil; mix well and set aside.

Bring the stock ingredients to a boil, then simmer for 20 minutes, uncovered.

Place a layer of sliced potatoes in a large pot or dutch oven. They will serve as insulation for the yalanji, ensuring they don't scorch.

To wrap the grape leaves, place a leaf flat in your palm, vein side up with the leaf points towards your fingers. Put 1 tbsp (15 ml) of the rice filling in the centre, fold the bottom half over, fold the sides in, and roll up tightly. Layer evenly in the pot (or tie in bundles, Zaatari-style, using butcher string), dousing the layers with olive oil and lemon juice. When the pot is ¾ full, add the tomato and onion slices and the chicken or meat (if using). Pour in the stock to cover. Place the lid on the pot and bring to a boil, then simmer for 1 hour. Remove from heat and transfer yalanji using tongs to a serving platter and garnish. Refrigerate leftovers.

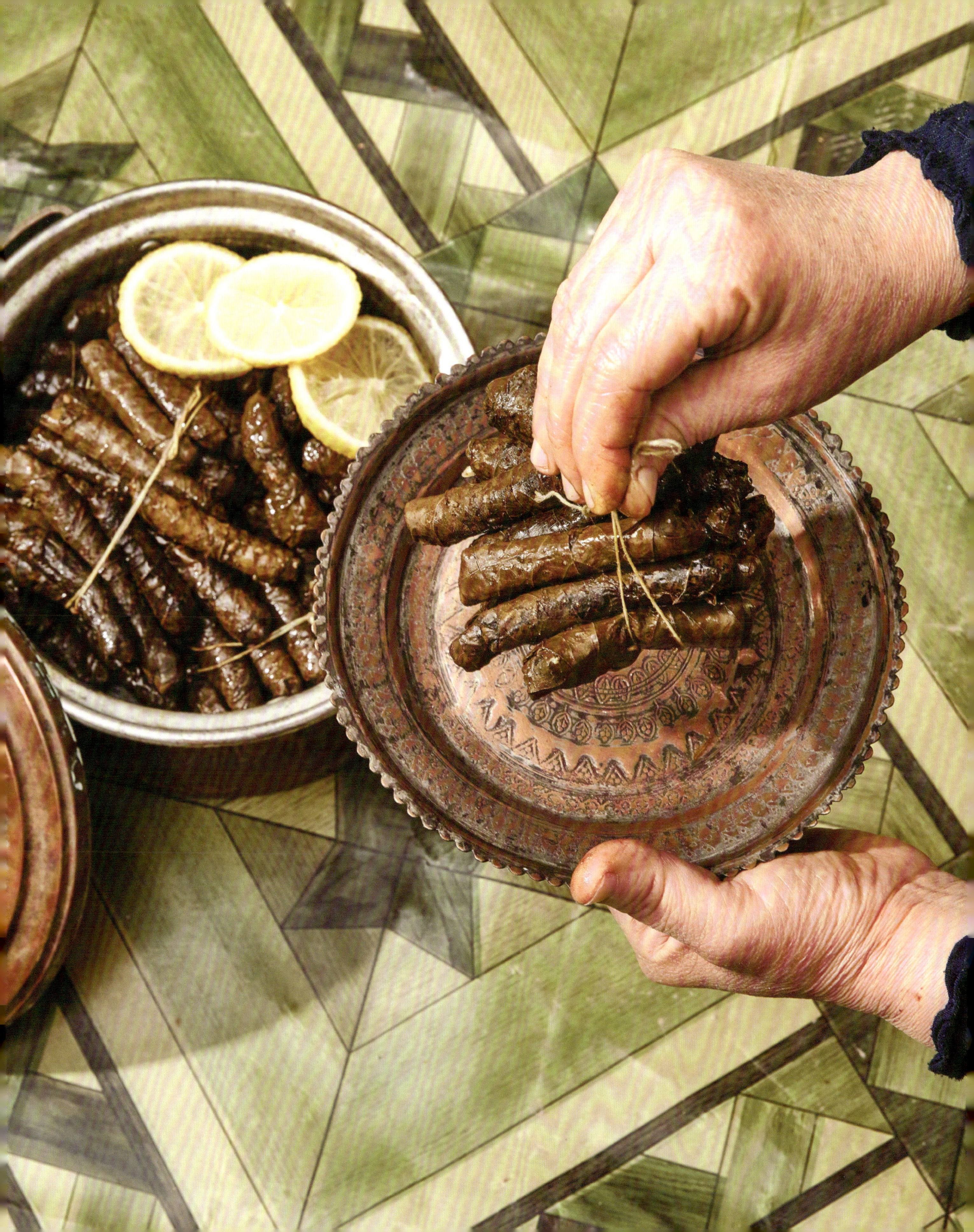

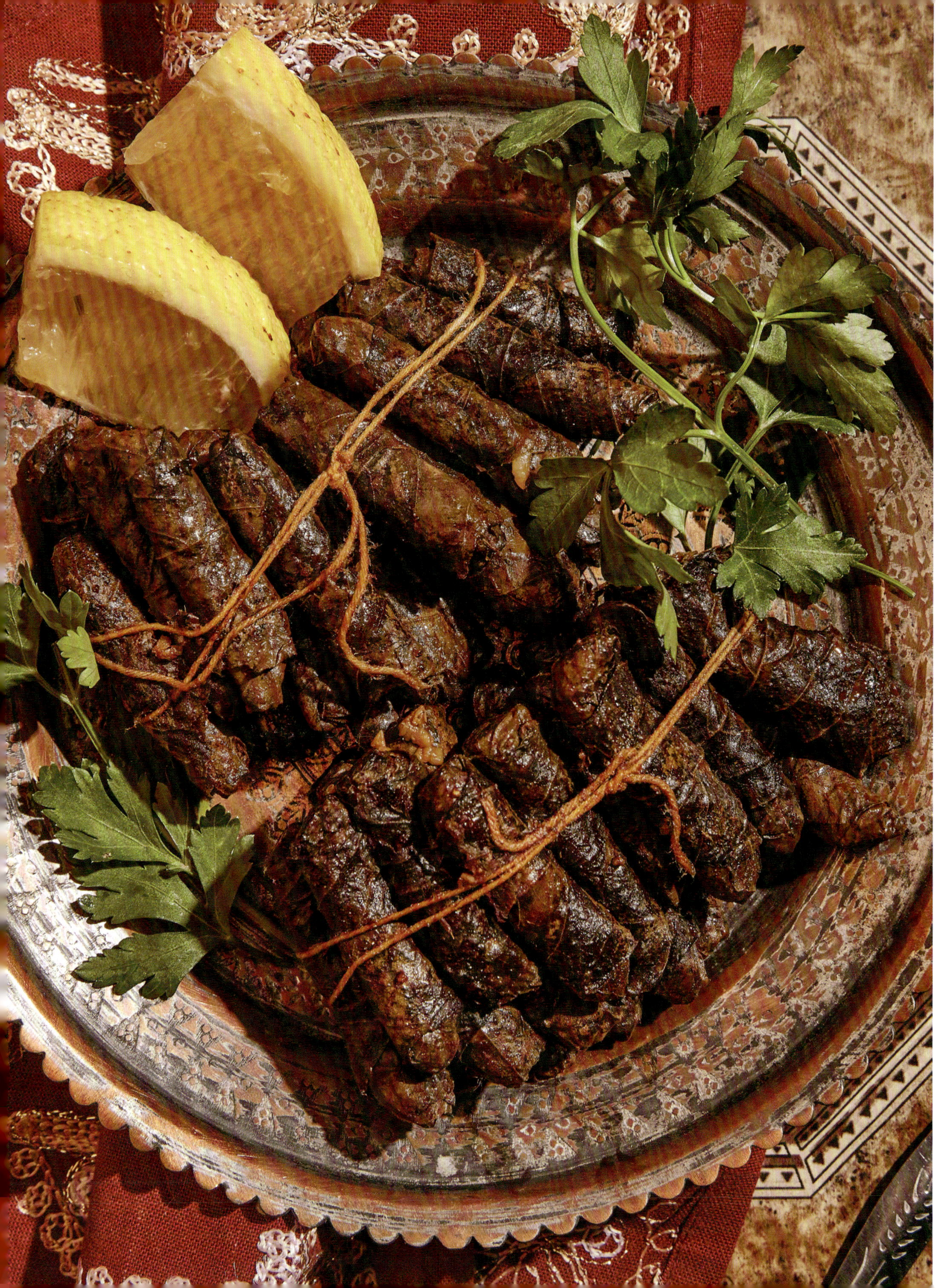

Yabraq

UMM BARAA, Tasil

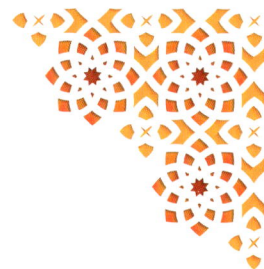

Umm Baraa explains, "We use lamb with yabraq, but beef or poultry are fine. As with yalanji, we tie the rolls in bundles using butcher string, making them easier to handle—and place a heavy rock on the lid to aid steaming. We like to serve yabraq warm with laban."

❖

Rinse the grape leaves carefully, ensuring not to tear them, and set aside.

In a large skillet over medium heat, warm the olive oil, add the ground lamb, and cook until no pink (about 8-10 minutes), breaking up large pieces with a spoon or spatula. Drain and discard any remaining oil, and set meat aside.

In a large bowl, cover the rice with water and swish with your hand. Drain water and repeat 3 times, until water runs clear. Drain the rice, place in a pot, cover with water and bring to a boil. Reduce heat to low, cover and simmer 20 minutes. Remove from heat and let sit covered for 5 minutes. Remove lid, put rice in a large bowl, fluff and add the parsley, cumin, chili, salt, lemon juice and rind, oil, and cooked meat. Mix well and set aside.

For the stock, bring the water, Maggi, and oil to a boil, then simmer for 20 minutes.

To wrap the grape leaves, place the leaf flat in your palm, vein side up with the leaf points towards your fingers. Place 1 tbsp (15 ml) of the filling in the centre, fold the bottom half over the filling, fold the sides in, and roll up tightly. Tie the bundles (10-15) with butcher string.

Place the bundles in the pot and layer with the sliced tomatoes, onion, and garlic. When the pot is nearly full, pour in the stock. Cover, bring to a boil, then simmer for 1 hour.

Transfer the yabraq to a serving platter and garnish.

1 lb (450 g) grape leaves

1 lb (450 g) long-grain rice, such as basmati

3¾ cups (927 ml) water

1 tbsp olive oil

1 lb (450 g) ground lamb

½ cup (12.5 g) parsley, minced

1 tsp ground cumin

1 tsp chili powder

1 tsp salt

1 tbsp lemon juice

1 tsp grated lemon rind

3 tbsp (45 ml) olive oil

4 tomatoes, sliced

1 onion, halved lengthwise and sliced ½" (1.25 cm) thick

½ head garlic, unpeeled and broken into pieces

STOCK

6 cups (1.5 l) water

2 tsp Maggi powder

2 tbsp olive oil

Garnish: fresh lemon juice, chopped parsley

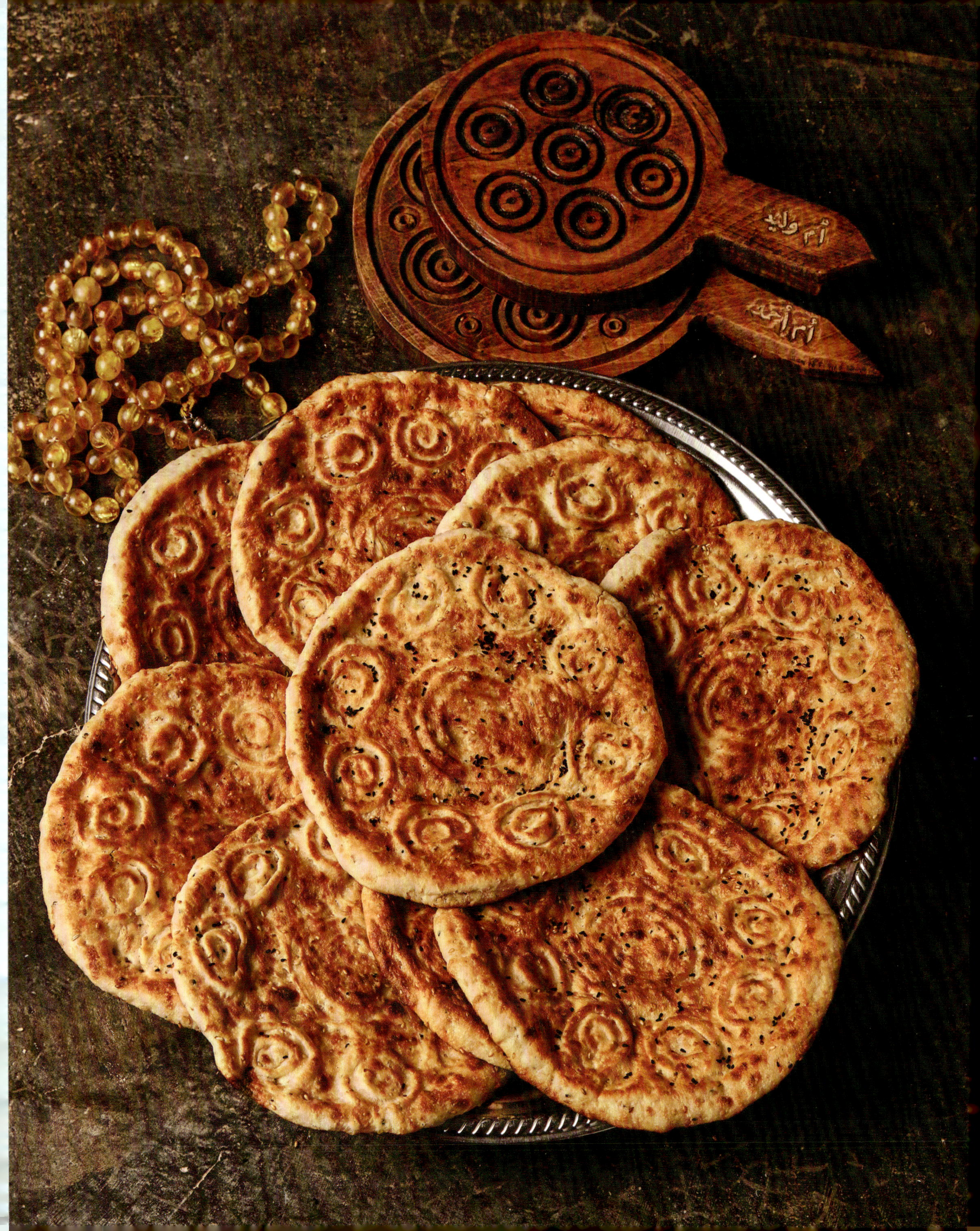
أم وليد
أم أحمد

Eid Bread

UMM MOHAMMED, Busra

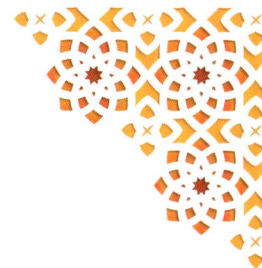

Eid bread is available only during Ramadan, especially at Eid al-Fitr and also at Eid al-Adha. Eid al-Adha is called the "greater Eid," or the "celebration of the sacrifice" that marks the end of the Haj pilgrimage to Mecca (one of the 5 pillars of Islam), and commemorates when the prophet Ibrahim (Abraham) was going to sacrifice his son Ismail (Ishmael) as a sign of obedience to Allah. Allah switched Ismail for a sheep, saving Ismail, and that sacrifice and its celebration are echoed by the sacrifice of sheep and camels with meat distributed to family, neighbours, and the poor, lasting several days.

Umm Mohammed learned to make eid bread in Syria from her mother and brothers, and she has passed on the recipe to her own daughters in Zaatari. She explained, "Eid bread reminds me of home and family every time I bake it." The fragrant, slightly sweet, savoury yellow breads are formed in traditional round wooden Eid moulds, patterned with whorls said to represent clouds, and decorated with black sesame seeds and nigella seeds as raindrops—Houran farmers' gratitude for a bountiful harvest. The unique flavour of eid bread comes from a mixture of spices, including ground mahlab (the seed kernels inside of sour cherry stones) and ground mastic (dried resin from mastic trees).

Cooks alter the thickness and cooking times according to their preferred fluffiness and crunch. Eid bread can be made without a mold by rolling to 6" (15 cm) circles and decorated using the tines of a fork or by making patterns with a small cookie cutter. Eid bread stays fresh for days, wrapped and refrigerated.

❖

Mix the yeast with the sugar and water until it foams and bubbles.

Mix the dry ingredients together. Add olive oil until the mixture resembles wet sand, then add the yeast mixture and knead. Gradually add water until the dough is smooth. Cover and let rise in a warm area until doubled.

Preheat the oven to 500°F (260°C). Slice the dough into 20 small balls. Brush olive oil on the bread mould and roll each ball over, re-greasing the mould as needed. Alternatively, roll each ball into a 6" (15 cm) circle and decorate using the tines of a fork.

Place the breads on an oiled baking sheet and decorate with the black sesame and/or nigella seeds. Bake until the bottoms are golden. Turn on the broiler to brown the tops. Brush the hot breads with oil and enjoy with sweet chai (black tea).

1 tbsp dry yeast

2 tsp sugar

½ cup (125 ml) water

6 cups (750 g) flour

1 cup (125 g) powdered milk

2 tbsp anise seeds

2 tbsp toasted sesame seeds

1 tsp fennel seeds

1 tbsp ground anise

½ tsp ground turmeric

1 tsp powdered mahlab (or ground cardamom)

1 tsp ground mastic (or **½ tsp** vanilla extract)

⅔ cup (160 ml) olive oil

2 cups (500 ml) water (approximately)

4 tbsp (35 g) black sesame seeds and/or nigella seeds, for decorating

Maamoul

UMM QAIS and Anseh Mais, Ghasm

6 cups (1 kg) fine semolina

1½ cups (375 ml) melted saman (or salted butter)

½ cup (125 ml) melted butter

¼-½ cup (60-125 ml) vegetable oil

1 cup (125 g) flour

1 tsp ground mastic (or **½ tsp** vanilla extract) with **½ tsp** sugar

1 tsp ground mahlab (or ground fennel seeds, or ground cardamom)

1 cup (125 g) powdered milk

2 tsp ground anise

1 tsp baking powder

1½ tsp instant yeast

½ cup (125 ml) water

1 tsp sugar plus **½ cup (100 g)**

1 cup (250 ml) full-fat (whole) milk

Maamoul are the sweet reward for fasting all Ramadan, eaten particularly at Eid al-Fitr and Eid al-Adha (explained in Eid Bread). Umm Qais described how Daraa women would gather to prepare maamoul using 22 lb (10 kg) of *sameed* (semolina) because the whole extended family as well as acquaintances would be coming. Sharing the tasks and the expense, the grandmothers rubbed the semolina with oils early in the morning, then let it rest all day. Others would arrive, arms laden with dates, nuts, spices, homemade jams, and their maamoul moulds—their shape and patterns specific for date, pistachio and walnut, hand-carved generations ago, patina darkened from age and use. Over coffee and chai, they worked all night, filling, pounding, baking; sharing stories and news over much laughter, as sweet smells of maamoul enveloped their village from house to house. Maamoul made with flour, available year-round at sweet shops and commercial bakeries, pales in comparison to handmade Eid sameed maamoul—lacking the crunchy texture and richer taste, so if you're at a shop remember to ask for "maamoul sameed."

◆×◆

To make the dough, put the semolina in a large bowl, pour in the hot saman, hot butter, and oil and rub well with your hands until the semolina is completely soaked. Cover and leave for 8-10 hours at room temperature.

In a large bowl, mix the flour, mastic, mahlab, powdered milk, anise, and baking powder. Add to the semolina.

Proof the yeast with 1 tsp sugar in ½ cup (125 ml) water; set aside for 10 minutes or until foamy. Combine the remaining sugar with the milk; add with the yeast to the semolina. Knead the dough gently until it clumps together. Cover and let rest for 1 hour, then shape into balls according to mould size.

To prepare the date filling (maamoul tamr), mix the ingredients well and knead to make a paste. Shape into balls. To prepare the nut filling (maamoul joz), mix the ingredients together.

To assemble, flatten the dough balls and place the filling inside. Shape the dough around the filling, seal, and flatten. Grease the mould with oil, wiping out the excess. Place the maamoul inside and whack against a hard surface to release them. (Or use the tines of a fork to make pretty patterns.)

Bake at 350°F (175°C) for 8-10 minutes. Broil for 2-3 minutes to brown the tops. Cool on wire racks. Dust with icing sugar and decorate with pistachios.

MAAMOUL TAMR

2.2 lb (1 kg) finely chopped pitted dates

2 tbsp saman or butter

1 tbsp ground cinnamon

1 tsp ground cardamom

1 tsp toasted sesame seeds

MAAMOUL JOZ

1½ cups (225 g) finely chopped pistachios or walnuts

½ cup (100 g) sugar

2 tbsp orange blossom water

2 tbsp butter or saman, melted

1 tbsp ground cinnamon

MAAMOUL MURAABA

1½ cups (475 g) rose, fig, or apricot jam (see p. 251)

SYRUP

2½ cups (500 g) sugar

1 cup (250 ml) water

1 tsp fresh lemon juice

2 tsp rosewater, or **½ tsp** orange blossom water

PANCAKES

1½ cups (187 g) flour

½ cup (100 g) coarse semolina

2 tbsp sugar

2 tbsp powdered milk

1 tsp baking powder

½ tsp salt

1 tsp instant yeast

2 cups (500 ml) warm water

1 tsp vanilla extract

saman or vegetable oil for frying

JOZ FILLING

1 cup (140 g) fried nuts (pine nuts, walnuts, hazelnuts)

1 tsp ground cinnamon

2 tbsp sugar

1 tbsp saman

Qatayef

UMM ABDALLAH and UMM FIRAS, Damascus, al-Hara

You know it's Ramadan when *qatayef* (small, round pancakes) appear in bakeries begging to be filled with *joz* (cinnamon-infused nuts), then deep-fried, bathed in sugar syrup, dusted with icing sugar, and served with *qishta* (rose-infused sweet cream). Remember, the qatayef should not be flipped, because the filling must cling to the soft side. Filling them is a great job for both young and old, using dried fruit, coconut, and other flavours. Try filling unfried qatayef with qishta by pinching one end to form a cone, sprinkling with nuts, and drizzling with syrup—an easy, lovely variation. Uncooked qatayef can be frozen and fried right from the freezer.

First, prepare the syrup. In a saucepan, combine the sugar and water. Bring to a boil and add the lemon juice, then lower the heat and simmer for 8-10 minutes. Remove from heat and stir in the rosewater. Pour into a deep bowl and cool to room temperature.

For the pancakes, in a large bowl mix the dry ingredients. Add half the water and the vanilla. Stir well and gradually add the remainder of the water. The batter should be velvety smooth and liquid; if it is thick, add more water, tablespoon by tablespoon. Cover and set aside for 1 hour or until bubbly and slightly risen—this helps tenderize the semolina.

Heat a large frying pan over medium heat and add saman or vegetable oil. Stir the batter well. Pour 2 tbsp into the pan, using a spoon to make small circles 3 inches (8 cm) apart. Cook for 1-2 minutes or until bubbles form on top and the pancakes are brown underneath. Place in a single layer on a linen tea towel and cover with another to keep the qatayef from drying out.

For the filling, in a small bowl, combine the nuts, cinnamon, and sugar with a fork. Add enough saman so that the mixture is crumbly and glistens.

For the qishta, in a medium saucepan, whisk together the cream, milk, cornstarch, and sugar until smooth. Over medium-low heat, whisk constantly until it boils and thickens. Stir in the rosewater. Pour into a bowl and cover with plastic wrap with the plastic touching the cream to prevent a skin from forming. Refrigerate for at least 2 hours. Stir before using.

Place 1½ tsp of the filling in each qatayef, bubbly side up and brown side down, fold in half, pinch the sides to seal, and set aside.

In a large pot, heat 3 inches (8 cm) of oil over high heat. Fry the qatayef in batches, 2-3 minutes on each side until browned. Drain on a paper towel and dip the hot qatayef in the cold syrup.

Place on a platter and dust with powdered sugar. Garnish and serve with the qishta.

Qishta

1 cup (250 ml) heavy cream

½ cup (125 ml) full-fat (whole) milk

2 tbsp cornstarch

1 tbsp sugar

½ tsp either rosewater, orange blossom water, vanilla, or ground mastic

Garnish: coconut (sweetened or unsweetened), finely chopped nuts, dried rose petals

Tamr Hindi

ABU ENSAAF, Inkhil

1 packet (12 oz/350 g) tamarind pulp

8 cups (2 l) cold water

2 cups (400 g) sugar (or to taste)

1 tsp orange blossom water
or rosewater (or to taste)

ice

Chop the tamarind paste into small pieces. Place in a large bowl, add water, cover, and let sit for 7-8 hours until the paste is dissolved in the water. Stir the mixture occasionally, breaking down the chunks with a spoon. Alternatively, to speed up the processing time, you can cover the tamarind paste with hot water and let sit for 3-4 hours, or until the paste dissolves.

Strain the tamarind using a sieve, discarding any seeds leftover from the pulp. Using a blender, pulverize with the sugar and flower water.

Serve in metal cups with ice and additional cold water and sugar.

During Ramadan nights, clad in tarboosh and colourful folk dress, tamr hindi street sellers clang symbols while carrying heavy copper pots filled with tamarind-based, sweet-tangy juice on their backs and metal cups belted around their waists. Loaded with nutrients and known for its blood-thinning properties, tamr hindi is Arabic for "Indian Fruit," the pod-shaped fruit of tamarind trees that is both sweet and tangy.

Abu Ensaaf learned to make tamr hindi at age seven by soaking tamarind pulp in cold water for 7-8 hours, and adding sugar and flavouring. While the soaking time can be shortened by using hot water, Abu Ensaaf advises against boiling the tamarind paste because high heat reduces the nutritional benefits of this beverage. Abu Ensaaf recounted, "When the revolution started, I was working in Damascus and unable to stay, so I returned home to Houran—it was two days before Ramadan. I bought a trolley and began selling tamr-hindi in the streets from the start of the holy month. People drink it a lot in the evenings, after fasting, because it helps with fasting and makes you feel quenched, in addition to its extensive health benefits. Tamr hindi is my preferred beverage."

Qamar al-Din

ANSEH ALA'A, Ghouta

Qamar al-din is a drink made in Syria from sun-dried apricot paste and is sold everywhere during Ramadan. It's easy to make, and orange blossom water adds the nicest touch.

10 oz (300 g) apricot paste

2 cups (500 ml) water

2 tbsp sugar

1 tbsp orange blossom water

Cut the apricot paste into small pieces. Place in a bowl with the water and sugar and soak for 1-2 hours or until soft.

Beat by hand for 2-3 minutes or with a mixer until smooth. Stir in the orange blossom water and refrigerate until cold.

Shaneena

ABU TAREK, Sayda

3 cups (750 ml) full-fat yogurt

1½ cups (375 ml) water

½ tsp salt, or to taste

½ cup (125 ml) sparkling water or club soda (optional)

2 tbsp chopped fresh mint (optional)

Combine all the ingredients and shake well. Serve cold.

Shaneena is a frothy, salty yogurt drink that is simple to make at home. We love it year-round in the morning, with barbecue, and at night it's said to bring good dreams. We buy it in the souk in large bags, similar to milk bags in Canada, and shake it vigorously to create a bubbly froth before pouring.

Haleeb wa Tamr

UMM SAAD, Keswa

Haleeb wa tamr, or date shakes, are nutritious and loved by young and old and are popular all year but especially during Ramadan. Try substituting almond or soya milk for whole milk.

1 cup (150 g) pitted and chopped soft dates

2 cups (500 ml) full-fat (whole) milk

½ tsp vanilla extract

1 tsp honey or sugar, or to taste

¼ tsp ground cinnamon

Blend all the ingredients with a little ice. Sprinkle with cinnamon and serve cold.

Habibi My Love

Arabic has over fifty words for "love." Summer, after Ramadan, is the start of wedding season. Zaatari weddings celebrate shy, courtly poetic love and being smitten, but also the uniting of families and tribes, the sharing of happiness among friends and neighbours. Virtually nothing is known by outsiders about Zaatari weddings as they occur after camp hours and require family invitation to attend.

Dress-shop mannequins in the souks advertise fairytale wedding gowns and glitzy party dresses. The dresses are for rent and the back room is a beauty salon for hair, makeup, sugaring, and henna. Similar home-based shops, with subtle or no advertising, can be found across the districts. But how do couples meet? It's not easy. There's no dating app, and camp culture, as in much of the Arab world, has gender-based norms where boys and girls attend school at different times, socialize with family and their own gender, and wear modest clothing and hijab. Love happens in fleeting moments, such as seeing your future wife with others on the street, at a community centre or gathering, or as the groom's relative at a wedding. Emboldened, the young man asks his mother and sisters to learn about her and report back. If they like her, the female relatives propose to the girl's family.

If her parents and the girl accept, then the male family members draw up a wedding contract that stipulates *mahr* (the bride's dowry). In Syria and Zaatari, the groom's family provide the mahr, *jihaz* (trousseau), and house furniture. Depending on their means, mahr is typically 1,500–2,000 Jordanian dinar (JOD, about USD 2,000–2,500). About JOD 500 (USD 700) is paid each for jihaz and for al-Tallah gold (the visit gift), along with the wedding entertainment and food expenses, which can run into a couple of thousand as hundreds of guests are invited. The families may follow al-Hasakah, where mahr is divided into immediate—paid upon court approval of the contract—and deferred—more than JOD 2,000, paid in the event of divorce or widowhood, unless a different date is stipulated or as a symbolic dowry if the families know each other well.

The groom's jihaz payment covers bridal clothes, makeup, and perfumes. The bride's parents are responsible for items like bedding and clothes. Agreement is also reached on the living place and the time of the engagement party and other parties. According to Hourani tradition, the bride and groom first meet at the engagement party, where the sheikh signs the wedding contract. Because Zaatari is in Jordan, Sharia court approval is required. After health checks at the medical centre, the groom, bride, and their parents go to the court at base camp to make the contract official. Legal approval is necessary before the formal engagement, as the groom needs to touch his betrothed's hand in order to place the wedding ring.

For the *khutuba* (engagement celebration) at the bride's house, the groom buys sweets, juices, and Arabic (welcome) coffee, while the bride buys clothes and gold. Meanwhile, both families prepare for the wedding. The groom and his mother and the bride and her mother shop for wedding rings paid for by the groom. The bride's ring is gold, the groom's silver. According to the hadiths, the Prophet Mohammed (PBUH) believed gold was ostentatious for men and wore only a small silver ring engraved "Muhammed Rasoolullah" (Muhammed, Messenger of Allah) for judicial purposes when sending letters. Muslim men today wear silver rings weighing less than 4.35 grams with no inscription. Gold is fine for women, as it enhances their beauty and financial security, though it should not be ostentatious.

The khutuba is attended by both families. The groom and bride exchange rings, which they wear on their left hand until switching to their right hand at the wedding. Al-Fatiha, the first Surah of the Holy Quran, is read aloud, along with Surah 30, Ar Rum "The Romans":

وَمِنْ ءَايْتِهِ أَنْ خَلَقَ لَكُم مِّنْ أَنفُسِكُمْ أَزْوَٰجًا لِّتَسْكُنُوٓا إِلَيْهَا وَجَعَلَ بَيْنَكُم مَّوَدَّةً وَرَحْمَةً إِنَّ فِى ذَٰلِكَ لَءَايَٰتٍ لِّقَوْمٍ يَتَفَكَّرُونَ

And of His signs is that He created for you from yourselves mates that you may find tranquility in them; and He placed between you affection and mercy. Indeed in that are signs for a people who give thought.

—The Holy Quran, Ar Rum "The Romans" 30:21

Mleihi

UMM ABDALLAH and UMM FIRAS, al-Hrak

4 lamb shanks or bone-in shoulder (fat trimmed) in 6-8 pieces, or
1 chicken, skinned and quartered

3 tbsp (45 ml) olive oil

1 onion, chopped

1 tsp salt

1 tsp pepper

2 tsp ground curry

2 tsp Maggi powder

In a large pot, heat the oil over medium heat and brown the meat slowly on all sides. Add the onion and seasonings and cover with water. Bring to a boil, then reduce the heat and simmer, uncovered, for 75-90 minutes (depending on the cut) or until the meat falls from the bone. Take the pot off the heat and remove the meat from pot; keep both the meat and the broth warm.

Mleihi is arguably the best-known Hourani dish, dating back centuries and reflecting traditional Bedouin and agrarian culture. Mleihi comprises cuts of lamb cooked in spices and placed atop bulgur, drizzled with tangy *kethi* (dried yogurt sauce, p. 175) and melted saman. Steam-fried kibbeh (known as kibbeh mohabbala) and fried kibbeh are typically arranged around the sides or on top. Mleihi is eaten using the right hand to shape neat balls of bulgur and meat and any remaining kethi is served alongside in bowls for dipping or as soup.

As kethi stones can be difficult to find, store-bought liquid kethi (jameed) found in Arab food shops can be substituted to make kethi sauce. For everyday occasions, chicken is often used. As a shortcut, our recipe uses store-bought chicken stock; in camp, the stock would be homemade using a whole chicken and spices. Mleihi is served at celebrations such as weddings for which up to 22 lbs (10 kg) of mleihi are prepared. Women prepare kibbeh the day before, while guests of the groom bring sheep, bulgur, kethi, and cooking pots. The guest of honour will pour a large ladle of kethi sauce and saman over the mleihi platter.

Jordan's version of mleihi is called mansef and it is Jordan's national dish. Mansef differs from mleihi in several ways, notably by using rice in place of bulgur, putting tanoor Arab bread underneath the rice, omitting the kibbeh, and adding the meat to the kethi sauce, which Jordanians call "jameed." According to Jordanian lore, mansef was invented when the Christian bishop of ancient Madaba asked his cook to prepare a dish that would enable him to distinguish between his Muslim and Jewish guests. Knowing Jews would refuse an un-kosher dish comprising dairy and meat, mansef was created.

◆×◆

3 cups (570 g) bulgur

1 tbsp salt

Rinse the bulgur and put it in a separate large pot. Add the salt and top with 4 inches (10 cm) of water. Simmer for 25-30 minutes or until cooked, adding warm broth from the meat pot as needed. Remove from the heat and cover to keep warm.

Stir the bulgur with a large spoon and transfer to a large platter. Smooth the top of the bulgur flat with your hand. Heat the remaining saman over medium heat. Ladle half of the kethi sauce (p. 175) over the bulgur. Top with the meat and ladle the saman over it. Serve the remaining kethi in bowls alongside the platter.

Kibbeh Mohabbala

UMM KHOLUD, al-Sawara

DOUGH

2.2 lb (1 kg) bulgur

2.2 lb (1 kg) ground lamb or beef

1 tbsp curry powder

1 tbsp ground cumin

2 tsp ground marjoram

2 tsp Maggi powder

½ tsp ground turmeric

2 tsp salt

1 tsp pepper

FILLING

2 medium onions, minced

1.1 lb (500 g) ground lamb or beef

1 tbsp salt

1 tbsp pepper

½ cup (125 ml) oil

1½ cups (200 g) pine nuts or walnuts, fried in oil

1 cup (140 g) pomegranate seeds, or **2 tbsp** pomegranate molasses

oil for optional frying

Garnish: whole green onions, laban

Kibbeh is adored across the Arab world. Syria's is the most renowned, with over sixty types! Kibbeh varies according to the dough (which often contains ground meat), filling, and whether it is eaten fried, boiled, or raw (Lebanon is famous for kibbeh nayeh, or raw kibbeh). Some people bake kibbeh filling, with or without the bulgur-and-meat dough, while others poach it in a kethi-based yogurt soup. In Syria and Lebanon, kibbeh meat mixture was made outdoors using a "jurn kibbeh"—a giant, heavy mortar cut from solid rock with large wooden pestle that today is used as garden décor, if one is lucky enough to find one.

Zaatari women have a hand signal for "come to my house, let's make kibbeh," and, a kibbeh novice, I accept every invitation. It takes years—decades—of practice to perfect kibbeh's elements and shaping. Kibbeh-making is social. At Zaatari and in Syria, women make kibbeh sitting on the floor, strategically positioned around a hot platter of cooked meat, a platter of bulgur dough (kept soft in a plastic bag), and a third platter for placing the perfectly shaped kibbeh. I've had many teachers at Zaatari and my kibbeh, to everyone's mirth, always stand out—one of these days they won't!

Kibbeh is an art that cannot be replicated by machine or in a factory. Zaatari women mould each palm-sized kibbeh perfectly, in a shape reminiscent of an American football. The thin, delicate shell gives way when you bite into it—never shattering or having a chewy texture—gently releasing fragrant steam and the moist meat inside. Kibbeh is a feat of engineering.

Kibbeh mohabbala, a Houran specialty, is popular across camp for its healthful bulgur with pomegranate seeds and pine nuts. Kibbeh is served as a side dish or in kethi soup at ghada', or presented atop a main dish such as mleihi. Many Zaatari cooks use the traditional large pestle and mortar to pound the bulgur and meat, using their hands and eyes to judge texture and readiness, but feel free to use your food processor. Kibbeh can be made ahead and frozen. Kibbeh mohabbala is traditionally fried in steam by placing a lid ajar—this can also be done with a false lid made from parchment paper known as a cartouche. It covers the surface of the kibbeh, trapping steam and reducing evaporation. To make a cartouche: fold a large square of parchment several times to form a triangle. Trim the length to fit your pot, snip the tip (to create a small hole), unfold the paper and place on top the kibbeh.

Soak the bulgur in 6 cups (1.5 l) of warm water for 30 minutes, then drain. Using a food processor, pulse the bulgur until it reaches a fine texture. Add the meat and seasonings to the bulgur, and pulse until well combined. Remove bulgur-meat mixture to a large bowl. Give the mixture a few good kneads by hand—it should be soft and yielding. Cover the bowl with plastic wrap to keep the dough from drying out.

For the filling, over medium heat, fry the onion, meat, and seasonings in ½ cup of oil until fully cooked. Stir in the pine nuts and fry 5 minutes longer. Remove from heat, stir in the pomegranate seeds (or pomegranate syrup) and let sit until the mixture is cool enough to touch.

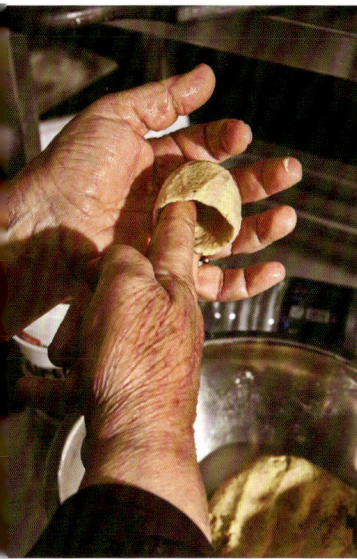

To assemble the kibbeh, position the bulgur mixture near the meat mixture. Tilt the meat pot so the oil/juice drains to one side of the pot. Dabbing your hands well in the meat oil/juices, scoop up an egg-size piece of dough. Roll it into a smooth ball and, pressing it into one palm, use your fingers to shape a very thin cup with high walls, dabbing the dough with more oil if it sticks. Fill the cup with 3 tbsp (45 ml) of meat. Close it up and gently roll it into ball, shaping the ends to resemble an American football. Place on a greased, large flat skillet and repeat.

Place the skillet over medium heat with the lid ajar (or use an inverted plate or cartouche made from parchment paper) and cook the kibbeh for 20-25 minutes, until lightly browned underneath and the shell is crisp, no longer doughy. Remove cooked kibbeh to a large bowl, cover with plastic to keep it warm and moist.

Alternatively, deep-fry the kibbeh in vegetable oil at 375°F (190°C) until golden, making sure they are dry before placing them in the hot oil.

Serve with green onions and laban.

DOUGH

2.2 lb (1 kg) bulgur

6 cups (1.5 l) warm water

2 tbsp flour

1 tbsp salt

2 tbsp ground marjoram

1 tsp ground cumin

1 tsp white pepper

FILLING

1.1 lb (500 g) chopped onion

3 tbsp (45 ml) olive oil

2.2 lb (1 kg) ground lamb or beef

1½ cups (225 g) finely chopped walnuts

1 cup (140 g) pomegranate seeds (optional)

1 tbsp salt

1½ tsp ground cumin

4 cups (1 l) vegetable oil for deep frying

Fried Kibbeh

UMM ANWAR, al-Hara

In this classic version, meat is omitted from the shell. The filling contains ground lamb or beef, onion, and finely chopped walnuts. Uncooked kibbeh can be frozen and deep-fried.

Soak the bulgur in 6 cups (1.5 l) of warm water for 30 minutes, then drain. Using a food processor, pulse the bulgur until it reaches a fine texture. Add the seasonings to the bulger, and pulse until well combined. Remove bulger mixture to a large bowl. Give the mixture a few good kneads by hand—it should be a soft dough. Cover the bowl with plastic wrap to keep the dough from drying out.

Next, prepare the filling. In a large pot, fry the onion in the oil over medium heat until softened, about 5 minutes. Add the meat and continue to cook over medium heat for about 10 minutes or until meat is no longer pink and the juices are absorbed. Add the remaining ingredients, stir, and cook for 3 minutes. Remove from heat and set aside until the meat is cool enough to touch.

To assemble the kibbeh, position the bowl containing the bulgur mixture near the meat pot. Tilt the meat pot so the oil/juice drains to one side of the pot.

Dabbing your hands well with the oil/juices, scoop up an egg-size piece of dough. Roll into a smooth ball and, pressing it into one palm, use your fingers to shape a very thin cup with high walls, dabbing the dough with more oil if it sticks. Fill the cup with 3 tbsp (45 ml) of meat, close it up, and gently roll into a ball, shaping the ends to resemble an American football. Place the kibbeh on a large cookie sheet and repeat with the remaining dough and meat mixture, placing the kibbeh so they do not touch each other.

In a large pot, deep-fry the kibbeh in batches, in a single layer, at 375°F (190°C) until golden. Remove to a platter and serve.

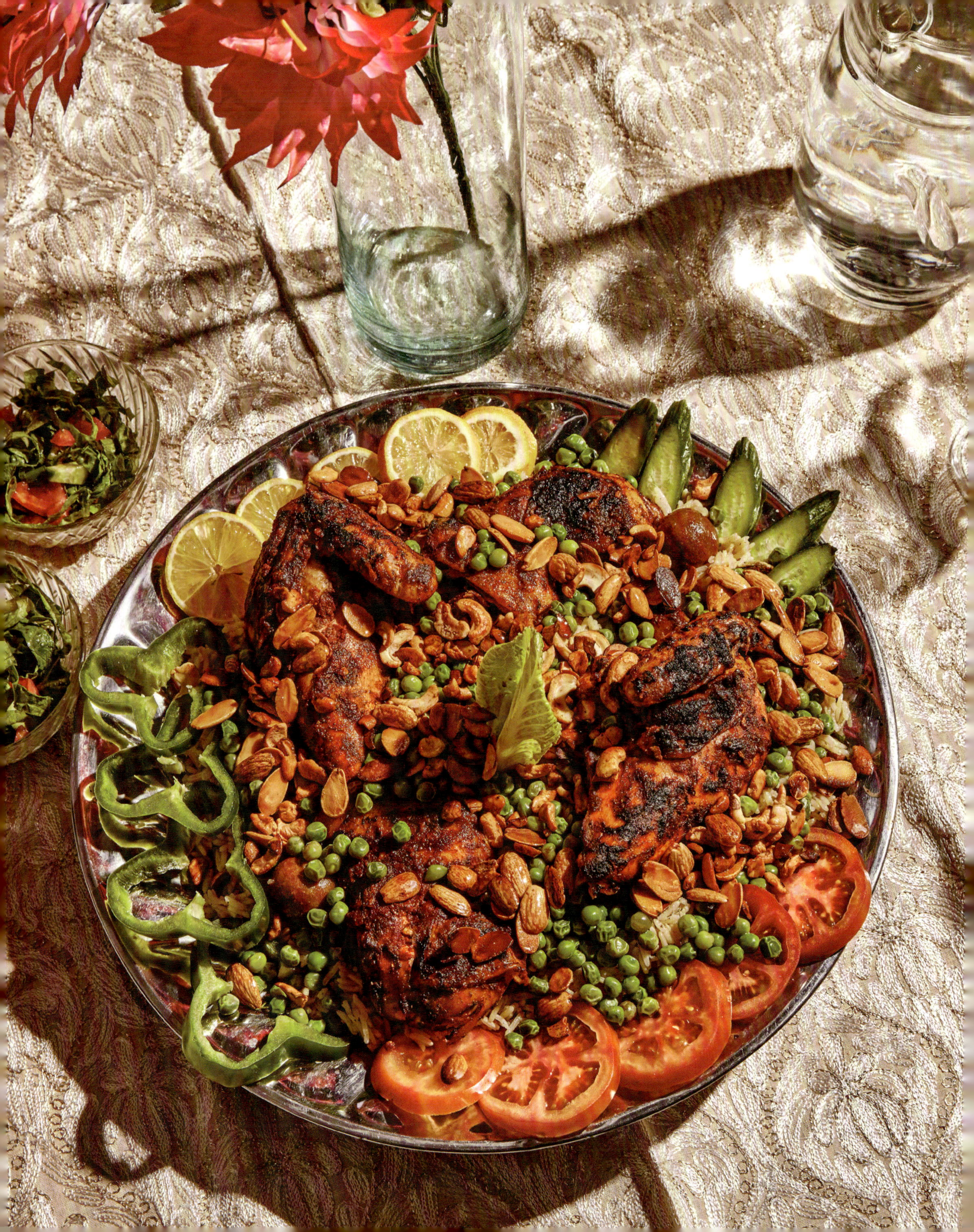

Oozy

UMM NADEEM, Simlin

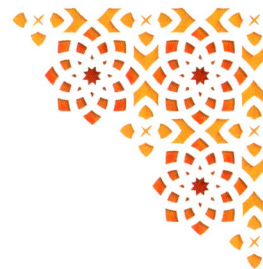

Oozy likely originated in Iraq and is served at weddings and other important events. It is a centrepiece dish for communal sharing, made with chicken or a single meat such as lamb, beef, or camel, or sometimes with chicken and ground beef—as in the below recipe. Oozy was one of the first dishes I enjoyed at Zaatari; Umm Nadeem smoked the boiled chicken using a tin can filled with hot coals. Oozy is served on a giant platter with side bowls of laban.

In cities, restaurants serve individual-sized oozy wrapped in puff pastry filled with chopped chicken or meat. Make it at home by brushing with saman/butter and baking at 375°F (190°C) for 30-35 minutes.

✧

In a large pot, cover the chicken with water and add the Maggi and salt. Bring to a boil, then add the onion, 1 tbsp (15 ml) baharat, the other seasonings, and the carrots and beans. Simmer for 25-30 minutes or until the chicken is cooked, skimming off the froth. Transfer the chicken to another pot and cover. Remove the carrots/beans and keep warm. Transfer the chicken (reserving 3 cups [750 ml] of the chicken stock) to a greased baking dish, brush the skins with a little oil, and bake at 375°F (190°C) until browned. Remove chicken from oven and cover to keep warm.

In a frying pan, brown the ground meat with a dash of salt and the remaining 1 tsp (5 ml) of baharat.

Rinse the rice 2-3 times, until water runs clear. Put in a bowl with cold water to cover, let soak for 30 minutes, drain well and set aside.

In a large pot, add the saman, oil, and reserved 3 cups of cooking stock. Add the drained rice and bring to a boil. Reduce the heat to low, cover tightly, and simmer for 15-20 minutes, until all the water is absorbed and rice is tender. Remove from heat and let sit covered for 5 minutes. Remove lid and fluff with a fork.

On a serving platter, first place the rice, then the beans and carrots, meat, and nuts. Top with the chicken pieces. Garnish, arranging the lettuce leaves on the sides.

VARIATIONS

For extra flavour smoke the cooked chicken by placing a tin can containing 1 tbsp of cooking oil and hot coals (or mesquite, apple wood) in the centre of the chicken pieces inside a large pot; cover with the lid for 10 minutes.

1 whole chicken, cut up

3 tsp Maggi powder

½ tsp salt

1 medium onion, chopped

1 tbsp plus **1 tsp** baharat (seven spice)

1 tbsp ground cumin

1 tsp ground cardamom

1 tbsp ground turmeric

1½ cups (190 g) carrot, chopped

1½ cups (190 g) green beans, halved, or peas

2.2 lb (1 kg) ground meat

2 cups (450 g) basmati or other long-grain rice

1 tbsp saman

1 tbsp olive oil

1 cup (140 g) fried almonds and pine nuts

Garnish: chopped cilantro or parsley, romaine lettuce leaves

Lahm bi Ajeen

UMM TAREK, Buser al-Harir

DOUGH

2 cups (500 ml) warm water

1 tbsp sugar

1 tbsp dry yeast

1 tbsp salt

6 tbsp (90 ml) olive oil

5 cups (625 g) flour

FILLING

2.2 lb (1 kg) ground lamb or beef

2 medium onions, minced

1 tbsp baharat (seven spice)

1 tsp salt

3 cups (675 g) minced tomatoes

¼ cup (60 g) shattah, or **1 tbsp** hot pepper

olive oil for drizzling

Lahm bi Ajeen, a type of open-face meat *mana'eesh* (flatbreads), are truly amazing. Enjoyed at ftoor and sold in pastry shops in the souks, in camp we also serve them at weddings as an inexpensive alternative to mleihi and oozy. You can make them spicier by increasing the shattah or pepper.

❖

Dough: In a large bowl, dissolve the sugar in the water and add the yeast. Leave it for 10 minutes or until the yeast bubbles. Add the salt, olive oil, and flour gradually, mixing well to form a soft, smooth dough, adding more water if needed. Turn onto a lightly floured board and knead for 15 minutes. Cover and let rise for 1 hour or until doubled in bulk.

Filling: Mix all the ingredients well in a large bowl or use a food processor.

Divide the dough into 4" balls. Roll into oblong shapes, ⅛ inch thick, on a floured surface. Place on baking sheets and dimple each piece with your fingers. Top each piece with a generous ¼ cup of filling, spread to the edges.

Bake at 450°F (232°C) for 10-12 minutes and then broil for a few seconds to further brown. Drizzle with olive oil and serve hot.

Baqlawah

ABU MAROUF, Damascus

SYRUP

1 cup (250 ml) water

1 cup (200 g) sugar

½ cup (125 ml) liquid honey

1 tbsp lime juice

1 cinnamon stick

BAQLAWAH

2.2 lb (1 kg) pistachios or walnuts

3 cups (600 g) sugar

1 tsp cinnamon

½ tsp ground cloves

2 tsp orange blossom water
or **1 tsp** rosewater

2.2 lb (1 kg) phyllo, thawed

1 cup (250 ml) saman or butter,
melted

Garnish: finely ground pistachios

Baqlawah is synonymous with Sham (Damascus), with Aleppo green pistachios, cashews and walnuts, rosewater and orange blossom water, cinnamon, and qishta. No wedding or celebration is complete without baqlawah. Several sweet shops deliver, outside camp too. Inside, their near-ubiquitous gold and pink décor, the practised eye knows each baqlawah's name by its shape, type of nut, filling, and delicate flavouring. Beloved green pistachios are not always afford-able, so our sweet makers may use peanuts or coconut, sometimes dyed green to children's delight.

In Amman there is fierce debate over who makes the best baqlawah: Syrian versus Palestinian—with all other nationalities viewed as distant runners-up. Everyone has their favourite shop, and they judge based on nuts; sweetness and flavouring of the syrup and the amount used; qishta or jibneh quality; and tightness of rolling. In fact, debate continues for most sweets, with the most heated debates reserved for what and how the best knafeh is made.

For the syrup: Combine all ingredients in a medium pot and bring to a boil. Reduce the heat and simmer for 10 minutes or until thick. Remove from heat, discard the cinnamon stick, and let cool completely.

For the baqlawah: In a medium bowl, combine the nuts with the dry ingredients and flavoured water.

Using a sharp knife, cut the phyllo stack to the size of a 9 × 13 × 2 inch (23 × 33 × 5 cm) baking pan with steep sides. Working quickly and keeping the phyllo covered to prevent drying, place a phyllo sheet in the pan and brush with butter. Add 7 sheets, brushing each sheet with butter. Sprinkle generously with nuts. Top with 2 sheets, brushing in between, then sprinkle with nuts. Repeat with sheets and nuts until all the nuts are used. The top layer should be 8 sheets thick. Using a sharp knife, make a diamond pattern.

Bake at 350°F (175°C) for 35-40 minutes or until golden.

Once the baqlawah is baked, remove from the oven and immediately pour cool syrup over the top. Let cool for 4 hours and garnish with finely ground pistachios.

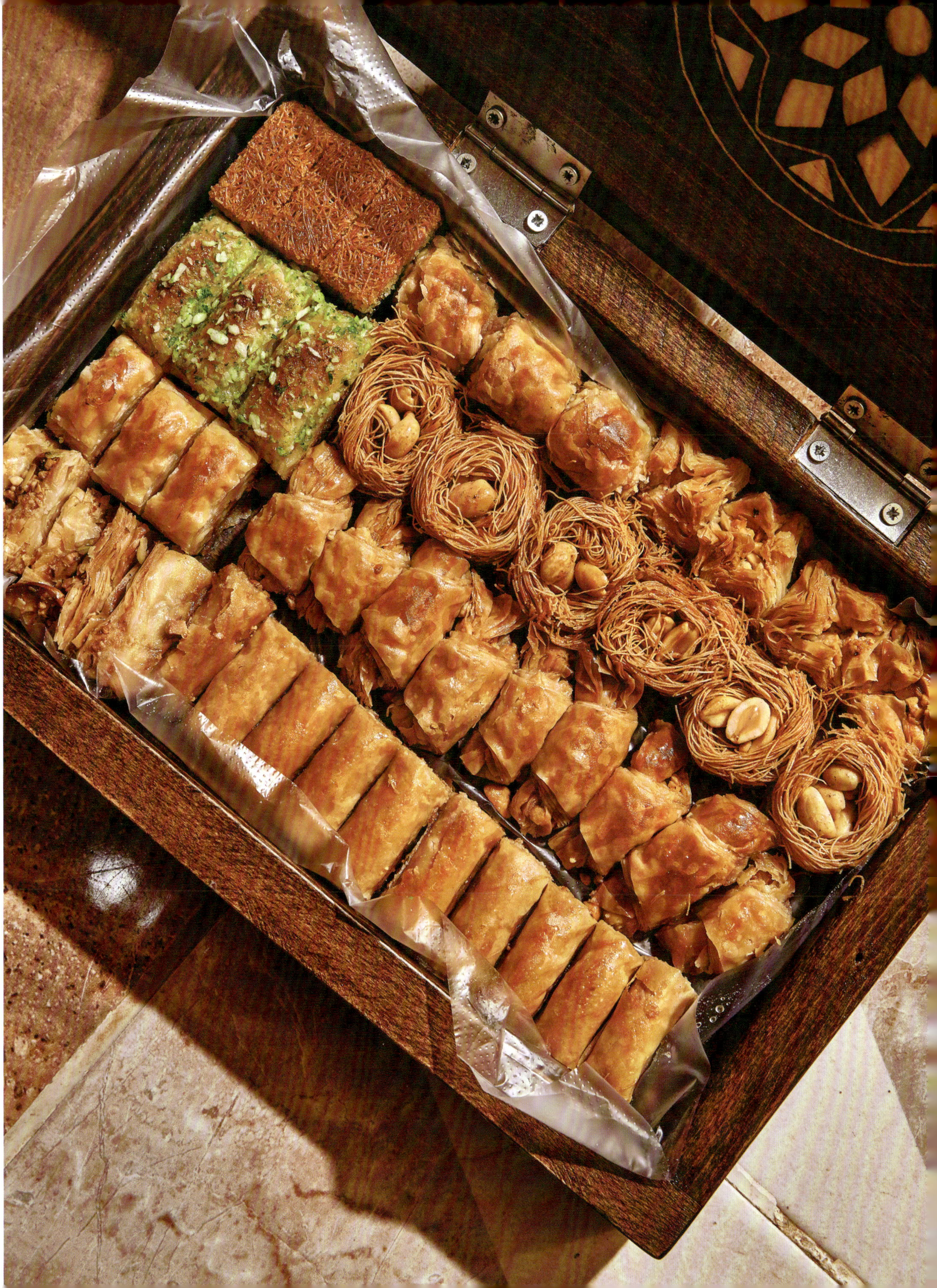

Basbousa

UMM HASSAN, Tal Shihab

Basbousa, a co-winner of the Zaatari Camp Best Chef Contest top prize, sweet-ens any joyous occasion, especially weddings and graduations. The creamy filling is what distinguishes these rich little semolina cakes—soaked with lemon and rose-infused syrup and topped with pistachios—from the less fancy, every-day versions of harissah and nammorah that omit the cream filling, and eggs (in the case of nammorah).

Though Egypt claims to have invented basbousa, a little sleuthing reveals that the cake, called Revani, was first baked by Ottoman chefs in the 16th cen-tury to celebrate the conquest of Armenia, and later spread across the Arab world. Regardless of its origins, the plethora of recipe versions differ by includ-ing flour (to make a finer, smoother cake), and using butter or saman for oil. At Zaatari, we like the coarse texture from using semolina and thus omit flour.

Prepare syrup by boiling the sugar and water, then let simmer for a few minutes. Remove from heat and add the flavourings. Cool to room temperature.

Preheat the oven to 350°F (175°C) and grease a 9-inch (23 cm) square pan using butter.

In a medium pot, mix the milk, cornstarch, sugar, and cream together over medium heat. Bring to a boil, then whisk over low heat until very thick, careful not to scald the cream. Remove from heat and stir in the rosewater or vanilla.

In a large bowl, mix the dry ingredients. In a separate large bowl, beat the eggs until frothy, add the remaining wet ingredients and beat well.

Add the dry ingredients to the wet in 3 batches, mixing well after each addition so the batter is smooth with no lumps. Turn half the batter into the greased pan and bake for 15-18 minutes, until the top is dry to touch. Remove from the oven and spread with cream. Add 1 tbsp (15 ml) of water to the remaining batter, stir well, and pour the batter over the cream, ensuring to fully cover the cream and sides of the pan. Return the cake to the oven and bake for 30-40 minutes or until the top is golden and firm to touch. Pour cold syrup over the hot cake and decorate it with pistachios. When the syrup is completely absorbed (about 30 minutes), cut the cake into squares or diamond shapes and serve.

CREAM

2 cups (500 ml) full-fat (whole) milk

¼ cup (30 g) cornstarch

2 tbsp sugar

½ cup (125 ml) cream

½ tsp rosewater, or **1 tsp** vanilla extract

CAKE

1 cup (180 g) coarse semolina

½ cup (100 g) sugar

½ cup (45 g) dried coconut (sweetened or unsweetened)

½ cup (60 g) powdered milk

2 tsp baking powder

3 eggs

¾ cup (187 ml) vegetable oil

1 cup (250 ml) full-fat yogurt

1 tsp vanilla extract

SYRUP

1 cup (200 g) sugar

1 cup (250 ml) water

1 tsp rosewater or orange blossom water

1 tsp lemon juice

Garnish: chopped pistachios

Abu Rustom's Heritage Band

I am from Homs, one of Syria's largest cities, where I was an antiques dealer in copper and silver. In the evenings I worked as a performer for henna parties and weddings, with audiences of over two thousand people. In June 2013 I had to leave Syria because of the war. My ancient city suffered badly.

When we arrived in Jordan, my family and I lived in Amman. Every Thursday and Monday I went to Zaatari to visit the aid agencies to see their activities and life in the camp. I noticed that many children born in camp knew little about Syria and that adults missed the joy of live, traditional Syrian music. In 2016 I returned to Zaatari to live and started Abu Rustom Heritage Band to preserve Syrian heritage and earn livelihoods.

In the beginning, the band was three people—me and my children. Then I started training youth and we increased to seven people. Currently we are fifty-four people, divided into four bands: two specialize in arada for henna parties and weddings; the other two specialize in hospitality. For sorrowful events, I bring Arabic coffee prepared by myself, served by band members in the mourning tent with dates, chai, and water.

The band's traditional Syrian dress is difficult to obtain because the war disrupted production and because of the logistical challenges of purchasing. It is a real struggle. I found a way to buy the Syrian costumes from Turkey. Every two months, when I save enough money, I buy one for 165 dinars (USD 235). I currently have thirty-six costumes and am trying to obtain one for each member. The rest of our equipment—swords, drums, tambourines, cymbals, speakers, microphones, torches, cooker, large coffee boiler, cups—is available in Jordan but is very costly, and most of our items must be Syrian.

Our band provides one of the camp's biggest joys for henna days and weddings. We also play for visiting delegations and camp celebrations. Our fame spread in Zaatari; now we play outside camp, in Amman, Irbid, and other places, helped by one thousand business cards that I printed. I coordinate the bands' events and the players by Whatsapp.

I love this work and the meaning it brings to the lives of our audiences and the players. To further preserve our important, unique Syrian musical heritage, I am now training children aged nine to eighteen at the Makani centre in the art of arada singing and dancing.

190

Sara's Beauty Salon

Since childhood, hairdressing was my hobby. I started my hairdressing career at age eighteen in Syria. Alhumdillah, my work was very good and when we took refuge in Zaatari Camp, I brought all my tools: scissors, apron, combs, hair dryer, brushes, curling irons, hair bands, hair dyes, highlights, et cetera.

After one year in Zaatari, I started hairdressing services in my tent—this was before we had metal caravans. I brought a small chair and a very small mirror. I faced many difficulties with electricity, bathroom, water, and heating.

Later, I bought a caravan for JOD 450 (USD 634) and a generator to use as my salon, attached to our family caravan. My work increased and I hired assistants, whom I trained in hairdressing and beauty. After two years, I opened a boutique for renting wedding dresses with a beauty salon in the Shams Élysées. Customers have many obstacles with prices and rental of dresses et cetera.

Then I expanded my home salon by buying another caravan to provide full service: hair, makeup, nails, henna, and dress rental. Dresses are large and take up much space—a Zaatari bride rents two or more dresses for her wedding.

Alhumdillah, I succeeded in this work, but I faced difficulties with my family because work takes all my time—some days I do not see my husband and children. I start at eight a.m., some days at seven, and when there are a lot of brides with their wedding parties, I close at nine p.m.

There are some people who say I do not laugh or smile when I am working. This is because I am busy focusing on my work. I am an artist, a perfectionist, and a businesswoman. ❖

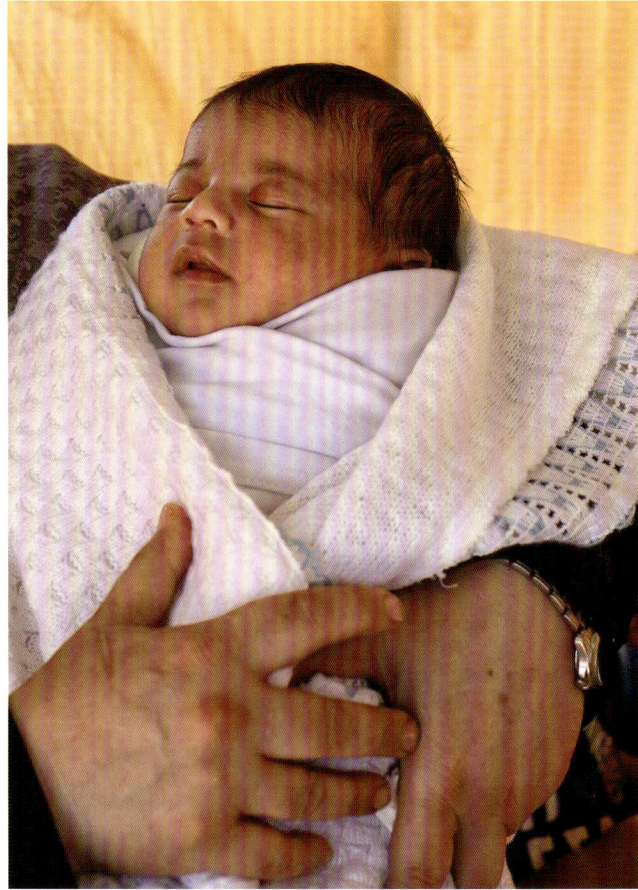

Aqeeqah, Welcoming Newborns

On the way to visit Umm Laith to meet her new baby girl, we stop for pistachios, walnuts, and coconut. The items are for *chai carawea*, a caraway drink that aids postpartum recovery and is enjoyed by guests (p. 194).

Shahad (pure honey) is a beautiful name for Umm Laith's dozing angel, her second child. Mothers choose girls' names, drawing on friends, flowers, and goodness. Male names are chosen by the father, after his father or grandfather or from the Quran. Before the birth, her mother-in-law Umm Ali prepared vats of *qarfa* (cinnamon chai, p 195) from fresh green and red ginger, cloves, and anise, to support delivery and postpartum care. Dates, parsley, and castor oil with cinnamon are also used in abundance to promote breastfeeding and care. We bring gifts of homemade saman and *halaweh*, a confection of tahini, powdered sugar, and nuts (p. 197), that provides extra nutrition as we drink sesame seed-laden chai carawea with Umm Laith and other guests.

I catch whiffs of cha'acheel (p. 198) brewing. Following Umm Ali's wink to the kitchen and the cracks of brilliant noonday sun, I wondered how they found ja'adah, a leafy green from the Houran region used for pregnancy and postpartum care. The light reveals spiced balls of ja'adah and lentils simmering in her homemade kethi. Baby Shahad is very blessed.

About eighty babies are born every week here; twenty per cent of the population is under four. When a baby is born at home or in hospital, the father or grandfather sings the adhan (the first call to prayer) in the baby's right ear, followed by the iqama (the second call) in the baby's left ear.

The baby is thus called to Islam. Seven days later, the baby's head is shaved, the symbolic weight of the baby's hair given in gold or silver to the poor. Shaving promotes hair growth; olive oil is used for the skin; and anise or *argel* (from the solenostemma plant) herbal chai is used to treat colic. When the child is a little older and perhaps unable to sleep due to bad dreams, they will sip warm water from a *Tasa al-Raba*, a small fountain-shaped brass-silver bowl with Quranic verse on the inside and outside.

A frequent sight is sheep being led to a home for sacrifice and feast in thanks to Allah for the safe delivery of a child. *Aqeeqah* is the celebratory feast and an invitation cannot be refused. Two sheep are sacrificed for a boy, one for a girl, and the meat is shared with the community. Aqeeqah, like barbecue everywhere, is men's domain; men carry out the sacrifice following halal rules and barbecuing while women prepare marinades and salads. Aqeeqah is highly social, with neighbours helping to thread skewers.

The barbecues are three-foot-long troughs with charcoal and, sometimes, a rotisserie above. A hand or motorized fan regulates the heat and smoke. The word shoqaf, akin to the Turkish kebob, derives from *keba* (Arabic, means "roasted meat" or "to turn" and was first recorded in a tenth-century Iraqi cookbook). Every family has its own recipe. Meat and vegetables are never threaded together, as the vegetable steam and positioning would interfere with the meat's reaching perfection. Thus, skewers of shoqaf (p. 200)and kabab are flanked by skewers of whole, unpeeled onions and skewers of whole tomatoes.

Kabab is a fine art of portioning lean meat to fat and mixing with spice, threading and shaping onto skewers, and then sussing coal heat and wind while grilling to perfection (p. 202). As with shoqaf, every family has its own recipe. Threading and shaping takes much practice—experts one-handedly thread meat onto skewers, shaping and adding as they go, confident the kabab will not fall during grilling. Kabab is also oven-baked as *kofta* (p. 205) with endless variations.

As smoke billows, carrying the unmistakable notes of barbecue, friends and neighbours come by to assist with threading, drink coffee, and celebrate. Meat is pulled from skewers, tasted by all with nods of approval, then slid into bowls lined with bread; more bread is placed on top to keep it warm. The shoqaf and kabab meat will be placed on a large platter topped with grilled onion, tomato, and parsley, accompanied by salads, laban, and bread. Soon we will dine sitting on the floor and say "bismillah," and later say "sahtain" to our aqeeqah hosts for sharing this blessed day.

Chai Carawea

UMM WALAD, Alma

½ cup (60 g) powdered milk

5 tbsp (40 g) rice flour

½ cup (70 g) caraway seeds

½ cup (70 g) sesame seeds

1 tbsp ground cinnamon

1 tsp ground mahlab or ground cardamom

1 tsp vanilla extract or orange blossom water

1 cup (200 g) sugar

6 cups (1.5 l) water

Garnish: pistachios, walnuts, or cashews

Grind half of the sesame seeds using a mortar and pestle (or a spice grinder) and combine with the dry ingredients. Bring the water to a boil and add the dry ingredients and the vanilla or orange blossom water. Simmer for 10 minutes or until thick. Adjust the seasoning.

Pour into cups and garnish; the seeds will float to the top.

Caraway can be made a day ahead, reheated or served cold.

Delicious *chai carawea* (caraway chai) starring caraway seeds and *simsim* (sesame seeds) is sipped and enjoyed with a spoon. It is packed with fibre, iron, zinc, magnesium, and phosphorus, which helps new mothers recover from birth—compensating for blood loss—and induces milk flow, passing the rich nutrients on to the baby.

Qarfa Chai

UMM YASSER, Ghouta

Qarfa, cinnamon chai, is used to help women recover from birth. Umm Yasser learned to make qarfa from her grandmother and mother, who always prepared vast amounts. Key is the brewing method and using two types of fresh ginger, especially red ginger *(alpinia purpurata)*. Qarfa is said to help clean the womb and intestines and brings a feeling of comfort to the new mother. Umm Yasser says they always "thank God for the health and well-being of the baby and mother."

2 cinnamon sticks

6-inch (15-cm) piece yellow ginger, grated

6-inch (15-cm) piece red ginger, grated (or **1 tsp** of ground mace or allspice)

3 whole cloves

1 tbsp anise seeds

6 cups (1.5 l) water

1 cup (200 g) sugar

1 cup (140 g) walnuts and pistachios

½ cup (70 g) toasted sesame seeds

Boil the ginger, cloves, and anise seeds in the water for 30 minutes. Remove from heat and steep for 10 minutes. Once it is deep red, return to the boil.

Remove from heat and filter into another pot. Add the sugar, stirring to dissolve. Adjust the sweetness and flavouring.

Put the nuts and sesame seeds into glasses. Fill with the qarfa and serve hot.

Kabab

ABU SADAAM, al-Hrak

2 lbs (900 g) ground meat

10 oz (300 g) lamb or beef fat, finely chopped

1 cup (200 g) chopped grilled tomatoes

1 medium onion, minced

5 cloves garlic, minced

1 hot pepper, minced

½ cup (12.5 g) fresh mint, or **1 tbsp** dried

1 cup (25 g) minced parsley

¼ cup (60 ml) olive oil

½ cup (125 ml) lemon juice

1 tsp salt

½ tsp Aleppo pepper

1 tsp ground cumin

1 tbsp ground coriander

1 tsp ground cinnamon

1 tsp sweet paprika

1 tbsp powdered ginger

In the west, the word kabab is often used for all sorts of grilled meat (ground, sliced, or cubed), but in Zaatari kabab refers to spiced ground lamb grilled over wood or coals and served with separately grilled whole unpeeled onions and tomatoes, along with salad. There are spice variations, often guarded as a family secret. Try the Zaatari way of threading scoops of meat, shaping, and pinching.

In a large bowl, mix all the ingredients (except baking soda) well by hand, or use a meat grinder for a smoother texture. Cover and refrigerate for 12-24 hours, removing 30-45 minutes before grilling.

Pour 2 cups (500 ml) of water into a small bowl. Moisten your hand and scoop up 2 tbsp of the meat and thread onto a metal skewer, shaping it into a thin 2-inch (3.5 cm) oval, flattening as you go, denting and pinching the sides so they stick to the skewer. Repeat with the remaining meat.

Grill over hot coals (or using gas grill), turning occasionally and fanning the smoke, for 8-10 minutes or until browned yet moist inside.

Remove the meat from the skewers and place in a bread-lined pan; top with more bread to keep the meat warm.

Serve with grilled tomatoes and onion, accompanied by salads, bread, and laban.

Kofta bil Siniyeh

UMM ABDO, al-Shaykh Miskeen

Bringing back memories of family gatherings, this kofta is layered in a large, shallow baking dish. It is served garnished with tomato and cilantro and then scooped up with bread. Home cooks vary the spices depending on family preference, type of meat, and availability. Roasted sliced potato or rice makes an excellent side.

❖

ROASTED CAMEL VARIATION

If using camel meat, limit the amount of salt because camel meat is salty, by default of the desert, and remains a bit tough. "Roasted camel is a classic dish of the desert people, recommended by the Holy Prophet Mohammed (PBUH) for its healthy and nutritious content," says Abu Basmah of al-Summaqiyat, who learned to make kofta bil siniyeh with camel from his Bedouin grandmother.

2.2 lb (1 kg) ground camel meat

1.1 lb (500 g) minced onion

parsley, minced

1 tbsp baharat (seven spice)

2 tsp ground cumin

1 tsp salt

1 tsp black pepper

7 cloves garlic

vegetable oil or saman

salt, to taste

Mix all the ingredients together so the meat is well seasoned. Place the meat on a greased roasting pan and roast at 375°F (190°C) until well done, about 1 hour. Serve with lemon, laban, and rice.

¼ **cup (60 ml)** tahini

4.4 lb (2 kg) ground beef or lamb

1 cup (50 g) minced cilantro

1 medium onion, minced

2.2 lb (1 kg) tomatoes, chopped

2 green chilies (such as jalapeno), thinly sliced

1 tsp ground cumin

1 tsp curry powder

1 tsp salt

1 tsp pepper

¼ **cup (60 ml)** olive oil

½ **cup (125 ml)** water

Garnish: slices of tomato and pepper, chopped cilantro

Brush the bottom of a large, shallow baking dish with the tahini. Crumble the meat on top and sprinkle with the cilantro. In layers, add the onion, tomato, and remaining ingredients, ending with the water.

Bake uncovered at 375°F (190°C) for 50-60 minutes or until the meat is fully cooked and the sauce is thick and bubbly. Garnish and serve with rice.

Arab Medicine with the Elders

The golden age of Arab-Islamic medicine and pharmacy rose under the Abbasid Caliphate, which included most of modern-day Middle East and North Africa from the ninth to the thirteenth century, when scientific centres spread from Damascus to Baghdad, the new capital, and across the empire. In large medieval cities, physicians collected the biomedical doctrines of previous civilizations, translating from Greek, Persian, Syriac, Hindi, Hebrew, and other languages to Arabic—creating the base for Arab medicine, with over two thousand substances listed, such as herbs, roots, rhizomes, seeds, etc.

Insights were added from pre-Islamic Bedouin folklore, the Holy Quran, and the practices of the Prophet Mohammed (PBUH), such as washing with water before prayer and amassing knowledge about fruits, vegetables, and herbs. The establishment of medical schools, hospitals, and pharmacies radically changed the pre-Islamic practices of priests prescribing treatment. Techniques such as distillation, evaporation, crystallization, and the use of alcohol as an antiseptic are still used today. While Zaatari has pharmacies and a hospital, people use Arab medicine for beauty, health, and cures. Remedies are shared orally and through practice—ancient knowledge learned from Zaatari's elders.

BEAUTY AND HEALTH

facial: vaporize/steam with boiling water and chamomile, exfoliate with sliced tomato dipped in sugar and mask of yogurt or honey with cornstarch; use cucumber slices for dark circles

for smooth skin: rub body with milk, use loofah

for healthy hair: apply roasted, boiled date seeds, olive oil with green pepper

for longer eyelashes and fuller eyebrows: use coconut oil and castor oil topically

to strengthen eyesight: drink carrot juice

to strengthen finger and toenails: rub with lemon and garlic

oral hygiene: brush with coal or almond leaves, use miswak twig; rinse mouth and gums with salt water

REMEDIES

for headache: drink **1½ cups (375 ml)** water with **2 tsp** rosewater; drink peppermint chai

for a colon cleanse: crush dried lime (lumi) and take **1 tsp** upon waking; drink argel chai

for diarrhea: drink chamomile chai with pomegranate rind and rice water; eat yogurt, banana

for inflammation and joint pain: drink ginger chai

for back/muscle ache: massage with olive oil; apply capers as a paste on cloth to back

for sore throat: drink ginger-lemon chai

for flu and fever: put onions inside room; use onion or Nerium oleander flowers as shoe insoles

for toothache: place whole cloves near aching tooth

for bee, wasp sting: rub with garlic

for insomnia: drink chai with anise or shaneena (yogurt drink)

to maintain memory: eat honey, walnuts, thyme

to maintain healthy blood pressure: eat 1 clove garlic upon waking

The Artist

I am Mohammad Jokhader, a Syrian artist born in Homs in 1986, married and the father of three children. I am from an artistic family—two of my brothers and other family have this talent as well. I began as an artist at school, where drawing was what I always wanted to do most. I drew people cartoons, but next I sought more passion by drawing historical figures such as the teacher and gardener Ibn al-Nafis and other personalities. I developed myself; I did not enter the institutes to learn drawing and art. I was always searching and discovering. The support and encouragement of my family was the motivation to continue and develop my talent. I drew paintings from the work of Renaissance artists—landscapes and heritage. Then the war began and forced us to leave our country. We came to Jordan in January 2013 and entered the Zaatari refugee camp.

When I arrived, I was in a very difficult psychological situation, because leaving the country is the hardest thing to be exposed to, leaving everything behind—friends, home, and memories. After a while I started to return to drawing. I found wood to make a frame and used a piece of cloth from a tent because it was strong and stretchable. I made a painting. Of course, I started painting in another way, documenting our lives, because the artist is influenced by the environment in which he lives and is also responsible for the transmission of his art. The truth is as it is, and it drives me to draw what I have lived and cared about during this war.

I also draw murals. Supported by UNHCR, the most important project was drawing murals on the caravans on the perimeter of the camp and inside the districts. Each district carries its own colour and theme. One is brown, its theme heritage and civilization. It is one of the most beautiful districts for me, painting the heritage and civilization of Syria so that the new generation born in the camp knows Syria and its history. Other districts are on education and its importance, and health and water supply. At Zaatari and al-Azraq camp I teach courses for children and young people in drawing. I now work with Mercy Corps, which means inclusive education for the integration of children with and without disabilities. I teach art to children with disabilities.

I love the paintings. Close to my heart is my painting of an old woman named Umm Sadaam. She is the mother of my friend and I saw in her eyes strength and steadfastness despite all the wrinkles in her face. "I am a strong woman" represents the strength of the Syrian people and forbearance in the face of persistent suffering.

Thank you to my family who stood by me from the beginning, and to UNHCR and Jordan for your kind support and refuge. ◈

Easir Romaan, p. 231

Chai, p. 234

Breads, Sweets, and Drinks

Did you know that "sugar" is an Arab word? Refined from sugar cane plants, sugar appeared in India about 2,500 years ago. When the Persians invaded India in the 6th century BCE, they were amazed by the sugar cane plants that provided sweetness without honey or bees. In 642 AD, Arab Muslims invaded Persia and were equally astounded by the production of sugar from plants. The Arab Muslims brought the plants and refining process to the Arab world, including the conquered lands in North Africa, Spain and Sicily. Up to and through the Middle Ages, sugar — like saffron, nutmeg, cumin and anise — was a rare and highly expensive good, valued and viewed as medicine. Called "sharkara" in Sanskrit (for ground or candied sugar, like grit and gravel), sugar was called "shakar" in Persian and "sukkar" in Arabic, later translated in Medieval Latin as "succarum," then in Old French as "sucre" and finally as "sugar" in English.

Syrians are famous for sweets — sameed (semolina) cookies, cakes, and pastries with nuts drenched in syrup, and glorious puddings perfumed with lemon, rose, and mastic — enjoyed with chai or drinks made from fruit and sometimes yogurt. Sweets differ regionally, served for occasions: maamoul at Eid al-Fitr (p. 162) and baqlawah and basbousa at weddings (pp. 186, 189). As many sweets are linked to specific occasions, you'll also find sweet recipes in the chapters on Ramadan, weddings, and Aqeeqah. The chapters profiling the TIGER Girls and Shams Élysées also contain sweet recipes. Favourites are barazek (sesame-pistachio wafers, p. 223) and O-shaped ghraybeh shortbread (p. 78). Sweets are made while lunch simmers. Unique

Riz bil haleeb, p. 220

Houran lazza'eyyat (Bedouin crêpes layered with halaweh cream and nuts, p. 228) is everyone's favourite. Sweet dates are symbolic, shared to welcome guests and during bereavement and sad times, and to break the fast during Ramadan.

At Zaatari, three breads are enjoyed daily: khubz, a.k.a. normal bread, shraak (or saj bread, thin and perfect for wrapping), and taboon or kmaj bread — both dimpled and thick, baked in a taboon oven or atop stones (pp. 210-12). Every Syrian village had a communal taboon, partially underground and fired all day with tablets of dung and hay (also used for heating in winter). Fatayer and manaeesh were also baked in the taboon. Bedouins at Zaatari bake arbood bread — flour, salt, and water shaped into discs, dusted with flour, and buried under hot ash, turned by a stick; tapped for hardness and a hollow sound, the bread is eaten as is with the ash dusted off, or torn into pieces onto a dish, soaked in melted saman or yogurt. At night, leftover bread is hung outside or placed elevated off the ground in gratitude for God's blessings.

Syria is known for its cold and hot drinks (pp. 230-34), especially purchased from street vendors. There are tamarind, pomegranate, and watermelon drinks — and the favourite, limone wa naana (lemon mint). Herbal chai (pronounced shai) varies seasonally; hot milky drinks made from salab and mastic are enjoyed using a spoon to scoop the yummy topping. Finally, no visit or meal is complete without Turkish coffee — strong, brewed with cardamom, and served in small cups (p. 237).

Taboon and Kmaj

UMM KHALED, Ataman

In Syria every village had an outdoor oven that everyone shared for baking taboon bread and fatayer. This partially underground clay oven used stones for baking and was heated by *jala*—sun-dried tablets made from animal dung (sheep, goats, donkey) mixed with straw, also used for heating homes in winter as a wood alternative.

At Zaatari bakeries like Abu Muhanned's, an industrial taboon oven, long metal tongs, and *karaa*—canvas pillow made from UNHCR tent canvas—are used to bake taboon that is blistery, dimpled, and misshapen by the blasting flames. In their homes, Zaatari women like Umm Khaled make smaller, thicker versions called *kmaj* using stones in their ovens, hand-shaping the dough using a swinging motion. Both taboon and kmaj are used for msakhan and other dishes.

Taboon

Kmaj

1 tbsp yeast

1 tbsp sugar

1¾ cups (400 ml) warm water

3 cups (375 g) white flour

1 cup (120 g) whole wheat flour, more for dusting

1 tbsp salt

2 tbsp olive oil

¼ cup (36 g) nigella or sesame seeds (optional)

20 clean smooth stones, ½-1½ inches (1.3-3.8 cm) in diameter

In a small bowl, combine the yeast, sugar, and ½ cup (125 ml) of warm water. Let sit for 10 minutes or until frothy.

In a large bowl, combine the white flour, whole wheat flour, and salt. Make a well in the centre and add the stirred yeast, oil, nigella seeds (if using), and the remaining 1¼ cup (310 ml) of water, adding more water if needed.

Turn onto a lightly floured surface and knead for 5 minutes or until soft and springy.

Lightly grease the bowl and return the dough, turning to coat. Cover with a damp cloth and let rise in a warm place for 1 hour or until doubled. Punch down, knead for a few minutes, and return to the bowl for a second rise.

Cut into 12 pieces, roll each into a ball, and place on a large tray dusted with flour.

Preheat the oven to the highest setting and place the stones on a baking sheet on the lowest rack.

Roll one ball into an 8-inch (20 cm) circle, make a few dimples, and place directly on the stones. Bake for 3 minutes and then broil for 1-2 minutes. Remove and cover with a cloth. Repeat with the remaining dough.

Fatteh wa Haleeb

UMM RA'EDA, Mhajjah

Fatteh wa haleeb is comforting bread pudding made from day-old crusty bread. Zaatari cooks use any bread and fillings on hand. You can't go wrong with this excellent dish. For breakfast, try replacing the raisins with blueberries or dates, or serve as a dessert with ice cream on winter nights.

✦

Tear the bread into small pieces and place in a large bowl, reserving ½ cup (125 ml) for later.

Bring the milk, sugar, and seasonings to a boil, then simmer for 5 minutes. Pour half of this mixture over the bread. Add the rosewater and 3 tsp (30 ml) of the saman, stirring to coat well.

Transfer the other half of the mixture to a greased baking dish. Top with the nuts, raisins, coconut, and soaked bread. Brush with the remaining 1 tbsp (15 ml) of saman and let sit for 10 minutes to absorb. Top with the reserved dry bread, then the qishta or cream.

Bake at 400°F (204°C) for 20 minutes or until puffed up and bubbly, then finish under the broiler for 1-2 minutes or until golden.

5 cups (350 g) bread or croissants, torn into pieces

5 cups (1.1 l) full-fat (whole) milk

¾ cup (150 g) sugar

1 cinnamon stick

2 tsp vanilla extract

½ tsp ground mastic

½ tsp cardamom

2 tsp rosewater

3 tbsp (45 ml) saman or butter, melted

½ cup (75 g) raisins

½ cup (75 g) roasted nuts

½ cup (75 g) dried coconut

1 cup (250 ml) qishta or whipping cream

Khaleat Nahl

UMM ADHAM, al-Dhayabiyah

Khaleat nahl (honeybee or beehive) are airy, syrupy buns stuffed with date filling or soft cheese. Ironically, khaleat nahl contains no honey! We like making it while dishes are simmering for ghada'.

❖

5 cups (625 g) flour

5 tbsp (37.5 g) powdered milk

1 tsp baking powder

½ cup (100 g) sugar

1 tsp salt

2 tsp yeast

1 tsp vanilla extract

1 egg, beaten

¼ cup (60 ml) canola oil

¼ cup (60 ml) saman or butter, melted

1½ cups (375 ml) water

Egg glaze: 1 egg beaten with **2 tbsp** water or full-fat (whole) milk

¼ cup (36 g) nigella and sesame seeds

DATE FILLING

4 cups (600 g) finely chopped dates

2 tbsp saman or butter, melted

1 tbsp ground cinnamon

1 tsp ground cardamom

1 tsp toasted sesame seeds (optional)

SYRUP

1 cup (200 g) sugar

1 cup (250 ml) water

1 tsp rosewater or orange blossom water

1 tsp lemon juice

In a large bowl, mix the dry ingredients together. Make a well in the middle and add the vanilla, egg, oil, saman, and water. Mix well, creating a soft, smooth dough. Knead for 20 minutes. Let rise in a warm place for 1 hour.

Mix the filling ingredients together.

In a medium pot, combine the syrup ingredients. Bring to a boil, then reduce the heat and simmer for 10 minutes or until thick. Remove from heat and let cool completely.

Punch down the dough and shape into 1½-inch (3.8-cm) balls (oil your hands to prevent sticking). Flatten the balls and stuff each with 1 tsp (5 ml) of the filling, then wrap/pinch the dough to form a sealed ball. Place close together, seam side down, in a greased large round pan. Let rest for 30 minutes.

Brush with the egg glaze and sprinkle with the sesame and nigella seeds. Bake at 350°F (175°C) for 25-30 minutes or until risen. Finish under the broiler for 1-2 minutes or until golden. Remove from the oven and douse with the syrup.

Mahalabia

UMM MUHAMMAD, Ghasm

4 cups (1 l) full-fat (whole) milk

¾ cup (150 g) sugar

1 cup (250 ml) water

5 tbsp (37.5 g) cornstarch

½ tsp crushed mastic

1 tbsp rosewater or orange blossom water

2 cardamom pods, crushed

Garnish: honey, **1 cup (100 g)** chopped pistachios

In a large pot over medium heat, combine the milk, sugar, and water. Bring to a boil.

Pour ¼ cup of the mixture into a glass with the cornstarch. Whisk until smooth, then return to the pot along with the mastic. Reduce the heat and simmer until thickened. Remove from heat and stir in the rosewater and cardamom. Refrigerate until cooled, the pudding will be very thick.

Serve cold in small dishes drizzled with honey and topped with the pistachios.

Mahalabia, a flavourful milk pudding, dates back to the tenth century. This easy dish is lovely for any occasion and looks fancy in dessert bowls.

My Sewing Business

I am Umm Faisala. We left our village, al-Sawara, because it was being bombed, and we entered Jordan in January 2013. My daughter is still in Syria and I miss her very much. I have not seen her children, my grandchildren, and it is very difficult to talk by phone. I share my caravan, our little house, with my husband. We've been married forty-two years and Allah has blessed us with ten children, five daughters and five sons, and now thirty grandchildren. We lost some of our family in the war; some live nearby in Zaatari, others in Lebanon and Turkey.

In Daraa as a little girl I learned to sew and do Houran-style embroidery from my mother and grandmother. Money and jobs are scarce in Zaatari, especially for women. I began sewing at UN Women and received a monthly salary. After a year and a half of saving, I bought a sewing machine for my caravan and started working for customers I know from Syria. In appreciation, UN Women rewarded me with an additional sewing machine.

I borrowed a small amount of money from my girlfriend and bought an embroidery machine and a knitting machine, and expanded the caravan for all the machines. Then I started working for all the people of the camp. Today, I employ three women seamstresses and specialize in designing and making Qallabiyat and Hourani abayas, repairing all kinds of clothes, and sewing butterflies and things. My challenges as a Zaatari businesswoman are sourcing quality cloth at good prices, security entry of materials into the camp, the expense of generators, and the availability of electricity, as it is rationed.

I aspire to expand my business to the commercial market, but this is difficult because I am not experienced in marketing and sales. I invite you to my caravan shop! We will make you a custom Hourani embroidered abaya in your size. ◆✕◆

Riz bil Haleeb

UMM NAWRAS, Ghouta

1 cup (225 g) rice

4 cups (1 l) full-fat (whole) milk

½ cup (100 g) sugar

1 cinnamon stick

½ tsp crushed mastic

2 tbsp cornstarch

¼ cup (60 ml) warm milk or water

1 tbsp rosewater or orange blossom water

2 tsp vanilla extract

2 cardamom pods, crushed

Garnish: honey, cinnamon, coconut, raisins, chopped pistachios

A childhood favourite, *riz bil haleeb*—a rice pudding variation of mahalabia, also ancient in origin—is rich in flavour.

Rinse the rice. In a large bowl, cover the rice with water and swish with your hand. Drain and repeat three times, until the water runs clear. Cover with water again and soak for 2 hours. Drain and set aside.

In a large pot over medium heat, bring the milk to a boil. Stir and add the rice, sugar, cinnamon, and mastic. Reduce the heat, cover, and simmer for 30 minutes or until the rice is cooked.

Dissolve the cornstarch in the warm milk or water and add to the rice with the rosewater, vanilla, and cardamom, stirring until thickened, about 5 minutes. Refrigerate until cooled.

Serve in small dishes drizzled with honey and garnishes.

Lyali Lebanon

UMM YASSEN, al-Hrak

Lyali Lebanon ("Lebanese Nights") cold semolina pudding is topped with qishta or whipped cream, then syrup and pistachios. It's a popular make-ahead sweet that, for Syrians, brings back memories of visiting Beirut.

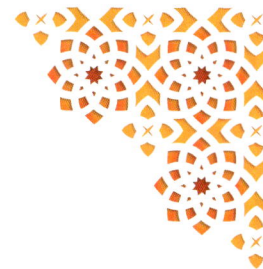

8 cups (2 l) full-fat (whole) milk

½ cup (100 g) sugar

1 cup (180 g) coarse semolina

2 tsp cornstarch

½ tsp ground mastic

1 tbsp orange blossom water or rosewater

2 cups (500 ml) qishta (p. 165) or whipped cream

SYRUP

1 cup (200 g) sugar

1 cup (250 ml) water

1 tsp rosewater or orange blossom water

1 tsp lemon juice

Prepare syrup by boiling the sugar and water, then let simmer for a few minutes. Remove from heat and add the flavourings. Cool to room temperature.

In a large pot over medium heat, warm the milk and stir in the sugar to dissolve. Add the semolina, cornstarch, and mastic, stirring well. Bring to a boil, then reduce the heat and simmer, covered, for 30 minutes or until thickened and the semolina is cooked. Stir in the orange blossom water or rosewater. Turn into a greased dish, smoothing the top. Spread with the qishta or whipped cream. Chill for at least 3 hours. Top with cooled syrup and pistachios.

Nammorah

UMM BESSAM and UMM WALAD, al-Karak

SYRUP

1 cup (200 g) sugar

1 cup (250 ml) water

1 tsp rosewater or orange blossom water

1 tsp lemon juice

CAKE

1 cup (250 ml) full-fat yogurt

2 tsp baking soda

3 cups (540 g) coarse semolina

1 cup (125 g) flour

1 cup (90 g) dried coconut

1 cup (200 g) sugar

1 tsp vanilla extract

2 tsp lemon zest

¾ cup (175 ml) saman or olive oil

Garnish: almonds, whole or halved

Nammorah, rich semolina-coconut cake—a simpler, egg-free version of haris-sah and basbousa—can be quickly made before company arrives.

❖

Prepare syrup by boiling the sugar and water, then let simmer for a few minutes. Remove from heat and add the flavourings. Cool to room temperature.

Combine the yogurt and baking soda and let sit.

In a large bowl, mix the dry ingredients together. Rub in the saman, vanilla, lemon zest, and yogurt mixture, ensuring that the semolina is well coated and adding more saman if needed.

Turn into a greased oblong baking dish, score into diamonds, and place an almond in the centre of each diamond. Bake at 400°F (204°C) for 30 minutes, then broil for 1-2 minutes. Douse immediately with cooled syrup.

Barazek

UMM ABOUD, Tal Shihab

Damascus is known for these buttery cookies with pistachios and topped with sesame seeds. A sweet shop mainstay, sold by the kilo, these crunchy, large-as-you-like cookies can be made at home.

✧

For the syrup, bring the water, sugar, and honey to a boil, then simmer for 8 minutes. Remove from heat and let cool.

For the cookies, beat the sugar and butter until fluffy. Add the egg, vanilla, and vinegar. Mix well, then add the flour, stirring to make a smooth, firm dough. Refrigerate for 1 hour.

In a small bowl, mix the sesame seeds with half of the pistachios and half of the syrup (reserve the remaining syrup for another use, such as with ice cream). Shape the dough into 1-inch (2-cm) balls. Flatten to a thickness of about ¼ inch (0.6 cm) and press one side into the pistachios, then turn and dip the other side into the sesame seeds. Place, sesame side up, on a greased or parchment-lined baking sheet.

Bake at 350°F (175°C) for 15-20 minutes or until the bottoms are golden, then broil for 30-60 seconds, making sure the seeds do not burn. Let sit for 1-2 minutes and transfer to a cooling rack.

SYRUP

1 cup (250 ml) water

1 cup (200 g) sugar

3 tbsp (45 ml) liquid honey

COOKIES

1 cup (200 g) sugar

1 cup (220 g) cold butter or saman

1 egg

1 tbsp vanilla extract

1 tbsp vinegar

2 cups (250 g) flour

¾ cup (75 g) finely chopped pistachios

2 cups (280 gl) toasted sesame seeds

Esh al-Bulbol

UMM ODAI, Damascus

SYRUP

1 cup (200 g) sugar

1 cup (250 ml) water

1 tsp rosewater or orange blossom water

1 tsp lemon juice

PASTRY

1 lb (500 g) knafeh threads

1 cup (200 g) pistachios

1 cup (250 ml) saman or butter, melted

Prepare syrup by boiling the sugar and water, then let simmer for a few minutes. Remove from heat and add the flavourings. Cool to room temperature.

Brush a baking sheet with saman.

Cut the knafeh threads into 8-inch (20-cm) lengths. Wrap a thread around your finger to form a bird's nest and press gently onto the baking sheet. Place 2 or 3 pistachios inside. Repeat with the remaining dough and pistachios. Pour saman into each nest, filling it halfway. Let rest at room temperature for 30 minutes.

Bake at 350°F (175°C) for 25 minutes or until golden. Transfer to a plate and pour cold syrup over the nests.

Esh al-Bulbol (nightingale nests) is knafeh pastry shredded and shaped into small nests, baked with green pistachios, and then doused in syrup. Kids love making and eating these confections; adults enjoy esh al-bulbol with coffee. Great with qishta, ice cream, or Nutella too.

My Brother Loved Esh al-Bulbol

Esh al-Bulbol has special sad memories. When I lived with my family in Syria, my younger brother Ahmad loved baqlawah, and esh al-bulbol especially. I made it almost every day and we'd eat it sitting around the heater, laughing.

In 2013 I was forced to leave and come here, my brother eating esh al-bulbol imprinted on my mind. I dared not make it. How could I if my brother was not with me?

In 2015 my brother died in the war. I felt choked, unable to see him, say goodbye. Sorrow withered me deep inside. After mourning for ten days, I woke early without knowing or feeling what I was doing. It was raining. I started making esh al-bulbol and made 20 kg.

I distributed it by hand to my neighbours and others I knew in the camp. I asked them to pray for my brother, for Allah's mercy, and for my parents' understanding. I felt like I walked and visited every house and street that day; my eyes did not stop crying. Every anniversary of his death I make esh al-bulbol and tell my parents Ahmad is happy in heaven, Alhumdillah. May Allah bless us and gather us with him.

Painting Is My Happiness

I am Malak Abu Alkhir. When I was 15, I wanted to be a pharmacist. That was ten years ago, but life has changed. Gone was our farmhouse where my family—me, my parents, and thirteen brothers and sisters—lived for generations. Gone was our garden where I played under the trees. Gone was our beautiful life, our security, our happiness. My only thought, every day, was how to safely return home. I'd always loved drawing, especially the flowers on wedding cards, and my sketchbook and paints accompanied me everywhere—they were my escape from the war, from my fears, from questions about the future.

When my family decided to leave Syria, I was shocked. They promised we'd return home in two months and my father stayed behind as proof. I said good-bye to my house, I kissed the walls and the garden earth. I left my new sweater—brown and white stripes—ready for my return.

Safety eluded us. We moved from city to city, from village to village. I cried so much in our car, my brother asked if it was raining. Arriving at Zaatari, I slept deeply from exhaustion. When I woke, I saw something white and asked, "Where am I?" It was the whiteness of the tent, the bleached desert, our gray future. I had no desire to explore the camp. I stayed in the tent with my notebook, drawing my beloved roses—neither of us suited to the desert clime. Soon my father joined us in Zaatari and I lost hope of returning home.

One day I went with my sister to learn handicrafts at Save the Children. Seeing my drawings, the centre volunteer asked me to participate in an initiative about early marriage—a topic very relevant to me as a sixteen-year-old girl. My paintings had an effect, convincing some mothers and daughters of the dangers of early marriage, and I learned that art could be stronger than words. Empowered, I attended Arabic calligraphy lessons taught by a painter. He believed in my talent and asked me to participate in an artists' committee. The committee gave me paints and tools. I was happy, like a little child, and my family supported me.

Painting is my happiness. I love sharing my talent and bringing joy through painting, especially with children. I paint walls in homes and the centers to saturate people's eyes with beautiful scenes. My dream now is to have an exhibition, to share my talent with all people, and support them when life's circumstances are difficult. People wonder why I have not married—I will marry when I choose, when I find the right person who supports me as a woman and artist.

Biskawit Sameed

UMM OBAIDAH, Damascus

These little semolina-milk macaroons disappear fast; thankfully, they're easy and quick to make.

2 tsp baking powder

1 tsp yeast

½ tsp ground mastic

1 tsp ground anise

2 cups (400 g) sugar

2 cups (250 g) flour

1 cup (180 g) coarse semolina

2 tsp rosewater

½ cup (125 ml) melted saman or canola oil

1 cup (250 ml) full-fat (whole) milk

Mix the dry ingredients well. Add the saman or oil, the rosewater, and the milk to make a firm dough. Chill for 1 hour.

On a floured surface, roll out the dough and shape it into 2 logs. Slice the logs into cookies ½ inch (1.3 cm) thick and place them on greased baking sheets. Brush the tops with melted saman and bake at 350°F (175°C) until golden, 8-10 minutes. Cool on a wire rack.

Lazza'eyyat

UMM MOHAMMED, al-Sawara

4 cups (500 g) flour

½ tsp salt

6 cups (1.5 l) water

6 cups (1.5 l) whole-fat (whole) milk or 3 cups (375 g) powdered milk dissolved well in 6 cups (1.5 l) of water

1 lb (450 g) halaweh, crumbled (p. 197, or use store-bought)

pinch of salt

4 cups (800 g) sugar

4 cups (360 g) dried coconut

4 cups (600 g) chopped walnuts

Perhaps the most beloved of sweets by young and old across Zaatari Camp is *lazza'eyyat*—layers of crèpes with homemade halaweh, sometimes adorned with coloured sugar and coconut for family celebrations. While crèpes might make you think of France, lazza'eyyat is Bedouin and these crèpes are cooked on a saj or a frying pan over fire. You can make small ones using a crèpe pan and experiment stylistically with folds and rolling. Lazza'eyyat is an old recipe, passed down through families from Daraa, and halaweh is the special ingredient—sometimes 1 cup of saman is substituted for the milk and the coconut is omitted. Other regions of Syria use honey in place of sugar, add raisins to the mix, and, sadly, omit the halaweh.

⁙

For the crèpes, mix the flour and salt with the water gradually until it becomes a smooth liquid; set aside in a jug.

For the sauce, bring the milk to a boil, remove from heat and let cool slightly. Add the halaweh, sugar, and a pinch of salt.

Lightly grease a frying pan and place it over medium heat. Pour the crèpe mixture into the pan thinly to coat the bottom. Cook each crèpe for about 30 seconds or until dry. Use your fingers (or a spatula) to flip it and cook briefly on the other side.

On a large plate, pour ⅓ cup of the sauce. Place a crèpe on top of the sauce and sprinkle with the coconut and walnuts. Repeat, building layers of crèpes, sauce, coconut, and walnuts, ending with sauce. Each layer will be about ½-inch (1.3-cm) thick, uneven in shape. On special occasions, decorate with sprinkles, sesame seeds, and whole walnuts.

Chai

UMM MASHREEF, Nasib

Syrian groceries have a vast range of *chai* (teas), sold as dried herbs and in tea-bags, prepared and consumed according to a person's health condition and the season—ginger with lemon is used to cleanse the stomach, for weight issues, and for sore throats/colds; chamomile promotes sleep and digestion; wild thyme (zaatar) is used for respiration and inflammation; cinnamon for menstruation and postpartum. All chai is usually sweetened liberally with sugar or honey.

CHAI MAGRIBI (MOROCCAN CHAI)

4 cups (1 l) water

¼ cup (60 ml) green tea

¼ cup (50 g) sugar

½ cup (12 g) fresh mint leaves

Bring water to boil. Add tea and sugar. Remove from heat, add mint, and steep for 5 minutes. Serve in small glasses with fresh mint.

ZANJABIL WA LAYMUN

4 cups (1 l) water

2-3 slices fresh ginger

1 sliced lemon or **2** lumi punched with holes

Bring water and ginger to a boil. Remove from heat. Add sliced lemon or lumi and steep for 10 minutes. Sweeten with honey. Serve hot or cold.

CHAI BADAWI (BEDOUIN CHAI)

4 cups (1 l) water

½ cup (100 g) sugar

3 tbsp (20 g) black tea

¼ cup (18 g) dried whole sage leaves

Bring water and sugar to a boil. Add tea and sage leaves, and steep for 5-7 minutes. Serve with sugar.

CHAI ZAATAR

4 cups (1 l) water

½ cup (12.5 g) fresh thyme

2 lumi punched with holes or **1** sliced lemon

Boil water with thyme and lumi. Steep for 10 minutes, then strain. Serve with honey.

CHAI WA NANAA

4 cups (1 l) water

½ cup (100 g) sugar

3 tbsp (20 g) black tea

Bring water and sugar to a boil. Add tea and steep for 5-7 minutes. Serve with sugar and fresh mint leaves.

MARAMEYAH

4 cups (1 l) water

½ cup (100 g) sugar

¼ cup (18 g) dried whole sage leaves

Bring water and sugar to a boil. Add sage leaves. Steep for 5-7 minutes, and serve.

BABUNJ

4 cups (1 l) water

7 tbsp (17.5 g) dried chamomile flowers

honey to taste

slices of ginger and/or **1 tsp** black tea (optional)

Bring water to a boil. Add chamomile flowers and simmer 10 minutes (adding ginger and/or black tea if desired). Add honey to taste and serve.

CHAI WA HIL

4 cups (1 l) water

1 tbsp black or green tea

¼ cup (10 g) dried rosebuds

5 cracked, roasted cardamom pods

2 tsp rosewater

Bring water to boil. Add tea, rosebuds, and cardamom. Steep for 10 minutes, then strain. Add rosewater and serve with honey.

Turkish Coffee

HALA (age 14), al-Midan

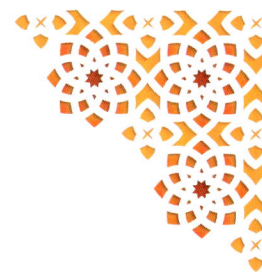

Turkish coffee is a misnomer—it's arguably Syrian. In 1554, Shams of Damascus and Hakem of Aleppo opened the world's first coffee shop in Istanbul's Golden Horn, serving their stove top-boiled, thick, dark coffee from Syria in small cups. What became known as Turkish coffee spread throughout the Ottoman Empire and the world. While coffee trees began in Ethiopia, the first coffee drinks as we know them today were made in 15th century Yemen by Sufis seeking to stay awake all night to pray.

At Zaatari we drink a lot of coffee. We start with Arabic (p. 27) or Turkish coffee, then drink chai, and have Turkish coffee before ending the visit. Coffee is said to change your mood—make it better. Umm Laith gave an example:

One day, I was exhausted and it was extremely hot. My daughters said the digger hit the fence of the caravan. I went out to have a fight with him, but I found a nice-looking guy, sweaty and tired. I served him a rakwah of coffee and cold water, we chatted, he finished work, and we said nice goodbyes.

Aromatic Turkish coffee—finely ground, powdery, dark roasted beans infused with roasted cardamom—is prepared in a brass rakwah (plural rakwat) and served in small finjeen cups with handles (unlike the handle-less finjeens used for Arabic coffee). Girls and women prepare coffee for guests served on beautiful Syrian hand-tooled, shell-inlaid wooden trays or etched brass trays. Handmade, weighty brass rakwat of different sizes are highly collectible because of their artistry and also because of the war. Imitation stainless steel rakwat are feather-light; the handles get overly hot and they are highly prone to tipping over.

As with Arabic coffee, Turkish coffee is served with a glass of water. If a guest drinks the water before tasting the coffee, it means they are hungry. If they drink the water after the coffee, it signals that they did not like the taste of the coffee. Don't worry about protocol—it's fine if you're just thirsty for water or need a palate cleanser.

FOR TWO SERVINGS:

1 cup (250 ml) water, filled to the brim

1 heaping tbsp Turkish coffee

Garnish (optional): cardamom pods

Measure the water into the rakwah. If you don't have a rakwah, use a small pot with high sides. Bring to a boil over high heat and add the coffee, stirring often with a long, slender spoon. Remove from heat when foam rises to the top. Place the rakwah on a tray. Fill cups halfway, then top up—the foam will rise to the top.

For foamless coffee, bring to a boil a second or third time, letting it settle in between by lifting from heat.

Traditionally coffee is served black (*sada*), but if you need sugar, add 1-3 tsp to the ground coffee when boiling.

Losing the Dear Ones

"The hardest thing in life is to lose what is most precious to your heart. My son drowned in Zaatari Camp; he was thirteen. My husband and family are in Syria, and the worries about my children are breaking me. Alhumdillah, I am very patient. Allah is my suffice and the best deputy."
—UMM MOAZ

When a person dies, the entire village supports the family, sharing the sadness and offering prayers to Allah for the person's soul. Condolences include "We come from God and to God we return. May Allah forgive him and accept him into paradise. May Allah have mercy and give patience to his loved ones." During the war, cemeteries on the outskirts of cities and villages were replaced by the cities themselves, with people buried amidst the destruction and in gardens, prayers shortened because of the sheer number of martyrs—and the fear, especially with civilians being targeted during Friday prayers and during Ramadan.

Traditionally in Syria, and at Zaatari, the deceased is buried within twenty-four hours to free the soul from the body. A mghassel, often a family member, washes the deceased, followed by ablution, and covering in a kafan (a shroud of two to four pieces of white linen or satin). Before tying the ends of the cloth, a male family member may ask if the deceased had any debts—which are paid by the oldest family member so the deceased's soul can properly rest. The body is laid in a wooden coffin, and the family see the deceased for the last time, saying goodbye. The al-Janazah (funeral prayer) begins with men carrying the coffin on their shoulders to the mosque (women do not attend funerals) where they place it in front of the worshippers. A rakah with al-Fatiha is prayed over the body followed by a rakah with a dua.

Between the Past and the Present, Tamr Jokhadder

The al-Janazah continues as male family members carry the coffin to the graveyard and place it in a grave facing Mecca. People pray to Allah for the person with special Duaa (prayers) for the dead and toss three handfuls of earth onto the coffin. The family accept condolences and return home to grieve—ending three days after the death, or a week after the death for people of high standing in the community.

People bring food to the al-Izza mourning tent (sometimes, separate tents for men and women). Arada performers, or a woman in a white headscarf, welcome mourners and serve bitter Arabic coffee and dates as the family sit in silence. People thank Allah for everything and recite al-Fatiha three times upon leaving.

Three days after the funeral, the family place flowers on the grave. Because a soul stays in the grave for forty days, the following day a white headstone with the person's identity written in black is placed on the grave so the soul will not become trapped.

The following week, the family make dishes and sweets loved by the deceased, inviting people for lunch and feeding the poor as charity for the mercy of the deceased person's soul. On the fortieth day, a male sheep may be slaughtered, with prayers offered first, and a blessing offered over the knife, to protect the deceased's soul. The sheep's meat is served with bulgur to the poor—repeated on the anniversary of the death. Male relatives may grow beards and refrain from washing while mourning. Female relatives wear black for a year or more; widows may wear black for the rest of their lives, remarrying only for livelihood and to support their children, often to a relative of the deceased.

On Eid al-Fitr, family often visit their deceased to lay favourite flowers. If the cost is not prohibitive, a sabeel (water fountain) inscribed with the deceased's name may be built, its users reciting al-Fatiha for the dear one's soul. Peace in loss comes from knowing that believers—people who walk the straight path—will be united in paradise and on the Day of Reckoning. ◆✕◆

A Star for My Father
BARAA

I lean back against the wall, tired
Holding my hands to your promises of returning.
I eye the doorknob
Eagerly, maybe your hand will touch one day.
Tell me, before you return so I extinguish the sun for you
So, I sleep closer to dreams.
Are there any dreams left, daddy?
When you come, I will pick a star and say to the moon
"Look, I have a star of my own now"
When you come, dad, I will tell my only friend
I don't want to learn the language of death anymore
I will ask my accompanying sorrows.
Is it true that my dad is gone?
Will he ever come back again?

أستندُ متعبةً إلى جدارٍ
حاملةً بين يديَّ وعدكَ بالرجوع
بلهفةٍ أرقبُ البابَ علَّ يدكَ على قبضتِه
أخبرني عندما تأتي كي أُطفئَ الشّمس
كي أنامَ على مقربةٍ من الأحلام
لكن هل مازالَ هنالكَ أحلامٌ يا أبي
عندما تأتي سأقطفُ نجمةً وأقولُ للقمر:
انظُر الآنَ لَديَّ نجمة
عندما تأتِ يا أبي سأقولُ لصديقتي الوحيدة
لم أعُد أرغبُ في تعلّمِ لغةِ الموتى
سأقولُ لصديقي النّدمِ،
هل حقاً رَحَلَ أبي؟
هل حقاً سيعود؟

Pickles, pp. 255-57

Muraaba al-Tiyn, p. 253

The Zaatari Pantry

وَهُوَ الَّذِي أَنشَأَ جَنَّاتٍ مَعْرُوشَاتٍ وَغَيْرَ مَعْرُوشَاتٍ وَالنَّخْلَ وَالزَّرْعَ
مُخْتَلِفًا أُكُلُهُ وَالزَّيْتُونَ وَالرُّمَّانَ مُتَشَابِهًا وَغَيْرَ مُتَشَابِهٍ كُلُوا مِن ثَمَرِهِ
إِذَا أَثْمَرَ وَآتُوا حَقَّهُ يَوْمَ حَصَادِهِ وَلَا تُسْرِفُوا إِنَّهُ لَا يُحِبُّ الْمُسْرِفِينَ

It is He Who produceth gardens, with trellises and without, and dates, and tilth with produce of all kinds, and olives and pomegranates, similar (in kind) and different (in variety): eat of their fruit in their season, but render the dues that are proper on the day that the harvest is gathered. But waste not by excess: for Allah loveth not the wasters.
—The Holy Quran, Al-Anam "The Cattle," 6:141

To understand a cuisine, it's often a good idea to understand its pantry, the staples that build flavour and reinforce the character of a dish. In knowing the *how*, *why*, and *when* an ingredient is used, home cooks (either in Zaatari Camp or wherever you are) can gain insight into how to prepare these dishes, no matter how well stocked your personal pantry is.

Whatever the culture or cuisine—let alone how or where they are expressed—cooking is an exercise in finding balance. Balance of flavours and textures, either within one dish or how one dish complements another. This list of pantry staples isn't just a shopping list, it's a primer on flavours, and how to use them judiciously.

At Zaatari, many items are bought by the kilo at the souks, along with items for special occasions, such as moulds for making maamoul and bread for Eid. In North America, many modern supermarkets today are thankfully expanding their offerings of international ingredients and pantry staples. You may be surprised at what you can find at your local grocer. If you're lucky enough to live in a city with Middle Eastern or Asian grocers, you'll probably be able to find most, if not all, of these ingredients. Otherwise, many small independent food and spice vendors have online stores, and will ship around the world.

The Zaatari pantry follows the seasons. In spring, yogurt, butter, cheese, and saman are produced. Summer brings the drying of kishk, kethi, and mloukhieh leaves; the canning of okra, tomatoes, and grape leaves; the making of fruit jams. Autumn brings the making of makdous, the pressing of olives, and plenty of pickling.

Before refrigeration, a *namlieh*, a wooden cabinet with drawers, cupboards, and shelving and fine mesh doors to keep insects out, was used as a pantry. The namlieh is in use once again at Zaatari, along with the Bedouin practice of suspending bananas and certain other foods.

In the same manner, keep all dry goods (legumes, grains, spices) in a dry cabinet or pantry, in well-sealed containers. Whole spices such as cumin and coriander seeds last for a year in this manner, while ground spices lose their freshness after three to six months. Dried herbs, such as mint, tend to last about a year as well. Note that dried herbs are not interchangeable with fresh herbs.

Fresh herbs are best kept in the fridge, with the stems (or roots) immersed in water. To keep them even fresher, cover the herbs with a plastic freezer bag. They should last up to a week in this manner.

Key equipment for many of these processes, and for cooking in Zaatari kitchens in general, is a large, heavy mortar and pestle. Invest in one, and you'll notice the difference it makes in crushing herbs and aromatics. A small spice/coffee grinder (for grinding spices as freshly as possible) is a good investment as well..

al-Qabas Spice Shop

I am Abu Yusef from Daraa. In Syria, I owned a shop that sold building materials. I left in June 2012 because of the war and living conditions. When I reached Jordan and registered with UNHCR, I lived in a city outside camp. I was buying spices and noticed the importance of spices in people's daily lives. I started thinking about opening a spice shop. I took advice and opened my shop in Zaatari Camp on the Shams Élysées. A simple shop with metal sheeting for walls above the dirt floor, I began with ten kilos of coffee beans, a small mill, and the main spices.

Now our shop is one of the best-known in Zaatari. It is where about eighty percent of residents buy their coffee and spices, as well as many people who work inside the camp (teachers, drivers, nurses, employees of organizations). We sell all kinds of coffee, chai, spices, herbs, and nuts, used for eating, cooking, beauty, and Arab medicine. Some of the spices have many varieties. Zaatar is a blend that is very healthy for you, used in many ways, and judged by its taste. We sell thyme dakka, regular green thyme, and royal green thyme, which is considered the best. Our most popular spices are zaatar, sumac, baharat (seven spice), curry, Maggi, kabseh, mandi grill, and Spanish.

We are always working to develop and expand our products in line with what residents need. Syrians consume large quantities of coffee, chai, and spices, and, of course, are demanding about quality. In Syria, our spices came from Aleppo, the spice capital.

Despite my great love for this serious work, I face difficulties purchasing stock, and with electricity. Our working hours are eight a.m. to ten p.m. My son and I take turns managing the shop and we have two workers. I wish to expand the business, to have more than one branch in the souk so it is easier for people to shop and to provide jobs for more people. ❖

Baharat

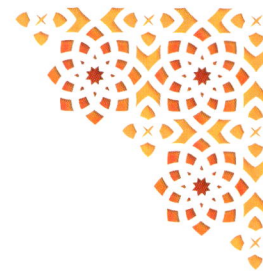

Baharat—seven spice—is key to Syrian cooking, with warm, highly fragrant spices and ratio varying according to taste and region. Some mixtures, like this one, have more than seven spices, but are still known as baharat. Buy at a shop or make at home by roasting and grinding with a machine or with mortar and pestle. Many Zaatari cooks include curry and Maggi.

1 tbsp black peppercorns

1 tbsp turmeric

1 tbsp cumin seeds

1 tsp coriander seeds

½ tsp whole cloves

2 tsp cardamom pods

1 tbsp ground cinnamon

1 tbsp paprika

1 tsp nutmeg

In a dry pan over medium heat, combine the first 6 spices and roast for 2-3 minutes or until fragrant, stirring constantly. Grind, adding the cinnamon, paprika, and nutmeg. Store in a glass jar and use within 6 months.

Saman

UMM QAIS, Jabab

Rich, nutty, golden saman (ghee) is known as "Syrian butter," and made from clarified cow's milk butter, the milk solids rendered from the butterfat. Warning: upon first taste, making saman becomes your life mission. Really, sample it from the jar or use it to fry an egg—the taste of homemade saman will change your life. Like sheep's milk butter, saman was traditionally made by shaking milk in a tripod-suspended goatskin, with the goatskin used as storage container. Its flavour depends on animal breed, grazing, and weather. Because of saman's high smoking point—over 450°F (232°C)—it is often mixed with olive oil, adding supreme flavour. Lactose/casein free, saman keeps on the countertop for over three months or a year refrigerated. Enjoy the remnant, separated solids on bread.

SMALL BATCH

1 lb (450 g) unsalted butter

Melt butter in a heavy pan over low heat, tilting the pan but not stirring, for about 15 minutes. The foam will disappear and solids will collect at the bottom.

Remove from the heat, cool for 5 minutes, then pour into glass jars using a cloth-lined mesh strainer. Refrigerate to solidify.

LARGE BATCH

For large quantities, bulgur is used to separate the milk solids. The buttery bulgur remnant is a most succulent treat.

4 lbs (1.8 kg) butter

2 cups (500 ml) water

1½ cups (285 g) coarse bulgur

Melt butter over low heat for 5 minutes. Add water and let sit for 3 minutes. Add bulgur and continue heating for 20 minutes without stirring. Remove from heat, let sit for 2-3 minutes, then pour into glass jars using fine cheesecloth or a cloth-lined wire mesh strainer.

Dibis Romaan

UMM KHOLUD, al-Kiswah

Lauded in the Quran, the super-food pomegranate is indigenous to the Middle East. Used in many dishes, sweet, tangy *dibis romaan* (pomegranate molasses) keeps forever. Zaatari women vary the recipe, tweaking the sugar and lemon to preference. Ripe pomegranates work well, but the women use sour, young pomegranates with green, smooth, thin skin for a richer flavour. Use store-bought pomegranate juice to skip preparing it from seed.

8 sour pomegranates, washed

½ cup (100 g) sugar

2 tbsp lemon juice

Remove the tops of the pomegranates, quarter, and remove the seeds.

In a heavy medium pot, simmer the seeds for 20 minutes, mashing with a spoon to release the juice. Remove from heat and strain using a mesh strainer or a cloth.

Return the juice to low heat, add the sugar and lemon juice, and simmer for 30 minutes, stirring occasionally and adjusting for taste. Remove from heat when the molasses is reduced to 1¼ cups (310 ml) and coats the back of a spoon. Let cool, then pour into a glass jar with a tight-fitting lid. Store in a cool place for up to 6 months.

Dibis Altamr

UMM FAREED, al-Dhayabiyah

8 cups (2 l) water

5 lb (2.2 kg) washed, pitted dates

Boil the water in a large pot. Remove from heat, add the dates, cover, and leave until soft, about 90 minutes.

Return to medium heat and bring to a boil. Lower the heat and simmer for 60-90 minutes or until syrupy and coats the back of a spoon. (For thicker syrup, reduce the water and increase the simmering time.) Remove from heat and let cool completely.

Using a large, lipped bowl, strain a cup at a time through a fine sieve or a cloth-lined strainer, pressing with your hand or a spoon.

Spoon into jars and store in a cool place for up to 6 months. Yields 4 cups (1 l).

Sweet *dibis altmar* (date molasses) is used widely as a meat marinade, as salad dressing, on bread, over yogurt, as a finishing molasses, or for preparing rose-infused jallab juice. Historically, it was covered with cheesecloth and sun-dried on rooftops until syrupy. Grape molasses is prepared and used the same way.

Shattah

ABU KAMAL, Nawa

Spicy red shattah is a key condiment to Syrian dishes, especially those with meat and dishes for ghada'. Try making it the traditional way or the fast, easy version by blending the peppers in a food processor, then stirring in the salt, pomegranate molasses, and ⅓ cup (80 ml) of olive oil. Either way, store your shattah in glass jars—it will keep for up to 6 months, no refrigeration necessary.

3 cups (275 g) red chili (such as ripe jalapeno) peppers

1 tbsp salt

2 tsp Dibis Romaan (pomegranate molasses)

olive oil

Wash and dry the peppers, then dehydrate in the sun for 3-4 days, rotating daily, until they are very dry. Remove the stems and grind finely, using a mortar and pestle. Add 1 tsp of salt and place in a strainer in the refrigerator for 3-4 days, adding more salt each day. Strain the paste and place it in a jar with the pomegranate molasses. Top with olive oil. Stir before using.

Jams and Pickles

❋

UMM OMAR, UMM FAISAL, UMM SADAAM, Simlin, Mhajjah, and Buser al-Harir

Zaatari chefs make Muraaba—spice-infused jam—with flower petals, fruits, and rinds, to be enjoyed with bread, cheese, and yogurt.

(left to right)
Muraaba al-Tamatim, Muraaba al-Mashmash,
Muraaba al-Burtuqal, Muraaba al-Tiyn,
and Muraaba al-Yaqtin

Muraaba al-Mashmash (Apricot)

In a large pot, layer the apricot
with the sugar and lemon salt and leave overnight.

Strain, reserving the fruit. Cook the juice over medium-low heat for 30 minutes or until reduced by half, skimming off the foam. Add the apricot to the syrup and simmer for 20 minutes. Transfer to a large dish and let cool. Dry in the sun for 5 or 6 days, then spoon into glass jars.

2.2 lb (1 kg) fresh apricots

4 cups (800 g) sugar

1 tbsp lemon salt, or **½** lemon, juiced

Remove the pits and quarter the apricots.

Muraaba al-Tamatim (Tomato)

Peel the tomatoes by hand or by blanching. Chop the tomatoes, discarding the seeds.

In a large pot, bring the water and sugar to a boil, then lower the heat and simmer for 10 minutes. Add the tomatoes and the remaining ingredients and cook for 1 hour or until set.

Remove from heat, discard the cinnamon stick, and spoon into jars.

2.2 lb (1 kg) tomatoes

1½ cups (375 ml) water

2 cups (400 g) sugar

1 orange, zested and juiced

1 cinnamon stick

1 tsp ground cumin

½ tsp salt

1 tbsp toasted sesame seeds

Muraaba al-Yaqtin (Pumpkin)

In a large pot, toss the pumpkin with half of the sugar and let sit for 3 hours.

Over medium-low heat, bring the remaining sugar and the water to a boil, then reduce the heat and simmer for 10 minutes. Add the pumpkin and all the remaining ingredients except the pine nuts and simmer for 20-30 minutes. Add the pine nuts and spoon into jars.

2 lbs (900 g) pumpkin, grated

2½ cups (500 g) sugar

2 cups (500 ml) water

1 tsp anise

5 grains mastic, crushed

1 cinnamon stick

4-5 whole cloves, crushed

1 orange, zested and juiced

½ cup (70 g) pine nuts or finely chopped walnuts

Muraaba al-Batiykh (Watermelon)

2 lb (900 g) watermelon rind in
1 × 2-inch (2.5 × 5-cm) pieces

4 cups (800 g) sugar

2 strips lemon peel, or **2** small pieces
of ginger, peeled

4 cardamom pods

2 tbsp lemon juice

In a large pot, cover the rind with water and bring to a boil over high heat. Reduce the heat and simmer for 30 minutes. Drain, reserving 3 cups (750 ml) of the liquid and the rind.

In the same pot, mix the reserved liquid with the sugar, ginger, and cardamom. Bring to a boil, then reduce the heat, add the rind, and simmer for 30 minutes.

Remove from heat, cover, and leave to cool for 8 hours in a cool place. Return to medium heat, adjust for taste, and simmer for 30 minutes or until thickened, adding the lemon juice for the last 5 minutes. Remove from heat and let cool. Store in jars in a cool place.

Muraaba al-Burtuqal (Marmalade)

1 lb (454 g) oranges (or **½ lb (225 g)**
each of oranges and lemons)

5 cups (1.1 l) water

4 cups (800 g) sugar

In a large pot over medium heat, boil the oranges in the water until tender. Remove the oranges (reserving the water) and let cool.

Remove the rind, and cut the rind into fine strips. Wrap the pits in a cloth and tie with a string. Return the rind and the pits to the pot, add the sugar, and bring to a boil, then simmer for 30 minutes or until thickened. Discard the pits and spoon the marmalade into jars.

Muraaba al-Tiyn (Fig)

If using dried figs, cut into quarters and leave overnight.

In a large pot, combine the figs, sugar, zest, anise, and mastic. Let sit for 4 hours.

Over medium-low heat, simmer, stirring often, for 2 hours or until the figs are very soft. Taste for sweetness. Remove from heat and stir in the lemon juice. Spoon into jars and top with the walnuts. Cool completely before sealing tightly.

3.3 lb (1.5 kg) green or purple figs, washed, stems removed (or use dried figs)

2 cups (400 g) sugar

1 lemon, finely zested

1 tsp toasted anise seeds

5 mastic crystals, crushed

2 tbsp lemon juice

¼ cup (37.5 g) finely chopped walnuts

Muraaba al-Ward (Rose)

Remove the petals from the roses, gently rinse them in a strainer, and dry them. Place in a large bowl, sprinkle with half of the sugar and crush using a mortar and pestle. Cover and leave for 8 hours.

In a large pot over medium heat, bring the water and remaining sugar to a boil, then simmer for 10 minutes. Add the sugared petals and the lemon juice, reduce the heat to low, and simmer, stirring constantly, for 20 minutes or until the petals are almost white. Add the rosewater and carmine (if using) and simmer, stirring constantly, for 5-10 minutes or until thickened. Remove from heat and spoon into jars.

4 cups (180 g) fresh organic pink Damask roses or wild pink roses

3½ cups (700 g) sugar

1¼ cups (300 ml) water

¼ cup (60 ml) lemon juice

1 tbsp rosewater (optional)

2-3 pellets carmines/cochineal (optional natural colouring)

Zaytun (olives)

UMM KHALED, Buser al-Harir

Brine for Olives

2 tbsp (30 ml) salt

4 cups (1 l) water

olive oil

Dissolve salt in water to make brine.

Green Olives

Rinse the olives and make 2 or 3 small cuts in each. Place in a large bowl and cover with water. Soak for 5 days, changing the water daily.

Place 2 tbsp (30 ml) olive oil in each jar.

Add the rinsed olives layered with the lemon slices along with 1 chili. Cover with brine.

Screw the lid on tightly and store for at least 1 month before serving.

1 lb (450 g) green olives

½ cup (125 ml) olive oil

2 lemons, sliced

2 or 3 whole green or red chilies (jalapeno)

brine

olive oil

clean jars with airtight lids

Black Olives

Rinse and dry the olives. Place in a large bowl, add the salt, and toss gently. Cover with water and leave for 4 days. Spoon the olives into jars with the lemon and garlic and cover with brine.

Screw the lids on tightly and store for a few weeks before serving.

1 lb (450 g) black olives

¼ cup (55 g) coarse salt

2 lemons, sliced

10 cloves garlic

brine

olive oil

clean jars with airtight lid

Mouneh

UMM KHALED, Tafas

2 **lb (1 kg)** cucumbers, cabbages, carrots, or turnips

2 chilies (jalapeno), quartered

1 head of garlic, peeled

1 beet peeled (optional, to be used for pickling turnips)

brine

olive oil

clean jars with airtight lids

Wash and dry the vegetables. If large, halve vertically.

Put in jars with two pieces of chili pepper and 4 garlic cloves.

If pickling turnip, include a few large pieces of peeled beet so the beet juice turns the turnip pink—its signature Syrian colour. Cover with brine.

Screw the lids on tightly and store for 1 month before serving.

Like zaytun (olives) and *zayt sagh* (olive oil), mouneh (pickled vegetables) are ubiquitous at ftoor and used in many dishes. Zaatari women gather to make mouneh in large batches that last for many months. Our favourites are cucumber, cabbage and turnip. The signature pickled turnips are made bright pink by adding beets. In all recipes, cover the jarred vegetables in brine, leaving 1" headspace and top with olive oil.

Makdous Houran

UMM QASSAM, Ataman

These pickled small eggplants stuffed with walnuts and spicy peppers take 8–9 days to prepare. An essential dish at ftoor, makdous are always a most welcome gift. Umm Qassam writes: "Makdous houran has a special taste and is very treasured. I was a volunteer at a camp organization and they asked for ideas to support the community. I suggested making products to offer for sale, especially makdous, pickles, and jam. It was very nice and successful, especially when most of my products became popular and sold out inside and outside Zaatari."

✦✕✦

On day 1: parboil the eggplants for 8-10 minutes, until softened. Rinse well, and transfer to a bowl with cold water until cooled. Use the tip of a knife to make a small vertical gash in the centre of each. Using your fingers, salt the inside of the gash and the outer skin. Place all of the eggplants in a plastic bag. Tie or seal the bag. Cover completely with a heavy weight and leave overnight in a cool place.

In a bowl, mix together the peppers, walnuts, and garlic. Add the olive oil and set aside overnight.

On day 2: drain the water from the eggplants. Stuff generously with the pepper mixture and layer them in jars. Turn the open jars upside down on large rimmed trays or baking sheets and leave until the remaining water drains from the eggplants; this will take 6-8 days. Every day, wipe the water from the tray using a sponge.

On day 8: remove the eggplants from the jars, wipe with a cloth, and return to the jars. Cover with olive oil and add the lids. The makdous houran will be ready to eat in about 12 days. Remember to always keep the eggplants covered in oil (the oil may reduce as you consume the makdous). Keeps for up to one year at room temperature but the eggplants will become tough if not consumed within a few months.

Serve the pickled eggplants whole or tear with khubz bread at ftoor.

20 small eggplants, 4-6 inches (10-15 cm) in length

2 tbsp salt

2 cups (180 g) finely chopped sweet red pepper

2 cups (180 g) finely chopped hot red chili pepper (jalapeno, or less, to taste)

1 cup (140 g) finely chopped walnuts

8 cloves garlic, smashed and minced

3 tbsp (45 ml) olive oil, plus more for filling jars

Labneh Modahbara

UMM FATIMAH, Tal Shihab

4 cups (2 l) full-fat (whole) milk at room temperature

½ tbsp (7.5 ml) full-fat yogurt

1 tsp salt

1½ tbsp nigella seeds

olive oil

Flavourings: zaatar, sumac, mint, crushed pepper flakes, finely chopped nuts, crushed rose petals

Drizzled with olive oil, zaatar, sumac, and more, labneh modahbara—strained yogurt balls—are a ftoor fixture. This low-fat snack is delicious in salads or on bread with cucumber and fried egg. If covered in oil, labneh modahbara keeps for 6 months refrigerated, but you'll likely use it up sooner. Roll the balls in flavourings for a beautiful presentation.

◆×◆

You can use store-bought yogurt, but if you're making your own, bring the milk to a boil, then remove from heat and let sit until lukewarm, 30–45 minutes. Stir in the yogurt, cover, and let sit at room temperature for 4 hours until slightly thickened. Refrigerate for 1 day. Add the salt, transfer to a triple-layered cheesecloth, tie at the top, and drain over the sink or a bowl, squeezing occasionally, until very thick. Transfer to a bowl and add the nigella seeds. Top with olive oil and refrigerate.

Serve as a spread, or shape into 1-inch (2.5-cm) balls and roll in the flavourings of your choice.

To preserve labneh, place 3 tbsp (45 ml) of oil in a large jar with a tight-fitting lid, add the unflavoured balls, and top with more oil to cover. Store in the refrigerator.

A Shami Goat Herder

I am Abu Ameer. When I was nine years old, after school in Daraa I would help my father care for our fifty sheep. Because of the war he sold the sheep and we arrived in Zaatari in August 2012. Like everyone, we lived in a tent. My father worked in construction and with NRC's maintenance team. My brothers and I attended school, but soon they got sick because of a lack of calcium. My father bought a *maaza* (goat) to meet my brothers' needs. When the goat had two kids, it inspired my father to get more goats and earn money selling milk. There was little fresh milk in camp and Syrians enjoy goat milk, especially for making cheese and yogurt. My father saved to buy four large Shami (Syrian) nanny goats and a billy goat, Abu Satr (The Cleaver). Soon, sixteen kids were born, which we divided into pure Shami goats and Shami-Baladi hybrids. An ordinary (municipal) goat is about JOD 200 (USD 280); a Shami goat costs JOD 500–2,000 (USD 700–2,800), depending on its quality. Shami goats are the most expensive because they bear multiple kids and their milk has a high fat content.

We have a small space next to our caravan for Abu Satr and his tribe. My brother and I take care of them with our sons, mixing barley with corn and leftover rice for their morning and evening meals. We share grazing them on desert herbs between the streets from nine to eleven a.m. and from four to seven p.m.; in between we return to the house. Depending on their food intake, they produce 2.5-5 kg (5-10 qt) of milk daily. Shami goats are the best, each has a personality and they produce the most milk; every five months each bears two or three newborns. As a herder, my daily challenge is finding good grazing space; also, our neighbours are disturbed by the smell. I hope to find a suitable place to raise goats and increase their number to produce large quantities of milk, yogurt, and cheese to meet the camp's needs. ◆✕◆

Mohammed Amaari, *Angel*

Me After Losing You

AMIRA

I'm emotionless like a stone against my window
Silent like a tomb, my tongue has dried
I gaze at the moon as if I'm guarding it
With a tortured soul and suffering heart
There's a brutal fight between my mind and heart
Are we going to meet again ever?
Will it be a thorny path away from you?
Who was unfair toward the other? Me or you?
What about the years that brought us together and
    didn't set us apart?
Are these years the cause of my pain?
Or is it Love?
It's our destiny
I started waking in nightfall
I have a growing fear of confronting people
I don't want them to ask me about the tears of my
    broken heart
Only my bed keeps my secrets
I told my bed a lot about you
And it never got bored
The bitter loss of you taught me an unforgettable
    lesson
It taught me how to take refuge in Allah
Thank you for guiding me to him
He provides me with strength without me noticing
Really, thank you

أتحدث عن نفسي بعد فراقك

جامدةٌ كالحجر أمامَ نافذتي
صامتةٌ كالقبرِ وكأن لساني جف
أتأملُ القمرَ وكأني أحرسه
بروح معذبةٍ وقلبٍ يتألم
ثمةَ شجار عنيف بينَ عقلي وقلبي
هل سنلتقي يوماً؟
البُعدُ عنكَ طريقٌ شائكة؟
ظلمتكَ أم ظلمتُ نفسي؟
السنواتُ التي جمعتنا ولم تفرقنا
أهي سببُ ألمي؟
أم أنهُ الحب ؟
لكن هذا قدرنا المكتوب
صرتُ أستيقظُ حينَ ينسدلُ الليل
لخوفي من مواجهةِ الناس
لكي لا يسألوني عن دموعِ قلبي
فِراشي كاتم أسراري
حدثته عنك كثيراً
ولم يمل
فراقك المرُ علمني درساً لن أنساه
علمني كيف ألوذُ بالله
فشكراً لأنكَ دللتني عليه
ليمُدني بالقوة دونَ أن أشعر
فشكراً لك .

ملك

260

Glossary of Pantry Staples

AKKAWI: A semi-fresh white and lightly brined cheese. A fresh mozzarella, patted dry, is an acceptable substitute.

ALEPPO PEPPER: Although named after the city, Aleppo pepper is used, grown and harvested throughout much of the Mediterranean and the Levant. This ground red chili is noted for being fruity on the nose, useful in both spice blends as well as a finishing touch. Heat levels vary, but generally a mild to medium-hot heat. Find Aleppo pepper in most Middle Eastern grocers, as well as in specialty food and spice shops.

BAHARAT: The word "baharat" means spices in Arabic, and the plurality of the word speaks to the various flavours and applications found in baharat itself. Also known as "seven spice," it is a warming blend of (usually) cinnamon, cloves, allspice, nutmeg, with variations including cardamom, mace, coriander, or cumin, depending on the vendor or home cook (recipe p. 243). Find baharat in most Middle Eastern grocers as well as in specialty food and spice shops.

BULGUR: Wheat kernels (usually durum wheat, a high protein wheat used in making noodles and pastas) that have been par-cooked and then "cracked" or broken into pieces. Available in the international or whole food sections of most grocers, as well as in Middle Eastern and specialty food shops.

CARDAMOM: A member of the ginger family and native to the South Asian subcontinent, cardamom is sold either whole (in green pods), decorticated (without the pods), or pre-ground. Buy whole or decorticated whenever possible. Incredibly fragrant, cardamom is used in both sweet and savoury preparations either on its own or in spice blends. Although related, black or white cardamom are not recommended, as the former is smoked, and the latter is bleached.

CHAI: Technically, "tea," though the word is used generically for any beverage where tea is the main star. Unless noted, black teas, like Assam, tend to be a good fit for the flavour profile of the chai drunk in Zaatari. It is often sweetened (recipes p. 234).

CHEESE: See *Akkawi, Nabulsi*

The main forms of **COOKING FAT** used in Zaatari are olive oil, saman, and animal fats, usually from lamb. Each have their own qualities and uses, based on the type of cooking being produced.

In Zaatari, **OLIVE OIL** is pressed annually, following the customs and uses that have been in the region for generations. For the home cook in the west, olive oils vary in price and quality, with the glut of olive oils coming from Spain or North Africa. Some good quality olive oils from California are hitting more and more grocers throughout North America.

SAMAN is clarified butter (recipe p. 244). Often sold as ghee in grocers, saman has a higher smoke point than regular butter due to the milk solids having been removed. Lightly nutty, saman is used in both savoury and sweet cooking. Not to be confused with *smen*, a Morrocan fermented clarified butter, or its Yemeni cousin *semneh*, both of which are funkier, almost cheesy in flavour. Ghee is sold in more and more grocery stores, and is available in many international food stores.

ANIMAL FATS are also used in Zaatari, with the majority of it being lamb fat, though beef fat can be used in these recipes. The fats used are often unrendered (meaning that they have not been melted), and often come from the tail of a specific kind of fat-tailed sheep. The fat from the tails of these sheep have been prized throughout the Middle East, Central Asia, and North Africa for centuries. Even the ancient historian Herodotus wrote about them in the fifth century BCE. Lamb fat and beef fat (usually in the form of suet, which surrounds the kidneys of the cow) are available from specialty butchers and butcher counters.

FREEKEH: Wheat kernels, usually durum, that are harvested before full maturity (often called "green" wheat), and have their hulls burned off. The result are wheat berries that are more vegetal in character than other forms of wheat berries, along with a pleasant smoky flavour. Most freekeh is sold already cracked, though whole is available. Use cracked for the recipes in this book. Available in the international or whole food sections of most grocers, as well as in Middle Eastern and specialty food shops.

JAMEED; KETHI; KISHK: No matter what you call it, or how you prepare it, these are all variations on a theme of how to preserve dairy, a highly perishable and nutritious food. Most often made from some form of fermented dairy, especially yogurt, it is sold either in small balls or "stones," or as a liquid. The dried balls or stones are reconstituted in various soups, stews, or dips, thickening the resulting dish.

For the purposes of this book, kethi refers to the small stones or balls of dried, often salted yogurt, while kishk is prepared with bulgur. In Jordan, kishk is often called jameed. All are found in Middle Eastern grocers.

LABAN; LABNEH: Laban is simply yogurt. For the recipes in this book, full fat yogurt is best. *Labneh* is made by straining out any excess whey or liquid from the laban.

LUMI: Also spelled *loomi,* or known as *limoo omani,* is a dried lime, often sold in Middle Eastern shops. Used either whole, or ground into a powder, it adds a pleasing acidity and a touch of salinity to stews and soups. When ground they are sometimes called ground lemon, or **LEMON SALT.**

MAGGI: Maggi is the brand name of a seasoning that is sold in both liquid and dried form throughout much of the world. It is a deeply concentrated, salty, and savoury ingredient that has become ubiquitous as a flavour booster for many a home cook. It is so popular that regional variations exist with varying flavour profiles, depending on where it is produced and purchased.

Owned by Nestlé, Maggi also produces other instant foodstuffs for various markets, but for the purposes of this book, when Maggi is mentioned, we are speaking specifically of the dried cube (technically a type of bouillon cube) that is used by those in the camp. The cubes are used either whole or crushed as an inexpensive flavour enhancer, in the same way one would use seasoning salt.

MAHLAB: Also known as *mahleb,* or *mahlap,* this spice is the seed of a type of cherry. It is used in Arab, Persian, Greek, and Cypriot desserts and baked goods. Reminiscent of bitter almonds or almond paste, a little goes a long way. It is

usually sold whole, as the perfume dissipates quickly once ground. The whole seeds can be used, like sour cherry pits, to perfume custards, jams, and more. Almond extract is an acceptable substitute.

MASTIC: Also known as gum mastic, it is the dried sap of a tree that is related to pistachios. This sap or resin is often used as (or the base of) chewing gums. The resinous flavour of mastic is mostly used in sweet preparations, though it is used sparingly in savoury preparations in spice blends. It is often sold by its Greek name, *mastiha.*

MLOUKHIEH: Sometimes spelled *mulukhiyah,* or Jew's mallow, the leaves are very popular in Syria, Lebanon, and Egypt. A mix of spinach and parsley, or amaranth leaves and spinach, is an acceptable substitute.

NABULSI: A lightly brined, semi-hard cheese, with a somewhat bouncy texture, similar to halloumi. Halloumi shredded with fresh mozzarella is an acceptable substitute.

NIGELLA: A small seed, reminiscent of sesame seeds in shape and size, nigella is commonly used in Arab, Persian, and South Asian cooking. Although it tastes mildly of onions, it is in fact related to carrots and fennel. Even more confusingly, it is often labeled as black cumin, or black caraway, or black onion seed. Sold in Middle Eastern grocery stores, you may also find it at South Asian grocers under the name of *kalonji,* or *siah denah* at Persian grocers.

ORANGE BLOSSOM WATER: Made via a steam distillation process using fresh orange blossoms, usually Seville or other sour oranges. Orange blossom water is common throughout much of the Middle East. Like rose water, it should be used sparingly, and judiciously, and as a finishing touch, as heat can kill the fragrance. Keep in the fridge once opened.

PURSLANE: A succulent that is prized in Arab and Persian cooking, in North America it is often viewed (and classified) as a weed. It is often served raw in salads, or cooked into soups. Hard to find at most grocers, ask around at farmers markets during the summer months.

QISHTA: Also written as *Qashtah,* it is a coagulated dairy product, very similar to clotted cream, and is sometimes translated as Arabic clotted cream. It is often eaten on its own, or used in desserts. See recipe on p. 165.

ROSES; ROSE WATER: Roses are used throughout much of the Middle East and North Africa in sweet and savoury preparations, most notably as rosewater (made via a steam distillation process using fresh rose petals) while the dried petals and buds are used for savoury spice blends.

Dried buds and petals are available from specialty spice shops, and occasionally in Persian and Middle Eastern grocers, as is rose water. Rose water, like orange blossom water, should be used sparingly, judiciously, and as a finishing touch. Refrigerate once opened.

SAMAN (see p. 261)

SEMOLINA: Made from durum wheat, semolina comes in both coarse and fine grinds, and has a texture similar to cornmeal. It is available in the baking aisles of most grocery stores, as well as international food shops.

SHATTAH: A type of hot sauce popular in Syria and other regions of the Levant (recipe p. 247). Substitutions such as zhoug (a Yemeni hot sauce) can be used, or even sriracha in a pinch, with a touch of pomegranate molasses added to it for acidity.

SUMAC: The dried and ground berries of a type of shrub, sumac lends brightness and acidity to dishes. It is often used in salads, as well as on poultry or fish, and is often a component in various zaatar blends. Found in well-stocked grocers, Middle Eastern and Persian grocers, as well as specialty food shops.

TAHINI: Sometimes spelled *tahineh,* tahini is a paste made from sesame seeds, used in both sweet and savoury preparations. Although available in both light and dark colours (as well as occasionally black), all of the recipes here use a light coloured tahini. Tahini does tend to separate, but just stir it well before using. Keep refrigerated once opened. Available from most grocers in the international or whole food aisles, as well as Middle Eastern grocers.

TAMARIND: In Zaatari, like in much of the world, *Tamr Hindi* (tamarind) is used as a souring agent in cooking, usually for stews and soups, or in drinks. A type of fruit, it is often sold in cellophane-wrapped bricks of the fruit's pulp, although it is occasionally sold while still in its pod. The cellophane wrapped bricks are used in this book. Find it in Latin grocers under the name of *tamarindo*, in Persian grocers under the name of *tambreh hendi*, as well as South Asian and Middle Eastern grocers.

ZAATAR: Sometimes spelled *za'atar*, this is a favourite spice blend of dried thyme, sesame seeds, oregano, marjoram, salt, and sometimes sumac, for which Aleppo and Palestine are famous. Zaatar (Arabic for thyme) is Zaatari Camp's namesake. The blend occasionally includes other dried herbs such as oregano, or even nuts, depending on where it is made. Its price varies in shops, depending on the quality and the source. Zaatar is used for cooking and for enjoying with olive oil and khubz.

Acknowledgements

Passion for family, for culture, and for food. For humanity and peace. Since its inception in 2016 *Zaatari: Culinary Traditions of the World's Largest Syrian Refugee Camp* was invaluably supported by the deep commitment of many individuals and organizations. My gratitude is eternal to my foodie family: my children for their understanding, their morale boosting, their love during my travels, and their commitment to supporting the people of Zaatari Camp. Deepest thank you to my mother and father in Newfoundland and my brother and family in Halifax, who inspired my passion for cooking and were bedrocks in this long endeavor.

My profound gratitude to UNHCR Zaatari Camp for inviting me in January 2015, approving our book mission in 2016, and your staunch support and shared vision that ensured the inclusion of thousands of voices and recognition of unsung women's work. Your commitment was boundless. I am indebted to Questcope, Blumont, UN Women, the UN World Food Programme, and to Zaatari's many iNGOs, especially Relief International, the Norwegian Refugee Council, the Nour Hussein Foundation, Lutheran World, International Medical Corps, and Peace and Sport. Thank you also to the Givaudan Foundation, who supported the soap making activities of Made in Zaatari.

There would be no book without Mohammed Shwamra, my Zaatari Camp Syrian project coordinator, who supported the logistics of our activities and translation and was intrinsic in leading our Zaatari brain trust with immense ingenuity and humour. This book also owes a great debt to Rob Firing, our literary agent bar none at the Transatlantic Agency (Toronto). Rob believed in our book since day one, guided me as an author, and spurred my creativity. Thank you to our publisher Goose Lane Editions in Atlantic Canada. To Susanne Alexander, Alan Sheppard, Julie Scriver, Jeff Arbeau, Ben Burnett, Simon Thibault, and team: thank you for believing in our book, for your commitment to refugees, and for bringing our book into the world.

My deepest appreciation to Salah Aldin Falioun for standardizing the Arabic transliteration and translating the bulk of handwritten recipes, stories, and poetry. A professional translator, a foodie, and a poet from Damascus, Salah instinctively understood our needs for capturing the essence of Zaatari. I am indebted to our Syrian camp photographers, UNHCR External Relations, Sam and Jack Powers and Michelle Heimerman of the Lens on Life Project, and Marshall Rawlings. Thank you for providing cultural images and searching through your collections for readers to get an insider view of camp. Eternal gratitude to food photographers Alex Lau and Jason LeCras, and food stylist Seersa Abaza for shooting over 130 dishes with camp youth assistants, guided by Zaatari cooks and styling à la Zaatari. Alex and Jason, thank you for leaping with us; donating your time, creativity, and passion—and for taste-testing every dish! Seersa, thank you for your attention to detail and integrating camp style. The collective organization and creativity of thirty cooks in their homes and the souks with fourteen youth assistants was sheer joy—an indelible reminder of the power of Zaatari.

Many others were intrinsic in our food photography. I am immensely grateful to the Embassy of Canada, the Embassy of Ireland, Jordan-Kuwait Bank, and Cozmo for financially supporting our activities: covering food costs (including ingredients from Daraa); the efforts of the camp cooks, youth assistants, and our food stylist; and the travel to Amman for photography in a professional kitchen. Thank you to Royal Jordanian Airlines for sponsoring travel to Amman, exemplifying Jordanian hospitality and the Kingdom's support of Syrian refugees. Our food photography would not have been possible without the kind support of the staff and the professional kitchen at the House Boutique Hotel on Circle 2. Thank you also to Umm Khalil Restaurant for staging a few dishes in your beautiful Syrian setting, and to Sufra Restaurant for loaning heritage props. My deepest gratitude to the Delegation of the European Union to the Hashemite Kingdom of Jordan for providing copies of our book to the many refugees who were instrumental in its creation.

I owe many people my gratitude for helping organize the Syrian heritage props in our food photography, through knowledge-sharing and sourcing. Many antique shops in Amman played a role—especially Heritage Antiques on Rainbow Street, who shared their vast knowledge and loaned precious items, including antique tablecloths and silverware.

My deepest gratitude to the Information School (iSchool) of the University of Washington for supporting our book since the early days, for financial support, inspiration and commitment to inclusion and making a difference in the world. Marie, Jesse, Apurva, Katya, and the GA Pool: thank you for organizing and digitizing the hundreds of recipes, paintings, stories, and poetry from camp. Thank you to the Grossman Family for supporting the students' work. And my global colleagues—Eeva-Liisa Eskola, Crystal Fulton, David Hendry, Jamie Johnston, Khadijah Khan, Patrick Oliver, Reem Talhouk, Gunilla Widen, Volker Wulf, and Eiad Yafi—thank you for your years of friendship and brilliance, your encouragement to co-design a Syrian refugee cookbook, and meeting urgent world problems through academic methods.

Many people provided invaluable insights, helped with translation, financial support, and provided encouragement through years of yummy conversation about Syrian and Arab food and culture. My heart to the many inspiring individuals who were pivotal on our journey: Norah Abokhdair, Mark Arar, Maram al-Athamneh, Nico Dingemans, Sherry Doyle, Hovig Etyemezian, Sophie Etzold, Mais Halim, Marwa Hashem, Mohammad Hawari, Siraj al-Hmoud, David Huchthausen, Abdullah Ibrahim,Rehab Khalifa, Kilian Kleinschmidt, Hisham Majali, Shatha al-Mashaqbah, Abdulqader al-Masri, Omar al-Muhaisen, Aya Musmar, Ayat Nashwan, Hani al-Naser, Irene Omondi, Carol Palmer, Omar Qawasmeh, Suna Qaisi, Matthew Reynolds, Maen Ryan, Omar Saleh, Hada Sarham, Rivkah Sass, Laith Shatnawi, Awad al-Sheikh, Cameron Stauch, Helen Storey, Mohammed al-Taher, Iris Vlachoutsicos, Eiad Yafi, and Rita Zawaideh—your kindness made all the difference.

I save my biggest debt to the glorious Syrian people of Zaatari Camp: thank you for your kindnesses, boundless creativity, enthusiasm, and generosity. It has been the honour of a lifetime to help bring your recipes and stories to the world. Thank you for welcoming me into your community, your families, your homes—your madafa and soufra. I hope to repay your love through our book. For safety I refrain from saying names—and the list is in the thousands, but know your stories are indelibly recorded on our pages. May Allah always guide you on the straight path and bless you with his infinite mercy and compassion.

Supporting

In partnership with
Canada

UNHCR
The UN Refugee Agency

Ambasáid na hÉireann | An Iordáin
Embassy of Ireland | Jordan

COZMO
It's a new day

البنك الأردني الكويتي
JORDAN KUWAIT BANK

European Union
Delegation to Jordan

الملكية الأردنية
ROYAL JORDANIAN

GIVAUDAN
FOUNDATION
For communities & nature

Index to Recipes

Photography Credits
Food photography by Alex Lau with Jason LeCras unless otherwise noted.

Other photographs appear courtesy of the following:
Mohammed Abazeed 22; **Mohammed Amaari** 18, 34 (hand writing), 62; **Mohammed al-Attewi** 44, 70; **Mohammed Abu Asaker** (UNHCR) 17; **Karen E. Fisher** 4, 16, 17 (contest), 19 (tent, house), 34 (drawing), 39, 46 (caravans, mural, cactus), 47 (children), 48 (Rahim and Iyad), 64, 73 (man and child), 88 (hands), 92 (dishes), 122, 136, 192 (dishes), 195, 226 (painting), 238, 259, 260; **Mohammed al-Ghanom** 88 (green heart soap); **Daham Khaled al-Hamed** 226 (Malak); **Shawkat Hesham al-Harfosh** 50, 140 (woman, sheep, prayer), 143, 191 (video still shot with Yousef al-Hariri); **Baraa al-Hariri** 88 (brushes), 90, 91 (pencil tip, mallet), 170 (bride); **Younis Hariri** 7, 45, 46 (man in garden), 51 (girls), 56, 73 (waving), 76, 88 (women walking), 96, 107, 128, 135 (woman), 140 (tamr hindi vendor), 158, 192 (baby, girl), 240 (spice bags), 242 (spices); **Yousef al-Hariri** 1 (caravans), 2, 6, 9 (sunset, boy and girl, boy running, maamoul), 10 (group walking to the mosque, woman, doves, man with walker, man with red scarf), 19 (girls), 24, 46 (football), 47 (sunset), 51 (imam), 68 (souk at night), 69, 99, 134, 161, 173, 191 (video still shot with Shawkat Hesham al-Harfoshi), 201, 264, 271; **Mohammed Hawari** 19 (boys); **Emad al-Kafri** 135 (horse), 142 (drummer); **Alex Lau** 8 (maqloubeh), 14 (woman cooking), 15, 27, 33 (process shots), 68 (vegetable market), 91 (Tarek), 92 (women), 132, 174, 175, 192 (meat skewers), 209, 219, 242 (old photograph, soap), 248; **Dina Luce** 172 (woman); **Ahmad al-Natour** 159; **Marshall Rawlings** 10 (fence), 33 (dish), 34 (Mohammed Amaari), 37, 49, 61, 68 (awameh), 192 (kababs over blue bowl), 208, 228, 240 (shelves); **Iyad Sabbagh** 17 (painting), 21, 48; **Qasem-ph al-Shahmehe** 9 (car), 10 (mosque, boys), 14 (woman with boys), 68 (shawarma), 83, 141, 142 (souk), 190; **Esra'a al-Soud** 46 (donkey cart), 170 (music, barber, bride and groom), 172 (drummer); **Helen Storey** 63, 88 (women in coats, coloured soaps); **UNHCR** 8 (souk alley), 9 (grocery cart), 13.

Goose Lane Editions acknowledges the generous support of the Government of Canada, the Canada Council for the Arts, and the Government of New Brunswick.

Goose Lane Editions is located on the unceded territory of the Wəlastəkwiyik whose ancestors along with the Mi'kmaq and Peskotomuhkati Nations signed Peace and Friendship Treaties with the British Crown in the 1700s.

Goose Lane Editions
500 Beaverbrook Court, Suite 330
Fredericton, New Brunswick
CANADA E3B 5X4
gooselane.com

Edited by Valerie Mansour and Simon Thibault.
Copy edited by Jane Broderick.
Translations from the Quran and hadith from the Saheeh International translation.
Recipes, interviews, and poems translated from the Arabic by Mohammed Shwamra and Salah Aldin Falioun.
Calligraphy (p. 1) by Iyad Sabbagh.
Project management in Zaatari by Mohammed Shwamra.
Cover and page design by Julie Scriver.
Front cover photograph of Siniyeh jaj wa batata by Alex Lau (recipe p. 123).
Back cover photographs by Qasem-ph al-Shahmehe (mosque) and Alex Lau (ftoor/breakfast).
Food photography by Alex Lau and Jason LeCras, with styling by Seersa Abaza.
Camp photography team directed by UNHCR External Relations, and Sam and Jack Powers and Michelle Heimerman of the Lens on Life Project in collaboration with Questscope, with contributions by independent camp photographers.
Author photograph (p. 272) by Baraa al-Hariri.
All images reproduced with permission.

Printed in China by MCRL Overseas Group.
10 9 8 7 6 5 4 3 2 1

Library and Archives Canada Cataloguing in Publication

Title: Zaatari : culinary traditions of the world's largest Syrian refugee camp / Karen E. Fisher ; food photography by Alex Lau with Jason LeCras ; Arabic text translated by Mohammed Shwamra and Salah Aldin Falioun.
Other titles: Zaatari (2024)
Names: Fisher, Karen E., 1966- editor, writer of added text. | Lau, Alex, photographer. | LeCras, Jason, photographer. | Shwamra, Mohammed, translator. | Falioun, Salah Aldin, translator.
Description: Includes index. | Some recipes and text translated from the original Arabic.
Identifiers: Canadiana 20230164676 | ISBN 9781773102351 (softcover)
Subjects: LCSH: Cooking, Syrian. | LCSH: Zaatari (Refugee camp) | LCSH: Refugees—Syria—Social life and customs. | LCSH: Refugees—Jordan—Social life and customs. | LCGFT: Cookbooks.
Classification: LCC TX725.S95 Z33 2024 | DDC 641.595691—dc23